I0213059

Beyond My Wildest Dreams

Beyond My Wildest Dreams

A Memoir

Ken R. Harewood

Keupid Publishers

Durham, North Carolina

Published in the United States by Keupid Publishers

Durham, North Carolina

Library of Congress Cataloging-in-Publication Data

Harewood, Ken R.

Beyond My Wildest Dreams: A Memoir / Ken R. Harewood, - 1st ed.

Paperback ISBN: 978-1-105-02035-3

Hardback ISBN 13: 978-0-615-48535-5

Printed in the United States of America

Acknowledgement

To my mother Annie who taught me to value family and faith; my father Glenville who instilled in me the desire to strive for excellence and dream big dreams; and my wife Eudine who inspired and encouraged me to pursue those dreams.

Table of Contents

Introduction

As he approached the age of seventy, Dad reminded my siblings and me that after he reached that important milestone he would be living on borrowed time. I vividly remember him saying that while he still had control of his mental faculties he wanted to be physically present when his grandchildren graduated from college. He also expressed a desire to live long enough to see me write a book that would chronicle my experiences as a biochemist, particularly my accomplishments during the time I worked as a discovery biologist in the pharmaceutical industry. Dad lived long enough to attend the graduation ceremonies of all of his grandchildren except those of my youngest sibling. I believe that those events provided him with some of the most gratifying moments of his life.

The desire to have his son the scientist write a book, however, remained a dream deferred. Although I shared Dad's vision about the importance of documenting my work as a scientist, I knew I could not take on such a demanding task at the time that he was making his request. I wanted to author a much more comprehensive manuscript that would include accounts of how family and community helped to shape my character and positively influence my development, especially during my childhood years. I was acutely aware of the fact that although I often talked to my siblings about family, none of us had ever taken the time to even construct an official family tree.

One of my reasons for wanting to broaden the focus of my book had a lot to do with the stark reality that, to my knowledge, there are no publications that capture what life was like in rural St. John during the time when the tiny island of Barbados was transitioning from being a British colony to an independent nation state. I was also mindful that very little had been recorded anywhere about the history of the black families that resided in the cluster of small communities that exist in the shadow of one of Barbados' major landmarks–Codrington College. I thought that my book could fill that void.

By writing this book, I knew that I would be forced to peruse old family records and talk to many of the elderly folk from my community to learn as much as I could about my ancestors, the Hayneses and Kidneys of St. John, and the Harewoods of St. Philip. I felt that it was important for me to document how the Hayneses and Kidneys benefited from the privilege of living on College Land and working at Codrington College. I believed that their stories would provide me with a framework upon which I could construct a more complete narrative about my own life. I also held out hope that through my own story, I could provide future generations of Harewoods with a better understanding of the critical roles that parents, family, mentors, community, and country will play in their own development.

While in my subconscious I felt that my family's journey from slavery to freedom might have mirrored the journey of many other Barbadian families, I was still convinced that there were some unique aspects to the Harewood family story that were worth telling. I particularly wanted to recount how I first learned about the importance of education in elevating rural Barbadian families from the depth of economic despair. Through this book I sensed that I could chronicle my own educational path, highlighting milestones, and whenever possible, stressing the value of mentorship and teamwork.

I knew that I could also use this book to show the power that teachers have to influence the development of young minds. In my case it was an elementary teacher who took note of my potential in the classroom and prodded my parents to take appropriate action. In another instance, it was a hardworking gamesmaster who helped my teammate Ronnie Hall and me transform the Lodge School Football (Soccer) Team into one of the most fearsome elevens in Barbados during the 1950s. It was through those early interventions that I was able to transition from student to soccer player and then to scientist, a development that Dad frequently talked about with considerable pride.

The family's move from Barbados to the U.S. in the 1960s profoundly changed my life, and I was convinced that by writing this book, I would need to invest a considerable amount of time gathering the material that best captures the essence of my American journey. The move to America unquestionably broadened my horizons, and sparked in me an insatiable desire to try to learn as much as possible about my Barbadian roots.

Over the years since Dad's passing, I became more and more convinced that I needed to take his advice and tell the story of my life. By telling my story, I would be keeping a promise that I made to him more than two decades ago. Another reason for writing this book has much to do with the fact that I grew up at a time of unprecedented change in Barbados and the rest of the world, and I wanted to provide my own perspective on what I experienced during that period. I was a student in high school when the Russian Satellite Sputnik crashed into the Atlantic Ocean within sight of Barbados. From my vantage point in the front of our home in St. John, as I looked in a northeasterly direction, I could see that incredible fireball disintegrating as it fell into the sea. It was one of those once-in-a-lifetime experiences that was both terrifying and exhilarating.

I was a science student during the decade of the 1950s when the secret of human inheritance was first revealed. The report on the structure of Deoxyribonucleic acid (DNA) appeared in the major scientific journals and daily newspapers when I was in high school in Barbados. I could not have envisioned then how that discovery would change the path that I would subsequently take to become an investigative biologist. Neither could I have imagined how the DNA molecules packaged in the chromosomes in the nuclei of all human cells could have the capacity to encode all of the genetic information that makes us who we are as individuals. It seemed heretical then to think that a DNA molecule could utilize a three-letter code embedded in its linear sequence to faithfully and reproducibly transmit genetic information from parent to offspring. The ability that DNA possesses that enables it to generate the incredible diversity of characteristics that are on display within and among human populations is unquestionably one of the genuine wonders of this world. I was mesmerized by that amazing reality as it unfolded during my teenage years, and I wanted to talk about it in this book.

Then, as my career in science unfolded, I served as a collaborator on the research team that discovered the first human cancer virus. I felt that I could provide a unique perspective on that initiative, and on the "War on Cancer" that was launched by the Nixon administration to investigate the biological basis of human cancer. And then there was the achievement of being the first scientist in the Central Research Division of Pfizer Inc. to have cloned a mammalian gene. That was a phenomenal accomplishment when it occurred, but for proprietary reasons, it was not widely publicized, and even if it had been, few would have understood the impact it would have on the company for which I worked. The success of my project alerted some of my colleagues to the fact that biotechnology could offer exciting opportunities to discover new drugs, and it certainly convinced many of them that biotechnology could become a very powerful tool for producing commercially important products and processes.

By recounting my role in those developments, I would in very tangible ways be repaying debts that I owe to my parents, grandparents, and the many outstanding individuals who mentored and advised me over the course of my career.

I began the process of preparing for this book by collecting information on my family history while Mum and Dad were still alive. Every chance I got, I probed them for details about family, friends, and community. I was particularly curious to learn as much as I could about their childhood and about family members whom I never had the opportunity to meet. I tape-recorded some of my conversations with them, and even videotaped others when it was convenient to do so. I reviewed the information I gleaned from all of my sources, and organized it in a way that provided me with an historical framework for the story I wanted to tell. I realized however, that I would have to take a special trip to Barbados in order to gather additional archival information. In 2009, I made arrangements for that trip back in time.

The night before my scheduled departure for Barbados, I stayed up late to pack my bags. It was a tedious process, because I wanted to include as much of the material I had gathered for the trip without violating any of the airline's rules for checked or carryon bags. I was also acutely aware of the fact that I needed to conform to size and weight limitations for all of my bags. Since 9/11, air travel had become very stressful, and I was not inclined to make my trip any more difficult than it had to be.

I was booked on the eight o'clock flight in the morning, so in my inimitable fashion, I calculated down to the last minute what I needed to do to ensure that after arriving at the airport, I would have at least two hours to negotiate the check-in and security processes before boarding my flight. I made the necessary arrangements with the airport taxi service, and I had devised a reasonable back-up plan in the event the taxi failed to show up.

I had the alarm on my BlackBerry set for three o'clock in the morning! I got out of bed around two o'clock after only a couple of hours sleep. My taxi was scheduled for a four o'clock pickup, because I wanted to have enough time to be ready and waiting for the short ride to the airport. I opened the garage door at ten minutes to four and stood there surrounded by all of my bags. It had rained overnight, and I could see the streetlights flickering in our cul-de-sac. The morning was dark and dreary. As I waited, four o'clock came and went and there was no sign of the approaching headlamps of my taxi. At a quarter past four, I placed a call to the dispatcher to express concern and was assured that the taxi was en route. Ten minutes later, I placed a second call to the dispatcher and waited for him to patch the call through to the driver who apologized profusely for his tardiness. He had apparently misread my address and was on the north side of town. He said that in spite of the error, he was confident that he could still get me to the airport on time.

The trip to the airport was short and uneventful. Check-in was routine, and I was finally onboard the aircraft. I closed my eyes as the plane left the gate and taxied onto the tarmac of the Raleigh-Durham International Airport in North Carolina. I waited patiently for the captain to announce that he had been cleared for takeoff. Shortly, I heard the roar of the engines as the plane rolled down the runway, and then within an instant, it was wheels-up and I was airborne.

I was on my way back to Barbados, back to St. John where I grew up, back to the neighborhood where my mother's family the Hayneses and Kidneys first settled in the nineteenth century. I began to plan for that trip back to Barbados sometime in August 2008. My itinerary included visits to: the Public Library; the Archives; and the Barbados Advocate, the daily newspaper that served the island during my childhood. I also made arrangements to talk to childhood friends and historians, and to do everything possible to make the narrative as comprehensive, interesting, and informative as possible.

When the plane landed at the Grantley Adams International Airport, I was pleased to have completed this first leg of my journey back to the place that I still call home. Barbados, the "Rock," the place where I grew up. The place that shaped my character, taught me values, and provided me with a true sense of self. A place where my parents along with the elders in my family and community instilled in me the principles that I still hold dearly.

The combination of information gathered from my parents and family members with the material collected from that trip I took in January 2009 made this book possible.

Chapter 1

The Kidneys from St. John

I drove the tiny, rented hatchback with caution along the narrow two-lane road heading east from Society Plantation toward Codrington College. I considered this highly revered theological institution that graces the landscape of Conset Plantation to be the most appropriate place for me to begin my journey back in time. For my entire life, I have been aware of the fact that this popular Barbadian tourist attraction, Codrington College, was the place where my ancestors the Hayneses and Kidneys began their long march towards freedom. It was a time when St. John, a mostly agrarian parish, and the rest of the island of Barbados, were emerging from the ravages of slavery.

I intentionally wanted to approach the college from the direction of Society Plantation. As a schoolboy, I traveled this route as I made my way from the Lodge School to my home on College Land. As I approached the top of College Hill, I knew that one of the most picturesque sceneries on display anywhere in Barbados was just moments ahead. Instinctively, I pulled the five-speed hatchback off the road, grabbed my digital camera, and selected a vantage point that gave me the best access to the panoramic view of Barbados' beautiful southeastern coast.

I remember standing on the same spot as a boy watching the lighthouse at Ragged Point and wondering who was responsible for choosing its location. I also thought of how difficult it must have been for the early settlers of Barbados to have constructed such an impressive landmark at a time when major projects of that type depended exclusively on manual labor. Although the view was now partially obstructed by an overgrowth of shrubbery, I was still able to see the spectacular bay at Conset Point that I frequented as a teenager to watch cricket or to buy fresh fish for the family dinner.

The tiny community of College Savannah visible in the distance, once a sleepy little village, was now dotted with a surprising number of modern, coral stone homes, attesting to the rapid pace of development that has occurred along this strikingly beautiful part of the Barbadian countryside. The azure blue Atlantic Ocean was on full display, hugging the rugged coastline as it embraced places with names like the Puff, Culpepper Island, Skeete's Bay, and Fortescue. I studied the landscape carefully, and just as I did as a teenager, I captured as many snapshots of this remarkable view as I could, and planned to add them to the photo history that I have been compiling of this uniquely beautiful part of the Atlantic coast of Barbados.

When I pulled the car back onto the roadway, I immediately shifted the transmission to low speed and prepared to make my descent down the steep hill that lay ahead. College Hill is perhaps the steepest hill in the parish of St. John, and the presence of three major curves in the road makes it challenging for motorists to negotiate. The most dangerous curve is located almost halfway down the hill at a spot known as Lazy Rock. I was well aware of the hazard the curve presented, so I reduced my speed to a crawl, inching forward slowly until I passed Lazy Rock, continuing carefully through the third and final turns until I reached the junction at the bottom of the hill.

The community that is nestled at the base of College Hill is called College Park. I used to know all of the families that lived in this sparsely populated neighborhood when I was a teenager. Mr. Bradshaw's shop, once the commercial hub was still there, presumably under new ownership, but still serving as the primary watering hole for many of the young men that are attracted to the Park to drink rum, play dominoes, and talk trash.

College Hill ends at the junction where it connects to Highway-3. I made a sharp left turn onto Highway-3 and headed north, traveling under the protective canopy of the cluster of mahogany trees that mark the beginning of College Woods. In less than a minute, I was approaching the main entrance to Codrington College. I made the right turn onto the Cabbage Walk, an immaculately landscaped driveway that forms the gateway to the old theological institution. The large sandbox tree I sheltered under when it rained was still there. Stately royal palm trees grace both sides of the paved driveway that slopes gently downwards to an enclosed breezeway to a main building that houses the Belfrey. Approximately fifty yards before the end of the Cabbage Walk, the entire façade of Codrington College came into full view. It's a spectacular sight that makes it easy to understand why this grand old building is considered to be one of the most frequently photographed attractions in the entire island of Barbados. I paused and tried to imagine what it was like for previous generations of Hayneses and Kidneys who walked along that same pavement to begin their day's work at the college.

My mother, aunt, grandmother, grandfather, and great-grandmother worked at Codrington College. They, like the many families that lived in this tiny corner of St. John, were totally dependent on the benevolence of that institution. Its imposing stone structure still casts a towering shadow across the surrounding communities.

Built in 1714 and opened in 1745, Codrington College became affiliated with the University of Durham in England in 1875 when it began to offer degrees in classics and theology. I remember thinking that it must have been a combination of the rich agricultural soil, the attractive terrain, and the spectacular vistas of the Atlantic Ocean that persuaded British landowner and prominent Barbadian Christopher Codrington II to choose the parish of St. John as the site of his two plantations, which he named Society and Conset. His son Christopher Codrington III who was born in Barbados and educated at Oxford University was the benefactor for whom Codrington College was named.

In his will he made two requests that profoundly influenced my life and the lives of many of my ancestors. His first request was to bequeath his estates in St. John to the Society for the Propagation of the Gospel (SPG). He instructed the SPG to establish an institution that was originally intended to provide Barbadians with training in medicine, surgery, and divinity. His second request was for the SPG to make necessary arrangements to ensure that his former slaves were retained on his plantation lands. It was as a result of that extraordinary action of Christopher Codrington III and the resourcefulness of my ancestors, that my family was able to stake a claim to this picturesque region of my island home. They, like most

Barbadians, were proud of the fact that their little island was affectionately referred to by many as "Little England."

My mother Annie Delcine Harewood (nee Kidney) was fortunate to be born on land that was formerly owned by Christopher Codrington III. Like most Barbadians, Mum firmly believed that our tiny island of Barbados was a blessed place to live. Located at thirteen degrees north of the Equator and fifty-nine degrees west of the Prime Meridian, this beautiful coral island, a member of the Windward Islands, has always been considered to be the gem of the Caribbean. It has been perpetually sheltered from the ravages of hurricanes and those dreaded tidal waves that I feared as a child growing up on a coral island that was widely reported to be below sea level. Can you imagine living in a country where there are no forests, no snakes or scorpions, no major rivers to negotiate, a water supply that was plentiful and naturally filtered by the coral stone? The Barbados where I grew up was a place where the weather was near perfect all year round, and the people, with some exceptions, generally respectful of the law, and deeply religious.

Settled in 1625 and claimed for King James of England, Barbados became a British dependency in the early seventeenth century and continued uninterrupted until independence was granted in 1966. The island is divided into eleven administrative units called parishes, two of which are landlocked. As a resident of the parish of St. John, located on the eastern or Atlantic coast, I felt doubly blessed–first to have the good fortune to be born in Barbados, and second, to have the unique opportunity to spend my childhood years on what I consider to be the most attractive piece of real estate available anywhere on that tranquil island.

Some of the most spectacular views of Barbados are encountered along its eastern coast in the parish of St. John. Rolling hills, sheltered picturesque bays with colorful fishing boats, and a landscape that cascades across verdant expanses of grass, with sugarcane fields gently sloping down towards the aquamarine waters of a very familiar ocean. This is the Atlantic coast of Barbados where bays with names like Martins, Congor, Bath, and Conset have for a very long time been at the center of the social and economic life of the very friendly people who lived on this windward side of the island.

My mother was born at a time when Barbadians of African heritage had not long emerged from the dark past of slavery, and the most resourceful members of the community were actively involved in establishing a foothold on the land that comprised the estate of Christopher Codrington III. They formed a small, close-knit village near to what is known as Sargent Street, and they constructed brightly colored chattel houses to replace the tiny shacks they once lived in on nearby College Tenantry.

Mum's family, the Kidneys of St. John benefited enormously from the largess of the college. They were able to escape from the rigors of plantation labor by seeking jobs within the college itself. My great-grandmother Jane Ann Haynes was the daughter of Margaret and Joseph Haynes. She was born in 1854. According to Mum's recollection, Jane Ann was the first member of her family to be employed at Codrington College. As a single parent, she earned a living as a maid providing laundry service for the students attending the Rawle Training Institute, a center for teacher preparation that was constructed approximately two hundred yards to the south of Codrington College. The Rawle was the only institution of its type that was established in Barbados during the colonial period, and was named after the Reverend Richard Rawle who was Principal of Codrington College from 1847 to 1864.

Jane Ann had three children, Clara Beatrice Haynes my grandmother who was born in 1881; Augustine Haynes my Aunt Mam who was born in 1885; and my great uncle Joseph Haynes Bradshaw who was born in 1889. My great uncle James was Clara's half brother and their father was Louis Firebrace.

My mother's maiden name was Kidney, and her father's family also lived in the parish of St. John. The name Kidney was and still is very unusual in Barbados. According to the Historical Research Center, the surname Kidney is believed to be of Irish origin. It represents an anglicized form of the Gaelic "O Dubhain," denoting descendant of Dubhan, a saint from the early Irish Christian era. A secondary meaning of Dubhan is Kidney from which the surname Kidney is derived.

In spite of the Historical Research Center's report on the origin of the name Kidney, my mother remained firmly convinced that the Kidney who settled in St. John was of

Scottish origin. Whether the early settlers from whom our family name was derived came from Ireland or Scotland, there were only two Kidney families in Barbados when I was growing up. One of them was white and lived on the west coast of the island, and the other was the black Kidney family, my relatives who lived on the east coast.

The Kidneys of St. John were originally from Newcastle, a tiny agricultural village located approximately four miles north of Codrington College. Mum told me that when she was a little girl her grandmother Jane Ann said that many years ago, a Scotsman named James Henry Kidney came to Barbados looking for a "good-looking dark woman to marry." He met and married Margaret Hurdle, a beautiful black young lady who fit the description of the woman of James Henry's dreams, and the family settled in Newcastle, St. John. The marriage between James Henry and Margaret produced four boys–Arthur, St. Clair, Joseph, and David Kidney; and two girls, Mary and Jane.

Information on Arthur, Sinclair, Mary, and Jane, the other children of James Henry and Margaret is very sketchy, but the record on Joseph and David is much better preserved. In fact, the images of Joseph and David were permanently etched in my memory from a photograph that hung in my maternal grandmother's home, and is now prominently displayed in my home and the homes of all of my siblings. The picture was taken in 1907 on the occasion of the wedding of Joseph Kidney to Millicent Smith. There was no photograph hanging in my grandmother Clara's home showing members of the wedding party when she married David Kidney. It was the union of David Kidney with Clara Haynes that introduced the Kidney surname to the small community at College Land, St. John. They moved in with Jane Ann, and the Kidneys remained in that home in the same community for more than one hundred years!

The family home was a small wooden house built at the base of a hill. That hill extended for approximately four hundred yards behind the Kidney family home, connecting College Land to lands owned by Haynes Hill Plantation. With its front entrance elevated and overlooking the Atlantic Ocean to the east, and its rear resting on the hill's bedrock, that house rose from the ground like a sentry assigned the task of keeping watch over the community of chattel houses that dotted the landscape around the college. Like most old houses of that era, the Kidney family home was constructed of flat board. I was told that the house was bought by my great-grandmother's brother Joseph Haynes who was a schoolmaster in Blades Hill, a small village about four miles to the south of Codrington College. To me it seemed like such a grand old house when compared to the other homes in our neighborhood.

The floor plan was typical of old Barbadian homes–a living room (fronthouse or drawing room), a narrow, central corridor (the passage) that separated the two main bedrooms, and a sunken dining room (shedroof) and kitchen on the north side of the house and connected to the living room by three wooden steps. A large cellar (basement) was located under the living room of the house. That house was a landmark for fishermen who sailed out of Conset Bay on their daily fishing expeditions, long before the era of the modern, diesel powered iceboats. With limited navigational equipment, local fishermen used the Kidney home that was visible from several miles out to sea, to guide their boats back from the vast expanses of the Atlantic Ocean into the narrow channel at Conset Bay.

After grandfather David Kidney married Clara, he got a job as a butler and housekeeper with Edward Rawle Drayton, British Administrator of Grenada from 1882 to 1915. Grenada is approximately one hundred forty-five miles southwest of Barbados. The newlyweds remained there for one year before returning to Barbados. Back in Barbados, Clara and David Kidney moved in with Jane Ann. David soon found a job as butler and housekeeper at Codrington College. The couple had two children during that period, the older, Mary Eudalie (Aunt Eude) was born in 1906, and the younger, my mother Annie Delcine, was born the following year.

David and Clara next moved to Panama where David worked as a butler and housekeeper. The move to Panama was not unusual. It occurred at the beginning of the twentieth century, a time when the desire for "Panama Money" enticed hundreds of Barbadians to seek employment in the Canal Zone. After two years in Panama, Clara returned to Barbados, pregnant with her third child. She gave birth in 1913 to her only son Lionel Haynes Kidney (Uncle Lionel). Her husband David remained in Panama, and was doing well at his profession.

Great-grandmother Jane Anne Haynes, who kept Eudie and Annie while Clara lived in Panama, was happy to have her daughter back home, and she adored her new grandson Lionel. The family continued its relationship with Codrington College during those very happy times.

Mum said that one day she was sitting on the step in the kitchen of the family home in St. John, when the mailman delivered a letter with a black border to her mother Clara. That brief, cryptic note informed her that her beloved husband David had died in Panama. There is no evidence of a funeral, a burial site, or even a death certificate. Clara did not even have an opportunity to see her husband's body before it was committed to the earth in a faraway place that no family member has ever visited.

After her husband's death in Panama, Clara took a job in Codrington College as a maid. Her duties included assisting with serving the meals to the aspiring priests, and laundering their robes and cassocks.

Aunt Eude was the fourth family member to be employed by Codrington College. As a young girl, she chose to work with Mrs. Dunlop who needed a maid to care for her children. Mrs. Dunlop was the wife of Mr. William Dunlop a professor of classics at Codrington College. Aunt Eude's job provided her with a unique opportunity to read the works of some of the world's greatest authors, as well as to become more familiar with the rules and conventions of the white, privileged class. Her preoccupation with etiquette throughout her life reflected the training and experience she gained while working with the Dunlops.

All of my siblings and I still have the photograph of grandfather David Kidney that was taken in 1907 when his brother Joseph married Millicent Smith. It is a photograph that we are all very proud of because it shows a very positive side of Barbadian family life in the early twentieth century. Joseph and his bride Millicent left Barbados in 1911 to live in Panama. After grandfather David's death the link between Barbados and Panama abruptly ended. In 1998 however, the Kidneys of Barbados and the Kidneys of Panama were finally reunited.

For most of her life Rose Kidney, the daughter of Joseph and Millicent, had limited knowledge of her Barbadian heritage.

When she was six years old, her father Joseph died, and all she knew about him was that he was a Barbadian from the parish of St. John. She, like most children born in Panama to Barbadian parents, had moved from Panama to the United States where she became a naturalized citizen. On two occasions she traveled to Barbados and tried to reconnect to her Barbadian roots, and each time she returned to the United States a disappointed person. Then in 1998 she returned to Barbados with her daughter Lois who wanted to take on the challenge of tracing her grandfather's roots. Because there are so few individuals in Barbados with the last name Kidney, it was easy for a resident from College Land to direct Lois and her mother to my sister's home in Atlantic Shores, Christ Church. My family had relocated to Atlantic Shores after Mum, Dad, Aunt Eude, and Joyce moved back to Barbados from New York in the early 1990s.

When Rose and Lois knocked at the door of Joyce's house and introduced themselves as the daughter and granddaughter of Joseph Kidney, they discovered that they had finally found their long lost relatives. It was a heart wrenching experience for everyone involved in that historic reunion. What Rose and Lois saw next was almost unbelievable. Hanging on the wall in Joyce's dining room was a ninety-one-year-old photograph of the wedding of Joseph and Millicent Kidney. It was the missing link that they were seeking. In the group photograph, Joseph and Millicent are surrounded by family members and friends all decked out in attractive wedding attire. Included in the photograph was Joseph's brother David, David's sister-in-law Augustine (Aunt Mam), and David's eighteen-month old daughter Mary Eulalie who was seated on Aunt Mam's lap.

Following the announcement of her father's untimely death, Mum used her entrepreneurial skills to help her mother Clara with the monumental task of supporting the family. As head of household, Clara now had to provide for three children. Mum would sneak off to pick pond grass at Haynes Hill Plantation during the school vacation. A typical workday for her started with her crediting a dung basket in the morning, pulling the pond grass up by the root, filling her basket and depositing her load. She repeated that process several times during the day until it was time to go home. At the end of the week she would be paid sixty cents for her labor!

Aunt Eude left for America in 1922, and Mum went to help with the Dunlop children. Her tenure with Mrs. Dunlop ended quickly, and she returned home to help Granny Kidney with chores around the house. She was also very protective of her younger brother Lionel. Mum told me that Uncle Lionel was very much a ladies man during his teenage years. He chose to become a tailor, learning the trade from Mr. Charles Thompson who lived on Chapel Hill. He later converted the cellar at the family home into a tailor shop, working with Harloyd Jackman from Coach Hill, Pappy Trust, Berry Sealy, and others from the neighborhood. Uncle Lionel was the consummate playboy who never moved out of his mother's home. His closest friends included some of the best musicians, cricketers, and artisans of the day.

Uncle Lionel played cricket for the local team, and their venue was a field located on a tiny patch of flatland down at Conset Bay. The field was bordered on its northern perimeter by sugarcanes, and by a stream on its southern side. The water in that stream flowed from the spring at Codrington College down to the bay. Over the years, the steady flow of slow moving water created a meandering brook that was a favorite haunt for the local boys who would wade ankle deep in the shallow water probing behind the mossy rocks for crawfish and eel. The hills to the west of the cricket field sloped gently up to Codrington College on the plateau. To the east there was an unobstructed view of Conset Bay with its rusting jetty and the beautiful Atlantic Ocean in the background.

Cricket was the most popular sport for Uncle Lionel and his teammates. I remember seeing local players like Sylvan Antrobus, Onenie from College Park, Reggie and Darnley Sealy, Shortie Beckles, Halman Wiltshire, Narvey Beckles, and others dressed in their traditional cream flannel pants with their starched white shirts making the trek down to Conset Bay to take on a rival team from Savannah, or Pool, or Gall Hill. These were magical days for my neighborhood friends and me. Those were times when discipline and pride were priorities for the men in our communities. Those men were role models that I would one day try to emulate.

When Uncle Lionel was not playing cricket or attending a local dance, he was courting the lovely ladies from the surrounding communities. There was Pearly from Welch Village, Muriel from College Savannah, Carmen from Jackson, St. Michael, and several others. Those friendships yielded my cousins Elsworth, Brenda, Isla, Victor, Odessa, and possibly others that I never got to know.

I was so proud of Uncle Lionel. He was an expert tailor who made my Lodge School blazers and gray flannel pants. I was astonished by the ease with which he could take several yards of a fabric like tweed and transform them into a beautifully tailored suit. Although I didn't spend a lot of quality time with him, I benefited immeasurably from his generosity and his compassion. When he became ill and was hospitalized, I remember visiting him in the Tercentenary Ward at the Barbados General Hospital. When he died in 1953, it was a major loss to his mother Clara and to the entire family.

Chapter 2

The Mason and The Golden Bangle

My father Glenville Rupert was a Harewood from St. Philip. I was told that all of the Harewoods in Barbados were originally from St. Philip. Dad's mother Drucilla Pilgrim was from Boson Hill, St. Philip. I called her Granny Harewood. She was born in 1874, and was in her seventies when I really got to know her. Diminutive in stature, with a full head of "salt and pepper" hair, she had spent almost all of her life working for the family that managed Bentley Plantation in St. Philip. Dad told me about how difficult her job was, and how little she received from them for her labor.

After Drucilla Pilgrim married Robert Henry Harewood Jr. in 1898, the newlyweds moved into the family home in Church Village. The Harewood family house was built by Robert Henry Harewood Sr. on an acre of land that he purchased on June 19, 1872, for fifteen pounds, twelve shillings, and sixpence. One of the family's prized possessions is the original deed to the property in Church Village. Handwritten on parchment paper, this antiquated document shows clearly that my great-grandfather Robert Henry Harewood Sr. was one of the few black Barbadians who became a landowner in St. Philip not long after emancipation.

The Harewood family home in Church Village was a modest, two-bedroom gable house. The fronthouse had a wooden partition that separated the living room from the main bedroom. A narrow doorway provided access to a small dining room behind the living room. A section of the dining room was partitioned off to form a second bedroom. On the other side of the dining room, two wooden steps led to a sunken family room that had a dirt floor. That room was mainly used as a pantry.

Contiguous to the family room was a small kitchen with a brick hearth.

One of the unique features of Granny Harewood's house was the miniature policeman that was perched on top of the roof of the fronthouse. The policeman's trousers were painted black with a red stripe, typical of the Barbados Harbor Police attire of that period. He wore a white tunic and white cork hat. That simple version of an anemometer had one arm up and the other down, and would rotate with every change in wind speed as well as direction.

The house faced south, across from a well-cared-for-patch of flowering plants, most of which were unique to Granny Harewood's gardens. I remember that many interesting trees surrounded her home. There were calabash (cup), plum, avocado, mango, breadfruit, pomegranate, guava, pawpaw, and coconut trees. I always enjoyed visiting Granny Harewood because I could climb the fruit trees in her orchard to sample the sumptuous mangoes, plums, and pomegranates.

Granny Harewood and grandfather Robert had four children–Camie, Stoddard, Glenville, and Ena. Robert, like many Barbadian men of his generation, joined the wave of emigrants seeking employment in the Panama Canal Zone, and just like my other grandfather David Kidney, he died in Panama. Dad was just seven years old when Granny Harewood received the news of her husband's death. Almost six years later, tragedy struck the family again when Dad's older brother Stoddard died. With Campbell living at his father's home in Four Roads, St. John, Dad was the only male in the Harewood household. His resolve was to try to fill his father's shoes, and this would propel him into a role that fundamentally changed the course of his life.

Granny Harewood was a gentle lady, short in stature, with a large mole on the left side of her nose. She loved her grandchildren with a passion. Granny always welcomed us with hugs and kisses. She would hold our heads between her hands and kiss us profusely on the top of our heads. It was a welcome that I could never forget.

Dad attended St. Philip's Boy's School. He entered at age five when Mr. Antrobus was headmaster and Mr. Blackman was his assistant. Every day when classes ended, he walked from

Church Village to Bentley Plantation to see his mother. Dad often talked about the years he spent at St. Philip Boys School. One of his favorite stories was about the incident with the school's water buckets. During those days, the school had two galvanized buckets. Dad was one of a small group of students that used those buckets to fetch water from the public standpipe. The routine was to fill the buckets with water, haul them back to school, and place them on the right side of the coral stone steps at the entrance to the building. On one occasion, after Dad and his classmates left the buckets on the step, one of the boys urinated in the water. Dad said that he and his classmates were so upset, that they reported the matter to Mr. Antrobus who quickly settled the problem by administering twenty-one lashes with the tamarind rod to the offending student! That disgusting student later became a very accomplished and respected St. Philip gentleman,

At age fourteen, Dad left school to become a mason. His preference was to be an electrician, but his mother made the decision for him based purely on economic considerations. After tallying the cost of tools for the various trades, Granny Harewood settled for masonry because she would only have to purchase three tools–a square, a float, and a trowel.

Masonry took Dad to all eleven parishes, first on foot, and later on his bicycle. He told me that he apprenticed for three years at Searles Factory in Christ Church with Earnest Brown. Mr. Brown was from Padmore Village, and he was such a skilled mason that his contemporaries called him Dr. Brown. Dad got his first job as a mason at Three Houses Plantation in St. Philip where he worked side-by-side with Dr. Brown. His assignment was to repair the scrambler and the chimney. He cut the bricks with a hatchet or bill. In 1920 he moved to Carrington Factory in St. Philip where his mentor was a man called Happy Roach from Brereton's Village. He stayed in that position until 1924. During his time as a mason, Dad worked on various family homes, as well as on buildings such as Thickets House, Three Houses Plantation, Carrington Factory, the Queen Elizabeth Hospital, and many other well known and not so well known places around Barbados.

Dad left his job as a mason in 1924 and took a job as a butler at Dalkeith House in St. Michael. He told me that he found that job to be very demeaning, because he was expected to stay and cleanup after every party. One Saturday night he left Dalkeith House and never returned! After a brief stint back at Carrington Factory, he next sought a job as a chauffer.

Dad received his driver's license in 1926, and shortly after he took a job with Mr. Garner working for twenty percent on the dollar. I can still see the excitement in his eyes as he told me that after Garner's chauffer resigned, he got to drive the Studebaker. His client was Mrs. Gladys Ince from Hopewell Plantation in St. Philip. Mrs. Ince later taught me at the Lodge School. His fee for driving Mrs. Ince was fifteen shillings per week!

Granny Harewood's only daughter was baptized as Muriel. Everyone called her Aunt Ene. She lived in the family home with Granny Harewood. Aunt Ene was a slim, elegant lady, who like Granny Harewood had spent most of her life working at Edgcumbe Plantation. She was hired as a seamstress, and I remember vividly the buggy with the driver decked out in his formal uniform and long whip coming to pick her up at the family home in Church Village for the trip to Edgcumbe Plantation. When I was a youngster, she was still working at Edgcumbe maybe one or two days per week. Whatever her schedule, they never failed to send the buggy for her.

Aunt Ene was a deeply religious person who spent most of her life worshiping with the Church of God denomination. She was an accomplished musician who owned an organ. One of the reasons Peggy and I loved to visit with Granny Harewood and Aunt Ene was to get to play the organ. It had two foot-pedals that our feet could not reach when we sat on the mahogany stool in front of the keyboard. Peggy and I solved that problem by taking turns depressing the foot-pedals with our hands while the other tried to coax the ivory keys to play a tune from the Smallwood book that Aunt Ene used to help us develop our musical skills. Aunt Ene was a great music tutor, and she taught me many of the favorite tunes that were written by musicians from an earlier era. Whenever I hear the tune "A Carnival in Venice" or any of the music from Smallwood's Piano Tutor, I always think of Aunt Ene.

Granny Harewood's home was a place where I also got to meet my cousins Graydon, Freddy, Pip, and Tony Sealy. These were my Uncle Cammie's children. They lived in Four Cross Roads, St. John with their older siblings Sylvia, Phyllis, Pauline, and Opal. Granny would invite us all to visit with her during summer vacation, including Dad's son Ivan. She tried her best to remind us of the importance of family and the value of maintaining strong connections with our first cousins. It was largely as a result of her efforts, that I have developed lasting relationships with all of Uncle Cammie's children.

I was always intrigued by the story Mum told me about how she met Dad. She told me that in 1926, she was attracted to a young man called Evelyn Hinkson. He was the son of Mr. Hinkson, a local butcher. She said that Evelyn was a handsome young man who had attended Combermere School, a secondary school in the City of Bridgetown. On leaving Combermere, he apprenticed with a Mr. John Codrington, a joiner who lived in Massiah Street. Evelyn and John were frequent visitors to the Kidney family home, and they even combined their talents to build a round table for Granny Kidney. The table provided Evelyn with the perfect opportunity to endear himself to my grandmother. Every time he visited the Kidney household, the table became the focal point of the conversation.

Mum's friendship with Evelyn grew as the frequency of his visits to her home increased. Her favorite color during the time of her friendship with Evelyn was green. She wore green almost every time she and Evelyn were together. She told me that she was wearing a beautiful green dress on the night her first child was conceived. She gave birth to a healthy baby boy and named him Douglas LeRoy. We all called him Roy.

Mum said that after Roy's birth, her affection for Evelyn began to wane when she learned that while he was seeing her, he was also courting two other young ladies, both of whom she knew. One night while attending a dance at the Society Model School she finally got her chance to get even with Evelyn. While dancing with a young man who was a friend of the family, she was confronted by a very jealous Evelyn. She said that in an effort to separate her from her dancing partner, Evelyn grabbed her by the arm causing her gold bangle to fall from her wrist to the floor. She said that she was very upset by his action, but before she could even say a word, a young man named

Glenville Harewood came to her rescue. He intervened, cautioning Evelyn to leave her alone. Then after he retrieved her bangle from the floor, Glenville offered to escort her home. It was an act of bravery that neither she nor her best friend Elaine McKeckney ever forgot. Mum later refused Evelyn's offer of marriage, preferring to raise Roy as a single parent. She also developed an aversion to wearing green that lasted for the rest of her life.

Dad's friendship with Mum grew stronger, and according to Mum's friend Elaine, everyone except Mum felt that marriage was just around the corner. Elaine said that she was so confident that the two would wed, that one day when Mum was grinding chocolate in the kitchen she told her directly, "Dell, I bet you that you are going to marry Glenville!" Mum accepted the bet believing that such a marriage would never happen. Elaine pledged that if she won the bet she would drink a glass of rum straight-up on the day the couple got married.

After a short courtship, Dad visited the Kidney family home at College Land with his mother Drucilla, his sister Muriel, and his great uncle Mr. Pilgrim from Parish Land, St. Philip to announce his engagement to Mum. The families talked about the arrangements for the wedding, and a date was set for the ceremony. Approximately four months later, Mum and Dad were married at Society Chapel, and the wedding reception was held at the Kidney family home on College Land. That day, Mum's friend Elaine celebrated her talent for predicting the future by drinking a glass of rum straight-up.

Mum told me that she got dressed in Massiah Street at the home of B. L. Barrow (BL). BL was a person who had attained significant status in the parish, as a member of the vestry and as a successful businessman. He was also Granny Kidney's cousin. Mum's eyes would always light up when she talked about her wedding dress. She was so proud of the fact that it was sent from New York by her sister Eudie. She described it as an all-white satin gown, accented by a long-sleeved, round-back bolero jacket made from lace. She said that she also wore white gloves and a white headpiece that were also sent from New York. She recalled that her longtime friend Gwendolyn Shepherd, who was a teacher at the Society Model School, was there to help her get dressed. Mum always liked to say that the first person to see her all decked out in her shimmering wedding gown was Marie Barrow, BL's youngest daughter. Apparently, Marie was so curious to see how Mum looked in her dress that she sneaked up the stairs, gently pushed the door ajar, and peeked through the narrow opening to take a quick look at the young bride.

After she was completely dressed, Mum said that she left BL's home for the ten minute trip by car to Society Chapel. BL was driving his sedate black American Ford automobile. I couldn't believe it when Dad pointed out that in 1934, BL was one of three black men from that region who owned cars. The other two were Mr. Garner from Church Village, and Mr. Maxwell from Bayfield. Mum told me that it was around four o'clock in the evening when BL's car arrived at the chapel. She said that he pulled the car to a stop in front of the main entrance to the building, got out and ran around to the passenger side to open the door for her. As she stepped out of the car in all of her bridal splendor, she remembered hearing BL cautioning the very large crowd that had gathered in front of the chapel not to take pictures or throw flowers, rice, or anything on the bride. Mum said that BL had heard that a local family was very distraught over the fact that Dad had selected her as his bride instead of their daughter, so BL did not want to take any chances.

Mum was always proud to tell me that her cousin Winnie Alleyne dressed the six flower girls who preceded her into the chapel. She said that they scattered rose petals generously on the aisle as BL escorted her up towards the altar. Mum remembered that as she was walking up the aisle she could see Dad waiting patiently at the altar with his bestman Mr. Garner. When she reached her place at the altar, she said that she stood quietly with her bridesmaid at her side. She was enthralled by the beauty of the anthurium lilies and bouquets of local flowers that seemed to be everywhere. Father J. C. Whipple, Principal of Codrington College conducted the ceremony in traditional Anglican style. After the service, the couple was escorted back to BL's car in preparation for the short drive down College Hill to Granny Kidney's house. Mum told me that there were twenty-two cars in the wedding procession that day.

The reception at Granny Kidney's house lived up to everyone's expectation. The food included two goats, one provided by Uncle John and the other by Elaine McKeckney's mother. Granny Kidney bought a suckling pig. It was baked by Gertrude Drayton, a relative, and had a potato stuffed into its mouth. Gertrude also baked a four-tiered cake that was cut up into small squares for distribution to the many friends and well-wishers in attendance. Iris Spence, a family member and teacher at the Rawle Training Institute, was given the top tier of the cake to be shared with the female student trainees. Flavius Knight and Sammie Hinds, both bailiffs from Church Village, and BL, were the speakers on that auspicious occasion!

The newlyweds did not go on a honeymoon. Instead, they retired to the modest two-bedroom home in St. John where Mum grew up. They took the smaller bedroom on the north side of the house, next to the shedroof. Dad continued to work for Mr. Goddard as a bus driver. He changed jobs twice during that period, first he drove for Mr. Lucas, of Parish Land, St. Philip, and later he drove for the Eckstein Brothers Company in St. Michael.

Mum and Dad's first child, was a six-and-a-half month, premature baby girl. One of the local midwives, Mrs. Cumberbatch, assisted Mum during labor, and she gave birth in the early afternoon. The infant was not doing well, and Mum said that she was very concerned. The day after the baby's birth, the Reverend J. C. Whipple, Principal of Codrington College was returning from a church function in Queens Park in Bridgetown, and when Mum saw his car she asked her mother to let the Principal know that she needed his help. He came into the house, saw the baby, and decided to admit her into the church by private baptism right there in Granny Kidney's house! Before proceeding with the baptism, he asked Mum what she wanted to name the child. Because she could not think of the name that she had chosen, the Nun who accompanied the Principal suggested that they could use her name, which was Mary Joyce. That is how my sister got her name. Fortunately, Joyce's condition quickly improved, and Mum was forever grateful for the decision she made that day to have the Principal bless her new baby.

Two years later, my brother Ralph was born. Mum was still living at Granny Kidney's house and Mrs. Cumberbatch again assisted with the delivery. In his excitement at the birth of their first son, Dad wanted to name the baby boy after a famous boxer Kid Ralph. Mum was not happy with naming her son Kid, and expressed her displeasure. As a compromise, they agreed to name him Ralph Kidney Harewood, but Dad always affectionately called him Kid.

During the same year that Kid was born, Dad learned that one of his friends who lived in Well House, St. Philip wanted to sell his house. Mum and Dad thought that it was a good idea to purchase the house and move the family to St. Philip. Mum said that she borrowed thirteen shillings from Ma-Ma Hart a relative, to complete the down payment on the house. The family moved to Well House in 1937, the same year that Barbadians took to the streets to express their displeasure with the deteriorating working conditions in that tiny British colony. It was the first and only time that Barbadians rioted to improve their social and economic conditions. Aunt Mam, Granny Kidney's sister, moved in with the family in Well House after an argument with her husband forced her to flee to a more secure location.

Joyce and Kid told me that the neighborhood in Well House was very charming. Over the years, Mum always reminisced about the wonderful times she spent there. Well House was a typical village in the Parish of St Philip. The open spaces were mainly flat, arid, grass-covered pastures that were generally used by the neighbors for grazing their sheep and goats. The stiff tradewinds that brought the early settlers to Barbados swept across the barren landscape every minute of every day, adding to the very special character of the Well House community.

A gentleman called Earnest Waithe had a small dry goods shop next door to our family home in Well House, and a very nice lady, Ma Harewood (not related) lived in the back. Mum adored Ma Harewood and considered her to be a valued member of the extended Harewood family. When Joyce was three years old, Mum enrolled her in Bailey's Girl's School, a primary school not far from the family home. A neighbor's child Coreen assisted Mum by keeping an eye on Joyce as she made her way to and from school everyday. Kid attended the Shrewsbury Boy's School and his chaperon was the son of a Mr. Williams who was one of Dad's colleagues at the bus company.

I was born in Granny Kidney's home at College Land. The events of that day were firmly etched in Mum's mind because my birth was by far her most difficult. Consistent with tradition, she called the midwife to assist with my delivery and the postpartum chores. On that occasion, however, Mrs. Cumberbatch who was a nurse at the St. John's Almshouse was unavailable to render her professional services as she had done so ably in the past. Instead Mrs. Smith who lived on College Tenantry was called to serve as midwife. Mum's account of what happened next is as follows. Mrs. Smith was working in the field when the call came for her assistance. There was no running water available to her as she made the trek across the sugarcane field, through the narrow grassy path to Granny Kidney's house, and in her haste to help Mum, she did not wash her hands properly. Mum said that she contracted an infection during the delivery and became gravely ill. The next day, Sunday, Granny Kidney called Dr. Muir from St. Philip. He arrived at the house around four o'clock in the evening and gave her a "tablet." Then he took my brother Roy with him to the dispensary and had a prescription filled.

Mum's recovery was slow. After my baptism at Society Chapel on June 11, she went to stay with Gertrude Drayton in Silver Sands, Christ Church. It was a well-deserved week of recuperation. I was sent to Granny Harewood's house in Church Village while Mum remained at Silver Sands. When she was fully recovered, she and I were reunited at Well House and the normal bonding between a mother and her young son began.

Tradition at that time required a member of the family to report my birth to the police station at District-C in St. Philip. Because the office at District-C was closed on the Saturday of my birth, Mum's friend Elaine transmitted the information to the police station on the Monday. The officer on duty erroneously recorded the Monday as my official birthday rather than the Saturday!

Two years later, Mum gave birth to my sister Peggy Irma in the family home at St John. Because of the difficulty encountered with my birth, Mum told me that she called Montel Ford who lived approximately one hundred yards away on the spot where the Butcher's later lived. Montel would run across the sugarcane field to call Mrs. Smith, the midwife. Peggy's birth was without incident, but later she caught a cold and Mum rushed her to Dr. Carter at Villanova. The remedy–massage her navel with castor oil. The treatment worked just as Dr. Carter predicted and Peggy made a swift recovery.

When my brother Roger was born, Mrs. Smith again took care of the delivery and as customary, Mum stayed indoors for nine days. Following this period of forced confinement, she was permitted to leave the bedroom daily to sit in the living room and go outdoors, returning indoors one half hour later each day. This was in keeping with the practice of having a staged return to normalcy to avoid catching what Barbadians referred to as a "lining" cold!

Sometime after Roger's birth, Mum and Dad opened a shop in Church Village. St. Philip. The shop was rented from the Knight family, and was located at the corner of the main highway and the road entering the Upper Village. They sold dry goods and liquor. I remember that shop very well. It was an old wooden structure, unpainted, and with a high, narrow countertop. It was separated from a modest residence by a three-foot space, and a block of coral stone was placed at the door to help us negotiate our way from the shop to the house. On the north side of the property was an unpaved shed where men from the neighborhood would gather on Sundays to exchange stories and play draughts.

I was about five or six years old when Dad left to go to America. He and several other Barbadian men were selected by the Labor Department to join the civilian effort that was directed at providing a steady stream of supplies to the Allied Forces fighting the Nazis in Europe. Dad talked at length about the dangers of their wartime travel to the U.S., and especially about the threat they faced from German U-Boats in the Atlantic Ocean. Joyce was a tremendous resource to Mum during the time that Dad was away in America.

When Dad returned to Barbados, he moved the business in Church Village across the street where he constructed a new shop and house. I remember the house was built from purple heart wood. The shop was much larger than the one Dad previously occupied, and it included a bar where the locals would gather to "fire" a rum or two. A one-bedroom house was attached to the shop. It had a spacious veranda that faced the road, a large living and dining area, and a kitchen and shedroof that were both unfinished. There was a ten-foot drop from the back door to the backyard. For some reason, Dad chose not to build a stairway that would have rendered the back door fully functional. The backyard was completely enclosed by a galvanized paling. The parcel of land on which the new shop and house were built was rented from Mr. Joy Moseley who lived adjacent to Dad's property.

As usual, Dad was very resourceful in executing the plan for that second family home. Along the perimeter of the paling, he planted marrow vines that bore beautiful, green marrows. He also built a pen for the special breed of pigs he purchased from the Grove Agricultural Station; and he installed an above ground pond for the flock of ducks he kept in the backyard. The one thing I remember best about our Church Village home is the Philips shortwave radio that Dad kept in the corner of the living room. It was my lifeline to the rest of the world. I would sit alone at night listening to programs broadcast from places like Quito, Ecuador, and London, and New York; or I could pretend that I had a ringside seat at one of Sugar Ray Robinson's exciting championship fights from New York. That reliable old radio, with its smoothly polished, mahogany stained exterior was perched on top of a dark brown swivel table that Dad built. It was powered by electricity that was generated from a wind mill that we called a "Wind Charger." It was positioned just in front of the veranda to take advantage of the strong easterly breezes that swept over the open sugarcane fields across from our home. The "Wind Charger" was not constructed like a typical windmill. Instead it had a simple two-blade propeller mounted on a forty-foot metal pole. A metal contraption formed the hub that connected the wooden propeller to the flat metal tail that was oriented vertically. It was the tail that enabled the "Wind Charger" to respond to changes in wind direction. A fan belt connected the propeller to a generator that was identical to those used in automobiles of that period. A wooden panel, replete with ammeters and capacitors assisted Dad with measuring and managing the current that was finally captured by and stored in a regular car battery that Dad kept in a corner of the shop. Our house was wired to facilitate distribution of the wind-generated electric current from the battery to the light switches and the receptacles that were conveniently placed throughout the house and shop. Dad always kept one battery connected to the "Wind Charger" to capture electricity, and a second battery off-line to supply current to the house and shop. Watching Dad manage that simple renewable energy system, taught me a lifelong lesson about the importance of science in our everyday lives, and provided me with a basic understanding of the principles of electricity.

When my brother Roger was an infant, Mum took him to live with her in Church Village. It was a very demanding time in her life. She was taking care of the family needs while assisting Dad with managing the business. During that period, she depended on Granny Harewood to help her with babysitting chores. Mum made arrangements with Darcus, a neighbor who would take Roger to stay with Granny Harewood during the day. One day, Granny Harewood had an appointment and could not keep Roger. Darcus volunteered to help, and from that day Roger stayed with her. Three other people lived in Darcus' house: her daughter Wrinkle; Wrinkle's husband Darryl; and a young man named Harry whose connection to Darcus was not clear to any of us. While at Darcus, Roger developed a bad rash at the back of his neck, which took a long time to heal. When Granny Kidney came to Church Village and saw Roger's condition, she asked Mum if she could take him with her back to College.

Granny Kidney was a gentle person, self-confident, and completely adjusted to living alone. She was no more than five feet tall, always neatly dressed, and known for her signature head tie. It was a white cotton scarf that was always starched, ironed, and neatly folded to cover her entire head. She was a loving lady, who was deeply religious. Like Roger, I spent a lot of quality time with her, and I especially liked it when she read selected passages from the Bible to me, or taught me one of her favorite hymns. Everytime I read the Old Testament story about Abraham and Isaac or hear it mentioned in church, I always think of Granny Kidney. I also experience a similar emotion whenever I hear the hymn "Beneath the Cross of Jesus." Those days that I spent sitting with Granny Kidney in her favorite rocking chair as she read the Bible or sang from her hymn book are permanently etched in my memory.

As a youngster, soon after it got dark, I would accompany Roger to Granny Kidney's house. As soon as we reached the walkway, without warning, he would take off at full speed, running across the rough surface, up the coral stone steps that led to the front door. I would keep watch until he was safely inside the house. I remember that ritual well, and was fully aware of Roger's fear of the dark. On occasion, I would even sleep over at Granny Kidney's house to convince Roger that there was no ulterior motive for him being the one singled out to live with our grandmother. Roger continued to sleep at Granny Kidney's house until he secured his first job in Bridgetown. I was always impressed by Roger's aggressive and independent nature. In order to avoid having to make the daily roundtrip between College and Bridgetown, he moved to live with his godmother Elaine in Villa Road, St. Michael in 1962.

Philip's birth was the one I remember the best. I was sitting on the front steps of our family home playing with my marbles when Mum went into labor. Immediately a call went out to the midwife, Mrs. Ersyl Jackman. It was amazing how effectively the communications network was then, because Mrs. Jackman would lose little time in responding to the call. I remained on the front step while she entered the bedroom to take care of the birth of my youngest brother. Mum went through the expected routine of remaining confined for nine days, and then adhered strictly to the procedure that enabled her to resume her role as homemaker.

I spent the first two years of my life in Well House. My memory of those early years is very sketchy, but Joyce and Kid have shared many interesting stories with me about their experiences growing up in that community. There were scary stories, like the time when Aunt Mam, Joyce, and Kid were drawing water from the standpipe using a homemade wooden cart. On the way back from the standpipe they claimed that they saw a two-headed turkey coming down from Bailey's School. It was an experience that Joyce and Kid always talked about at family gatherings.

Then there was the time when Dad took Joyce and Kid to Bottom Bay in St. Philip. His routine was to leave the children sitting on the sand while he tested the surf. That day, the sea at Bottom Bay was very turbulent, and Dad soon discovered that he could not leave the kids unattended. A huge wave rolled in and engulfed them, pulling them into the churning Atlantic Ocean. Dad rushed into action, retrieving Kid who was rolling with the rising surf. Joyce was also caught up by the surging tide. Dad rushed to her aid, grabbing the frightened youngster and racing with her to the safety of the shore. Relieved and exhausted, Dad packed all of his and the children's belongings and headed home. Mum said that Dad never took the kids swimming at Bottom Bay since that incident.

In 1941, Mum and Dad received some bad news from the owner of the land on which their house in Well House was located. Over the years Mum was firmly convinced that the owner's action was motivated by jealousy. Dad was a very resourceful husband, and he invested an inordinate amount of time in whitewashing the foundation to his home and painting the interior and exterior. He cleaned the yard and added a kitchen. He purchased a Coleman lantern and the glow from that lamp illuminated the entire neighborhood every night. The owner's envy seemed to increase with every improvement Dad made to the property. It soon became too much for him to bear, and it was then that he informed Mum and Dad of his intention to terminate their lease. Dad quickly made arrangements to relocate the family to College Land, St. John.

Chapter 3

Family Matters

Aunt Mam lived in Sargent Street with her husband Uncle John Antrobus. She was an amazing member of the family. Loving, self-confident, strong, healthy, god-fearing, generous with her love and service, and skilled in the art of self-sustenance. Her husband John was a giant of a man. He was the neighborhood's joiner. He made furniture for Harrison's, one of the up-scale department stores in Bridgetown. He and Aunt Mam also operated a shop on the spot where the Wilkerson's later built their home. Aunt Mam and Uncle John's rum shop was popular for its black pudding and souse that she made every Saturday.

Dad bought his pudding and souse from Aunt Mam. It was through this patronage that he first saw Mum, a young girl assisting Aunt Mam in the shop. The shop was originally located in Sargent Street across from a man called Sol Do who was a tinsmith. He handled cans and made kerosene lamps. Sargent Street was a prominent community at that time. It was a narrow street, dotted with small, well-appointed chattel houses. Mum told me that when she was a little girl, there were three small shops serving that neighborhood. They included Miss Kitt's shop, a three-door structure close to Bath Hill, Ma-Ma Hart's shop, and Mr. Marshall's shop.

Aunt Mam's marriage to Uncle John was fraught with problems that eventually led to their separation. He was an abusive husband who drank more than his share of alcohol, and threatened her constantly. On one occasion, a family argument escalated into threats of violence, and Aunt Mam sought shelter at Mum and Dad in Well House. Dad was so upset that he told her that she could stay with them for as long as she desired. She accepted Dad's offer, and moved into our family home at

Well House. She continued to live with us until her death on October 17, 1960.

My first memories of Aunt Mam are hazy at best. I knew that she owned a house across the street from our home in College Land. The house was an old weather-beaten wooden structure. There was a set of concrete steps leading from the public road to an unpaved landing at the perimeter of the property. The unusual thing about those steps was the fact that they were not connected to anything! They simply ended in that unpaved area of scrub grass and rock. Perhaps they were built to provide access to the entrance of a home that previously occupied that site and was much closer to the highway. The front of her house faced south towards Maud Barrow's house, where Lay-Lay and the Labbie lived. A small parcel of land with three large breadfruit trees separated the two houses.

As a young boy, I remember that Beryl Gittens lived in Aunt Mam's house. I was told that she rented the house. Beryl was a tough lady who worked hard to make ends meet for herself and her children, all of whom lived with her in Aunt Mam's house. There was Micey, and Mossa the older girls, and Nigel (we called him Old Man), and Pet, and Janice. Beryl was a fish seller. She went to Conset Bay every day and whatever fish the boats brought in, she would compete with the other fish sellers for her share of the catch. With her wooden tray filled with the day's catch and perched precariously on her head, she walked all the way from Conset Bay through our neighborhood "hawking" her load until the last fish was sold.

The most vivid memory I have of Beryl is from Sea Egg season. To most Barbadians, the white spiny Sea Urchin is a delicacy. Every year, from September through April divers went into the bay to catch Sea Eggs by the thousands. They brought the catch ashore, cracked the shells open on the beach, cleaned them, and harvested the delicate roes for sale. Fish sellers like Beryl took the roes and carefully pack them into the empty shell. A seagrape leaf, twisted to form a cone, was filled with the delicious roes and placed on top of the shell. When the catch was bountiful, Beryl would cook the Sea Eggs in her kitchen and sell them to the families in the neighborhood. One evening, I remember eating so many of her steamed Sea Eggs that I fell ill. I was bloated, nauseous and unable to eat anything for a while. It was a terrible experience that has forever shattered my appetite for the very tasty Sea Urchin.

Much like Beryl, Aunt Mam was a very resourceful lady. She was up at the crack of dawn gathering wood for the fire, "staking out" the sheep and goats, and feeding the pigs and chickens. She always taught me that "the early bird gets the sweetest worm!" Aunt Mam practiced what she preached. I don't know how she knew when there were potatoes for sale at Victoria Plantation or Bath Plantation, or that they were picking pigeon peas at Bryan Hill or Society. I accompanied her whenever I could, especially during the summer vacation. A plantation overseer coordinated the sale. Aunt Mam would try to find out which rows were "breaking well" meaning yielding the most sweet potatoes. She would then buy several rows and proceed to dig. As she dug, I would take the freshly harvested tubers and pack them in a crocus bag. When the job was finished and the bag was filled with potatoes, she lifted it onto her head with some assistance from me, and we began the long walk home.

Mornings in St. John were delightful. From the front window of our home, I could see the sun rising in the east. It resembled a brilliant spotlight creeping slowly upwards from below the grey horizon. It seemed to me that the sun also signaled the blackbirds in the trees around our home to begin their morning chatter. Aunt Mam told me to listen closely to what they were saying. She convinced me that those birds always chanted in unison, "Miss Betsy Jane, Miss Betsy Jane, the coffee sweeet, sweeet, sweeet!" The doves on the other hand were much more disciplined in their behavior. They were very reserved in their demeanor, and Aunt Mam would tell me that if I listened carefully I would hear them coo, "Moses, speak God's word."

Aunt Mam's entrepreneurial spirit never allowed her to go without having something in her wooden tray for sale. She sold sugar cakes, peanuts, bananas, ackees, sweet potatoes, breadfruits, golden apples, and anything that she could get her hands on. Her moneybag was always filled with coins, and she knew how to "cut and contrive." That moneybag was my ATM, my ticket to the Exhibition, the Civic, and to the movies in Bridgetown. It was the source of my lunch money and bus fare.

It was a virtual lifeline that she extended to me during those formative years that I spent in rural St. John.

Later, when I was a student at the Lodge School, Aunt Mam was very, very proud of me. I never fully understood the impact that my achievement would have on someone like Aunt Mam who grew up in the post-slavery era. To Aunt Mam and those of her generation, Lodge School was symbolic of the planter society that still had a firm grip on the lives of most Barbadians. People like Aunt Mam and others in her age group viewed Lodge School as the original gated community. Children of the white planter class and white expatriates felt like they had exclusive rights to attend that school, and reside in its dormitory. While the classrooms were integrated, the boarding school was reserved for whites only. So against that backdrop, Aunt Mam was proud of my achievement, and reluctant to do anything that she felt would embarrass me.

Selling her sugar cakes and peanuts on my school campus was something she could not bring herself around to doing. I can only remember one occasion when she came to Lodge School with her tray filed with goodies. On that day, she remained on the perimeter of the campus, not wanting to let anyone know that we were related. Yes, that was my Aunt Mam, a person who always put pride in family before money or anything else.

In the late 1950s after scrubbing the floor she complained of not feeling well. I found out later that she suffered a stroke that paralyzed her on her right side. The stroke confined Aunt Mam to bed for the remainder of her life. It was difficult for me to see her in that condition. This very independent lady having to wait for one of us to help her with the simplest task. When the day came for me to leave Barbados to travel to New York to enter college, I was torn apart. I had no idea if I would ever see my Aunt Mam again. We embraced and wept uncontrollably. I left Barbados in August, 1960, and it was in October when I learned that this gracious lady, my "Rock of Gibraltar" had passed away. Aunt Eude and I cried our eyes out. We both knew that one of the stalwarts in our family had been called home.

Mum's best friend was Elaine McKeckney. She was four years younger than Mum. She lived in a small wooden house that was perched on top of College Hill. I can still remember the view from the McKeckney house. It was spectacular!

Elaine once told me that her grandmother Augusta Matilda McKeckney was originally from the parish of St. George. She moved to St. John where she met and married Elaine's grandfather Mr. McKeckney. Elaine recalled that Mr. McKeckney came to Barbados from Scotland. Her family and my family therefore shared this Scottish connection. The admixture of genes was much more obvious in her family than in mine. Elaine said that her grandmother Augusta had five children. Her mother Louisa Matilda Baker was the fourth child. Louisa had three children, Elaine, Maude, and Viola. Elaine and Maude were mulatto, while Viola was dark skinned. Elaine met Mum when the two girls were in their teenage years, and they remained best friends for the rest of their lives.

By any measure, Elaine was a statuesque beauty. Her good looks combined with her vivacious personality were a combination that was hard to match. She was also a genuine extrovert, and an accomplished storyteller. The most hilarious tale she ever told me was about a lady called Boozing. One Sunday afternoon, Boozing and her sister came to visit Elaine. As they entered the narrow, unpaved walkway, it started to rain. Boozing was quite upset because she had just done her hair and was concerned about getting wet. So instead of following the regular course of the walkway, Boozing took a shortcut across the yard. Little did she know that the McKeckney's had an open pit in the yard that served as the family's outdoor toilet. The thin sheets of galvanized aluminum that covered the pit could not support Boozing's weight, and she fell into the pit. It was an unforgettable sight. Boozing in her lovely dress with her fresh hairdo, stuck in the pit of doo doo! The family members rushed to her rescue, and they took her to College Spring where they helped her wash her troubles away.

Granny Kidney was very fond of Elaine, and encouraged her friendship with Mum. Mum and Elaine spent a lot of time together. Elaine would walk the mile and a half to Granny Kidney's house, and she and Mum would exchange stories about their families and their personal aspirations. Their love for sewing brought them even closer. Mrs. Alleyne who lived on College Tenantry taught Mum how to sew. Mum in turn, shared most of what she knew with her dear friend Elaine. The two of them made cassocks for the students at Codrington College. They also sewed for many of the residents in the neighborhood.

In 1941, Mum and Dad received a note from their landlord informing them that he would no longer be able to rent them the land at Well House. They were both devastated. After sharing the news with Granny Kidney, she suggested that they should consider moving to an attractive plot of land close to where she was living. Dad agreed and lost little time in preparing the spot for the move. He constructed a foundation of coral stone, and reinforced it with two sturdy steel rails from the abandoned railroad track. He prepared an impressive entrance with a well-constructed limestone stairway that formed the gateway to the house.

On the day of the move, several of Dad's closest friends, under the leadership of an experienced carpenter, carefully took the house apart, section-by-section. Each of those sections was loaded onto a truck and transported from Well House to College Land where the team reversed the process, systematically reconstructing the family home.

The house with its bright green, French style entrance, and its neatly shingled gable roof was an imposing presence in that quiet hillside community. The front of the house faced east towards Conset Bay, In fact, I could see Conset Bay, College Savannah, and the lighthouse at Ragged Point from every window in the living room.

The living room was connected to the dining room (shedroof) by a narrow hallway that we called the passage. Initially the house had two bedrooms, one on the north side and the other on the south side of the passage. As the family expanded, Dad added a third bedroom on the south side of the shedroof in the space that had earlier served as the kitchen. That old kitchen had a brick hearth and a dirt floor. It also had a large barrel for storing potable water. The new kitchen with its cast iron wood stove was constructed on the north side of the house at the other end of the shedroof. The backyard was small but functional. A narrow pathway carved out of the bedrock from the hill traversed the back yard parallel to the shedroof. That footpath facilitated movement from one side of the yard to the other. Five-foot wooden gates secured each end of the back yard. Solid rock elevated approximately two to three feet above the footpath formed a permanent surface for the remainder of the back yard. The entire area was enclosed by a galvanized aluminum paling. A small outdoor toilet, a large pig pen, and multiple fowl coops decorated the inner perimeter of the paling.

Although Dad was not trained as a landscape architect, he had a great sense of how to layout the grounds surrounding our home. On the left or south side of the house he planted a cluster of flamboyant trees. These were gorgeous shade trees that bore a beautiful red flower. During their flowering season which began in May and ended around August, these trees would be ablaze with the most brilliant red flowers, accented by their uniformly green, fern-like leaves. I loved to play with the soft, pod-like sepals that I would fill with air and pretend that they were tiny, colorful balloons. Next to the flamboyant trees, Dad planted a soursop tree. That was a low branching, bushy tree that bore an irregularly shaped fruit covered with soft, pliable spines. Unlike the flamboyant trees, the soursop tree was unattractive, and to make matters worse, my siblings and I always believed that it was the spookiest tree that we had on our grounds. At night that tree made a noise that sounded like sand falling on its oblong, dark-green leaves. The children in the neighborhood always said that duppies were responsible for the noise the tree made. So every day after the sun went down, I always keep my distance from the soursop tree.

Bordering the north side of the property, Dad planted a row of olive trees. These were beautiful trees with narrow oblong leaves that bore a small fruit. It seemed as though they were resistant to attack from any of the insects that preyed on the plants that surrounded our home. In fact, branches of the olive tree were always used to keep the mosquitoes away. Dad also planted a grape vine that adorned the top of the carport that was at the front of the house. That plant bore a small greenish fruit typical of the grapes produced in the vineyards of northern California, and rarely seen in Barbados. I don't know where Dad got that plant, but I enjoyed eating the large bunches of white grapes it frequently produced.

The soil on the sides and front of our home was rich, deep, dark, and highly fertile. To the front, my siblings and I kept a kitchen garden. We planted parallel rows of cabbage, lettuce, string beans, shallots, carrots, and beets in neat, rectangular beds of soil that were raised six to eight inches above the ground. I was always awestruck when I saw the first signs of the tiny green shoots pushing through the clumps of dark soil seeking to access their primary source of energy–sunlight. Year-round, our kitchen gardens always provided us with plenty of fresh vegetables. The land on both sides of the house was used to produce spinach, pumpkin, corn, sweet potatoes, and okras. We planted pigeon peas along the perimeter of our land, and together with the other crops, we were able to grow a lot of what we ate.

A large flower-fence hedge ran along the front of our property providing privacy and security. No one would dare try to crawl through our flower-fence hedge. The thick branches were covered with thorns, and one encounter with those thorns was enough to discourage anyone from making a second effort. To the left of the hedge was a large evergreen tree.

The evergreen tree was a beautiful addition to the landscape. Its thick green foliage was on display all year round, providing lots of shade from the blazing morning and afternoon sun. Its extensive network of roots was visible at the base of the trunk, forming a convenient sitting area before they disappeared into the rich soil below. My friends and I spent many hours under the evergreen tree. I often enjoyed climbing that tree to scan the horizon for passing ships.

One day I was perched at the top of the tree when I spotted a warship on the horizon. I was so excited that I desperately wanted to share my excitement with Peggy, Roger, and Philip. I vaguely remember saying, "Peggy, Roger, Phil, look," and before I could say another work, I heard a dull thud, and found myself lying on my side in the gully below, narrowly missing a large stone. I had fallen from a distance of at least twelve to fifteen feet! All I could think of at that time is that I had died, and as I wailed in surprise and pain, I was distinctly heard muttering these words over and over, " Uh ded, Uh ded, Uh ded!"

Our neighbor Beryl came running to my rescue. My left arm was hurting badly but there was no way to fully determine the severity of my injuries. It was time for one of those trips to the clinic at the St. John Almshouse, approximately two miles from where I had fallen. My friend Elton Marshall took me to the clinic on Dad's bicycle, and I soon learned that I had fractured one of the bones in my left arm. I wore a cast for approximately six weeks before my arm finally healed. It was a lesson that I never forgot.

Chapter 4

The Model School

Mum told me that there were three schools that children of ex-slaves who lived on plantation lands formally owned by Christopher Codrington attended. There was a girls' school, a boys' school, and an infants' school. Together they occupied a single building that was called the Society Estates School. That building was erected in Chapel Hill on a parcel of land next to Society Chapel (now called Holy Cross Church). Prior to emancipation, there was little enthusiasm to educate black children, so the Society Estates School was initially used as a place where children who were too young to work on the plantation could stay. The curriculum was designed simply to teach those children moral lessons until their parents returned from the fields at the end of the day. Black children were kept in that school until they were old enough to be drafted into the third gang. After emancipation, the status of the schools that were established to prepare black children for the third gang, was upgraded, and the children were assigned to classes where they were taught to read and write.

In 1915, when the Reverend Arthur H. Anstey became Principal of Codrington College, he built a school at the top of College Hill and called it the Society Model School. He then made arrangements to transfer all of the black students from the Society Estates School to the Society Model School. Two years later, Principal Anstey renovated the Society Estates School and converted it into a new secondary school for white girls called Codrington High School. Every time Mum and I passed by that building with its high, coral stone walls and gated entrance, she would remind me of the time when that school catered exclusively to black children whose parents were living on lands that were part of the Christopher Codrington estate.

Mum, Aunt Eudie, and Uncle Lionel attended the Society Model School along with many of their friends from College Land. Mr. Crawford was headmaster then, and, the boys, girls, and infants shared the same facility.

Barbadian author Dr. Dan Carter in his book entitled "The Story of Society Primary School (1795-2006)" provides a detailed account of the development of the Society School System. I was pleasantly surprised to learn from his writings, that the Society Model School has the distinction of being the first elementary school for blacks in Barbados.

It was at the Society Model School, later known as Society Mixed School where I learned to read and write. The building was only two stories high, but from its perch at the top of College Hill, it seemed to a much taller structure. It was hemmed in on the north by an expansive sourgrass field, and on the west by a prominent ridgeline that stretched from Hackleton's Cliff in St. Joseph to Cliff Den Hill in St. Philip. The main entrance to the building faced east towards College Savannah where St. Marks Anglican Church was easily visible in the distance. In the foreground below the school, the buildings of Codrington College were almost completely hidden by the dense canopy of mahogany trees that formed a major part of College Woods.

One of the unique features of the school was the very steep, wide stairway that was constructed at its main entrance. The cement-covered coral stone steps began at street level and rose gradually until they reached the wide verandah that ran parallel to the first floor classrooms. There was a three-foot wall on either side of the stairway that enhanced its appearance and made it a safer place for students to use. With the exception of the headmaster's office and residence on the upper and lower floors, respectively, all of the remaining space in the building was dedicated to teaching. The upper forms were on the second floor, and the lower forms, including the infant school, were on the first floor.

There was a second entrance to the school. It was on the south side of the building and could be conveniently accessed from a small playground where I pitched marbles and occasionally played a game called "rounders" with my classmates. I remember the unpaved driveway that led from the public road to the playground. South of the playground was a sparsely wooded area that extended almost to a standpipe on the opposite side of the public road.

I entered the Society Mixed School when I was four years old. Joyce was my chaperone. I accompanied her to school, and because I was so young, I was not permitted to attend any of the organized classes. Instead of remaining downstairs in the Infants School, I was allowed to play with my marbles upstairs, or sit quietly until Joyce's classes ended. Miss Audine Codrington from Stuart's Hill was my favorite teacher during those early years. Mum had not yet cut my hair, and Miss Audine loved to play with my locks.

When I was old enough to attend formal classes, I was placed in A-bee-Ab. My class was on the first floor, and it was there that my classmates and I dutifully learned our alphabet and times tables. My day generally followed the same routine. The bell rang to signal the beginning of school. Students were required to line up in the schoolyard on the south side of the building. Once we were in position, the teacher would move meticulously down the line of students inspecting our heads and hands to make sure that we had combed our hair and cleaned our finger nails.

Caring about personal hygiene was as important as the attention we dedicated to academics, and we all learned that our shirts had to be clean and neatly tucked into our trousers. Our teachers were charged with ensuring that we were always in full compliance with the stringent standards of deportment that our school expected and the Barbadian educational system demanded. Mum always told me that "cleanliness is next to godliness," so my hair was always neatly combed and parted; my fingernails cleaned and clipped; and my shirt and pants clean, starched and pressed. I was never one of those students cited by my teachers for bad deportment. In fact, I always felt a kinship with all of my primary school teachers.

During the period from 1943 to 1948 while I was a student at the Society Mixed School, Mr. Fred Parris was my headmaster and he was assisted by Mr. Bernard Hall who served as deputy headmaster. My other teachers included Mr. Alban Brown, Mr. Freddy Gittens, Miss Lester Hall, and Miss Audine Codrington.

Class always started with a prayer, and then we would begin our daily routine, which almost exclusively involved rote learning. For arithmetic this meant rehearsing our times tables. All the teacher had to do was instruct the class to say the two-times table, and almost instantaneously we would respond with the familiar refrain, "two-ones-are-two, two-into-two one!" That was immediately followed by, "two-twos-are-four, two-into-four two!" And we continued that refrain until we reached "two-twelves-are-twenty-four, two-into-twenty-four twelve."

For English class, our textbooks were the Royal Readers. Those books were replete with stories that were obviously intended for British students. I routinely read about "Mr. Mike who rode on a bike;" or "Little Miss Muffitt who sat on a Tuffit;" or about the need to "Ride a cock-horse to Banbury Cross to see a fine lady upon a white horse..." My classmates and I always wondered what was a cock-horse!

My brother Kid, Elton Marshall, Carl Mapp, Earl Mackintosh, Evvy Rowe, and Carl Barrow (Woogie), and several other boys and girls from the neighborhood attended the Society Mixed School with me. Then there were boys like Rawl Maynard, Leaton, and Tackie from Massiah Street, Lassie Rouse from Sealy Hall; Keith Hoyte, Colin Antrobus, Wilson McKechney, and Snuffie and Cornelius Harewood from Chapel Hill.

There was a urinal on the north side of the school at the top of a series of coral stone steps that we would have to climb before we could relieve ourselves. I remember that we would have competitions to determine whose urine had the furthest reach or frothed the most. Those were considered genuine signs of approaching manhood!

Mr. Parris also kept a kitchen garden that the students helped him maintain. I was too young to be assigned garden duties, but could not help admiring the attractive beds of lettuce, cabbage, and string beans that clearly signaled the success of that project.

The mid-forties in Barbados was a time when slates and pencils were used to teach elementary students penmanship. Our slates were rectangular, almost the same size as an eight-by-ten sheet of paper. Some slates were neatly framed in wood, others were unframed. I learned to write on a slate that had a plain wooden frame. I used the same slate to solve problems involving addition, division, and subtraction. I am still proud of my handwriting and my ability to complete mathematical calculations using the rules I was taught at the Society Mixed School more than sixty years ago.

Once a year my classmates and I were invited down to Codrington College for a "treat." I competed in sac races, egg-and-spoon races, and wheelbarrow races. I always looked forward to eating as many hot cross buns and drinking as much ginger beer as possible. When the competition ended, the winners were all presented with prizes. I always enjoyed attending those annual school fairs. Mum told me that the annual fair in Codrington College got started after Principal Anstey decided to move the white students from the Society Model School to the more luxurious Codrington High School facility on the sprawling property at Chapel Hill. His compensation to the black families was to entertain their children at the fair that was held annually at College.

In those days, my classmates and I were served biscuits and milk for lunch. Because I lived reasonably close to the school, there were many days when Aunt Mam would meet my siblings and me with lunch that she prepared at home. When the bell rang for the lunch break, Kid, Peggy, and I would run down College Hill to Lazy Rock where we took the footpath across the rugged hillside down to the main road. When we reached the highway, we walked maybe another hundred feet down the Cabbage Walk where we took up position under one of the royal palms to wait for Aunt Mam. When she arrived, she would spread a little plastic tablecloth on the grass. After the tablecloth was neatly positioned, she placed her cabbage basket onto the clean surface and removed the goodies that she prepared for lunch.

Most days, lunch would include fresh pancakes that we called bakes, muffins, and sweet lemonade. I always preferred the lunch that Aunt Mam brought to the powdered milk and eclipse biscuits that were served back at school. Whenever I reflect on the time I spent at Society Mixed School, lunchtime on the Cabbage Walk always ranks high on my list of fondest memories.

As Peggy reached school age, Mum enrolled her in St. Philip's Girls School where Mrs. Yearwood was headmistress.

Mum wanted Peggy to be closer to her, so Peggy moved to Church Village to stay with Mum. When Roger reached the age to attend school, he, Phil, and Roy's daughter Sonia went to school in Welch, a little village that was approximately one mile north of our family home in St. John. Mrs. Thorne from Massiah Street, who was a friend of the family, was headmistress there, and I guess that Mum felt comfortable sending the younger children to her school. Roger later attended St. John's Boys' School where he came under the guidance of Mr. Marshall and Mr. Collis Bailey.

Occasionally, the dentist visited Society Mixed School. The Barbados Public Health System required all public school students to have their teeth examined by a dentist annually. Usually, the dentist's visits were unannounced. I would be comfortably seated in the classroom deeply engaged on one of my lessons, and suddenly the teacher would break the news. I recall her saying, "put away your pencils and slates, get up from your seats and form a single line, we are taking you to have your teeth examined." Those words always instilled fear in my heart.

I remember my first encounter with the school's dentist. I was a little boy, perhaps six or seven years old. I was lined up and escorted into the classroom on the first floor that was temporarily converted into a dentist's office. It was a traumatic meeting for me. I knew that the dentist had a reputation for pulling out any tooth that he believed would pose a potential problem for the student. As he looked into my mouth, I was silently hoping that he would find nothing wrong with my teeth. I was one of the unlucky students that day. After a cursory examination of my mouth, he decided that I needed to have one of my permanent teeth extracted. It was a molar from the left side of my upper jaw. Before I knew what had happened he yanked my tooth out.

I never forgot that day, I kept blaming myself for not following most of my classmates who, when they heard that the dentist was coming, jumped through the first floor window and made their exit from school. On subsequent visits from the dentist, Kid and I were the first to escape through the first floor window. We ran as fast as we could across the grass piece toward Howard Hill, and then down the hill to the safety of our home.

During summer vacation, I spent a lot of time at the beach. Those August days would be so hot that I could hardly walk on the pavement. I gathered a group of friends, and with permission from Mum and Dad, I headed down to Bath Hill. I then traveled along the narrow cart road that bisected the cane fields at Bath Plantation until I reached a rocky trail that gradually descended to Bath Beach. I continued along the old train line traversing a wooden bridge that straddled a deep gorge, before reaching the shady areas of the beach that were best for picnicking and swimming.

I had my favorite spots to bathe at Bath. I used a maypole or an inflated automobile inner tube to stay afloat in the shallow water. The beach was always filled with sea moss and as I walked along the water's edge, I had a lot of fun bursting the sea bladders with my bare feet. I enjoyed tiptoeing out to the shoal where I had to be very careful not to step on a lionfish or sea urchin that would be camouflaged in the thick seaweed. After I learned to swim, my trips to Bath Beach were even more special. I remember changing into my slick, blue Jantzen swimsuit behind one of the casuarina trees, and after performing a few acrobatics on the sand, I would wade into the warm Atlantic Ocean, advancing cautiously until the water was at shoulder height.

I always swam parallel to the coastline remembering my Mum's warning that "the sea don't have any back door!" My swim strokes were borrowed from talented swimmers like Rupert Jackman who could glide through the water like a fish. After demonstrating my backstroke, I practiced my dives expelling all of the air from my lungs and traveling so close to the bottom that I would scrape my chest on the sand. Occasionally I swam approximately twenty-yards out to the shoal, pausing to rest before returning to the shore. My friends and I were very careful however, to always keep our distance from an area called the Well Pit. It was marked by a rectangular piece of wood that warned swimmers of the dangerous rip currents in that location. I never heard of anyone who ever drowned by venturing too close to the Well Pit, but we always were led to believe that the waters in that area cascaded down like a whirlpool into a bottomless pit.

I spent most of my August vacation at the beach swimming, lying on the sand, or walking down towards a place called Sentize to pick welks off of the rocks. At the end of the day, I changed into my street clothing and made the trek back up the hill with my friends until we reached Bath Plantation yard. There was an active spring there, and the water emerged from a metal pipe and cascaded into a shallow concrete trough. I always stopped at Bath's Plantation yard to drink that refreshing water in preparation for the climb up Bath Hill to negotiate that dreaded section of the hill that we called man-stomach.

I was always confused about whether I lived in Sargent Street or College Land. In fact I used three different addresses on my official mail, and that was a direct result of the confusion that existed then. The first address I used was Sargent Street. Most people felt that the official name for our neighborhood was Sargent Street. After all, that was the name prominently displayed on the Route-7 bus. Sargent Street however, was a small community that was accessed by a narrow, unpaved footpath that originated from the public road near the McIntosh family home. That path gradually sloped upwards in a westerly direction toward Gerald Ward's house and shop. There were several families that lived on both sides of Sargent Street; these include Mr. Charles Bennett and the Wilkinsons at the street's entrance. Sonny Ming, and several others whose names I have long forgotten lived further along the path.

The second address I used was College Land. Mum and Dad paid a modest monthly rent to Codrington College because our home was built on land that was wholly owned by the SPG as instructed by Christopher Codrington. The third address I used was Near Codrington College. I considered this to be my most appropriate address because it indicated that my home was located near to one of the most prestigious landmarks in the island of Barbados.

Kid and I spent many nights in front of the Route-7 bus depot that was about fifty yards away from the entrance to Sargent Street. That was a popular place where the boys congregated to swap stories or ogle the neighborhood girls as they walked by. The bus depot was also a popular spot for the local evangelists to spread their tarpaulins, light up their gas lamps and start preaching. Those local preachers were legendary figures in our neighborhood, and I always enjoyed listening to their message.

Then there was the Mobile Cinema, a customized van that visited our community on a schedule that I was never able to figure out. Anyway, when I heard that the Mobile Cinema was coming to College Land, my siblings and I would set out early to make sure that we got an unobstructed view of the screen. The van parked in the middle of the Codrington College playing field, and around seven pm or as soon as it got dark enough, the entire neighborhood would be treated to Tom and Jerry cartoons, the latest newsreels of amazing things happening in far away places, and a short feature film.

For fun, my friends and I played marble cricket in the street, or bat-and-ball on Sabina Park, a pitch that was located under College Woods. There was also the marble games called Licking-off-Jades and Pitch-and-Spawn. I also played Nicks, Trademan, and Hop Scotch with the neighborhood kids. On moonlit nights, I played Hiddey-Biddey, Hide-and-Seek, and sang ditties such as “London Bridge is Falling Down” with my brothers and sisters and our cousins Janet and Pinky.

Good Friday was one of the holiest days in the calendar of the Anglican church when the women in our community would dress in white, purple, or black and attend church to re-enacted the stations of the cross. For us kids, Good Friday was the culmination of the kite-flying season. The season usually began in March, and by the time Good Friday rolled around the sky would be filled with kites of all descriptions. There were square kites, round kites, bat kites, box kites, and man kites. Kid and I made our own kites. We fashioned the “bones” or wooden frame from scraps of lumber removed from the paling. We purchased “pretty” paper from the kite shop in Bridgetown, and with a starchy paste or sometimes the fruit from the clammy cherry tree we stuck the paper to the kite frame to form very attractive patterns. Each kite then had what we called a “mad bull” affixed to the nosepiece as the final step. Once airborne, the force of the wind would cause the “mad bull” to vibrate and the frequency of vibration caused a high-pitched humming sound. The kite tail would be assembled from strips of old clothing that we gathered from around the house. I made the loop from marlin twine that I purchased from Mr. Marshall's shop on Coach Hill. I always liked to make a climbing loop on my kites. Armed with my kite, I ran up the hill behind our house to the top of Howard Hill and entered the competition.

Kite flying on Howard Hill was not an activity for the faint of heart. That was a real contest with guys like Earl Mackintosh and Carl Mapp commanding the respect of all comers. Their kites were built to fly, and their goal was always to ensure that no kite dominated the airways but theirs. The tactic used to remove the competitor's kite from the air was called hooking or raking. Hooking involved the use of some complicated maneuvers to entrap the competitor's kite usually by the tail. Once hooked, the kite hung almost lifeless from the victor's twine. Kites removed from the competition in such a fashion were usually an embarrassment to the owner who was humiliated beyond belief. If however, the hooked kite had razor blades in the tail, it wouldn't be long before the marlin twine would be severed, releasing the competitor's kite sending it floating like a parachutist that had just been released from a low flying airplane. Kites whose strings were severed in the heat of the competition would float for great distances, buoyed by the stiff winds that were typical on Howard Hill. They would eventually settle into the bosom of the Haynes Hill sugarcane field. I was always upset when that tactic was employed to eliminate my kite from the competition.

In addition to the kite flying competition, I looked forward to participating in several other activities on Good Friday. These all had to be performed exactly at midday. The first involved breaking an egg and placing it in a glass with its yolk intact. The glass was then exposed to the midday sun until the heat was sufficient to coagulate the white of the egg. I was led to believe that the midday sun on Good Friday had magical powers that would be revealed in the formation assumed by the congealed albumin of the egg. I was always intrigued by the images I thought I saw in the glass!

The second thing I did was to pick a young breadfruit from one of the trees in the neighborhood. Exactly at midday I made a fresh cut on the long green stem, and invariably I would see the letter "C." I was told that the "C" was the first letter in Cain's name, and it was a reminder of the fact that Cain had slain his own brother Abel.

The third activity I engaged in was to tap the physic nut tree with a stone at midday. I believed that if my timing was precise, I would see blood oozing from the site of the injury instead of the whitish sap normally produced by that tree.

As a scientist, I find it very interesting that I never thought of trying to prove that this was a phenomenon that occurred only at midday on Good Friday. In retrospect, I should have conducting those experiments at a different time on Good Friday as well as at midday on a day other than Good Friday. Who knows what I would have found. What I know for sure however, is that I have seen ships and coffins and faces in the images formed in the glasses containing eggs; I have observed the large, well-formed letter "C" on the freshly cut stems of the breadfruit; and I have seen blood oozing from the freshly damaged trunk of the physic nut tree!

Chapter 5

Growing Up

Growing up with my siblings Joyce, Kid, Peggy, Roger, and Phil was a real treat. Rainy days brought as much pleasure as sunny days. Just for fun, I would climb up to the top of the partition in our passageway and plunge five feet to the bed below. I played marble cricket in the passage, and I pitched marbles on the wooden floor with my siblings. Aunt Mam was our surrogate mother during much of my childhood. She taught me to take care of the goats and sheep. I learned to feed the pigs, and scatter scratch grain for the fowls. I took turns with my brothers and sisters in fetching water from the local standpipe, picking breadfruits, or digging potatoes and yams from College Land, and from other plantations in St. John with names like Villanova, Haynes Hill, Guinea, Bath, Victoria, and Kendall. Aunt Mam earned a living by selling potatoes, yams, breadfruit, sugar cakes, bananas, plantains, figs, and roasted peanuts. She would always know where the best deals were, and she was never afraid of hard work. She was also a good cook, and often made us traditional Bajan treats like bakes, muffins, and "old man hat,"–a cassava based pancake that was very popular with country folk.

Peggy loved to compete with Philip, Roger, and me at any sport. She played bat-and-ball with us, climbed the ackee and golden apple trees, and even pitched marbles competitively for buttons. She was fearless and was not bashful to take on any challenge. I vividly remember playing a game of cards with her in the living room one day when we both narrowly avoided serious injury. Dad had a very large six-foot mirror that leaned at a seventy-degree angle in the corner of the room. It was very heavy and had a four-inch wooden frame that was painted white. During our game, Peggy became so excited by the cards

I dealt her that she could hardly control her emotions. Confident that she had a winning hand, she began to celebrate by bouncing up and down, pushing her body backwards from her seated position. As her body lurched backwards she managed to push the base of the mirror closer and closer to the wall. I still don't know how she was able with her modest size to accomplish such a feat, and I didn't notice how precariously the mirror was positioned.

What happened next was unforgettable. I heard a very loud crash as if the house had exploded, and then there was glass everywhere, tiny shards of broken glass on my clothes and on the floor surrounding me. I was so stunned that I was unable to move. I looked at Peggy and saw that she was trapped under the frame of the mirror. It was obvious that she was scared as she tried to crawl out from under the shattered mirror. That was a hazardous proposition, and she paid the price by sustaining a deep cut on her elbow. I was unscathed, and consider myself lucky that there was a mahogany rocking chair directly in the path of the falling mirror, and it was that chair that saved the two of us from impending disaster. The chair absorbed most of the energy of the falling mirror, preventing it from crushing us under its weight. The crash was so loud that neighbors within a quarter of a mile from our home came running to see what caused the explosion.

The other incident I remember involving Peggy and me occurred one evening when she fell from the cart that we were pushing and split her lip. Dad had constructed the cart from flat board nailed together to form a small rectangular platform. Four wheels, one at the base of each corner of the rectangle rendered the cart mobile. A four-foot piece of wood attached to the front of the cart served as its handle. Peggy and I would take the cart out to College Park to pick up bags of charcoal that Mum sent by bus from Church Village to St. John. Because we had used the cart to pick up the charcoal several times before, we felt that we had our routine well worked out. On our way out to College Park, which was approximately one mile from home, we took turns riding on the cart or pushing from behind. After we picked up the bags of charcoal and loaded them onto the cart we set out for home. I was pulling the wooden handle and Peggy was pushing from behind. Whenever we got up to a good speed, Peggy would jump onto the bags of charcoal and ride until we lost momentum, and then she would dismount and push again. On what was perhaps her fourth or fifth attempt to hop onto the cart she missed her step and crashed to the ground sustaining a serious cut to her lip. I was devastated by that unfortunate accident and wished I could have done something to have prevented it from happening. Peggy never let me forget that incident.

Peggy and I shared so many memorable experiences during our teenage years that it is impossible to remember them all. I often think about our trips to visit her two godmothers during summer vacation. One of her godmothers Mrs. Davis lived in Rices, St. Philip near to Mrs. Keane's school, where Kid was enrolled as a student. I don't know who made arrangements for our visit, but somehow Peggy and I were told that her godmother was expecting a visit on a particular date and time. She and I set out on either Dad's or Kid's bike. She sat on the handlebar or on a wooden bar that Kid made and I pedaled the bike from our home in St. John all the way to Rices in St. Philip. When we reached her godmother's, we were ushered into the living room of her small but neatly furnished home. We would sit there for what seemed to be an eternity before her godmother had time to spend with us. It was a ritual that we acted out every summer.

Peggy's godmother and her husband were owners of a small shop that provided most of the goods and services for the residents of Rices and the surrounding neighborhoods. As self-employed owners, they could not take time off from the frontline of their business to socialize with us. Nevertheless, they were always very gracious hosts, providing us with as much time as they could reasonably afford, and at the end of the visit, providing Peggy with enough goodies to make the trip worthwhile.

The trip back from Rices had one highlight, a visit to Aunt Beets' dunks tree. I have seen dunks trees in my life, but there wasn't another dunks tree in Barbados that could compare with Aunt Beets'. That tree was umbrella shaped and low to the ground. It was always laden with lots and lots of the marble sized fruit. Peggy and I knew that as dunks matured they changed color from green to yellow to golden brown. We picked as many of the yellow and golden brown dunks as we could stuff into our pockets and the bags that were hanging from the bicycle handle, and we ate them all on the way back home. For some reason, Peggy and I always felt that we should have unlimited access to the dunks from Aunt Beets' tree.

Then there was the annual trek to her second godmother, Mrs. Hart who lived in St. Elizabeth Village, St. Joseph. That was always a more sanguine experience. Mrs. Hart was the wife of our cousin Frederick Hart who was the headmaster of the St. Elizabeth Village Elementary School. As headmaster, Mr. Hart and his family lived in the government provided headmaster's house. Mrs. Hart was a very gentle, lovable person. Because she was ill, our visit involved spending lots of time chatting with her in her bedroom. Highlights of that trip to the Hart's would be our opportunity to spend time with their children, Dudley, Anthony, Dorothy, and Pat.

The trip from College Land to St. Elizabeth Village was always challenging. Because of the hilly terrain, there was little opportunity to ride the bike, although we always carried one. Roads were uneven in some spots, and in others, the rains would have washed away the entire surface. When I visit that part of Barbados today, I am amazed at the fact that the original road is no longer accessible, and the route there is much more tortuous than it was when I was a kid. Traffic must now travel all the way down to Foster Hall Plantation, and then back up the hill in order to reach St. Elizabeth Village. When we were kids we could go directly to the Hart's via an unpaved road that was bordered on both sides with stately Royal Palms!

The fifth of November was Guy Fawkes Day in Barbados. That was the only occasion that our community would tolerate what at any other time was considered to be bad behavior. Guy Fawkes was involved in a plot to blow up the British House of Parliament. That was known as the notorious Gunpowder Plot. Barbados being a British colony at the time, always celebrated Guy Fawkes Day with spectacular displays of fireworks and other incendiary devices. Those parents that could afford to, bought starlights, bombs, firecrackers, and Roman candles for their children. We supplemented these with a number of homemade devices. We made Trashmen from sturdy, wooden sticks on which we stacked as many dried leaves from the seagrape tree that the five-foot wooden stick could comfortably accommodate. The Trashman was lit at the top and the flame moved slowly down the stick until it reached the last leaf.

Those of us who had access to old tires would set them ablaze, and the soft, inelastic shiny material that resulted when the rubber in the tire was completely burnt we called balata. "Carboil" was also a popular explosive substance that was used in our neighborhood. I had no idea where it came from or how it was produced. I suspect however, that it could have been a mixture of saltpeter, sulfur, and charcoal. Anyway, I needed a small can so that I could achieve the desired effect. I liked to use an empty Andrews Liver Salts can because of its convenient size, tight fitting lid, and thin metal bottom. I prepared the can by punching a small hole in the bottom. Then I removed the lid, placed the "carboil" inside and spat on it. I shook the can vigorously, and placed it in the street on its side. I then lit a match, and held the flame as close as possible to the hole at the bottom of the can. The flame ignited the volatile gases and triggered an explosion that blew the lid off. Following the explosion, the air would smell like rotten eggs. I did this against the concrete bridge so that I could easily retrieve the lid and repeat the process.

Another homemade device was called the "key." That was a U-shaped contraption made from wire. On one end of the wire I placed an ordinary, old-fashioned key that had its end hollowed out. On the other end of the wire I inserted a nail. I then stuffed sulphur from the heads of matches into the hollow opening of the key. The device was cocked and ready for action. When I slammed the device against the firm surface of the road, the nail entered the hole of the key at a speed sufficient to ignite the sulphur. The result was a loud, cracking sound.

On Guy Fawkes Day, I would wait patiently for dusk to set in. Then, without anyone giving the signal, the celebration would begin. I would take my Trashman out of storage, light it and run back and forth across the neighborhood yelling, "hip, hip, the fifth of November! Bombs would explode under my feet, and lids from Andrews Liver Salts cans would be crashing against the cement bridge that straddled the gully. It was mayhem in my neighborhood. Then the kids whose parents could afford to buy fireworks would light their starlights and their Roman candles, and everyone would join in the chant, "hip, hip the fifth of November!" When the outdoor activities subsided, I went home and ate Conkies with my brothers and sisters. Guy Fawkes Day was never complete without engaging in the ritual of eating Conkies. I always devoured my share of those delicious concoctions that Mum made from cornflour, grated coconut, sweet potato and pumpkin, and steamed to perfection in banana leaves.

Another exciting time of the year for my siblings and me was the annual Exhibition at Queen's Park. We had to get dressed up in our new outfits; take the bus from College Land to Bridgetown; pay the entrance fee at the gate; and spend the evening walking from one end of the park to the other viewing the art, culinary, agricultural, and other exhibits; and socializing with our friends. I remember there would always be a giant pumpkin, yam or potato that won first prize in the agricultural competition; and usually a masterpiece painted by one of Barbados' top artists that would win first prize in the art competition. At the end of the evening we exited the park, tired, and with our feet aching from the non-stop walking in our new shoes. I remember every year my friend Belfield would always ask me the same question as we walked to the bus stand, "Ken, are you coming back to the Exhibition next year?"

Christmas in St. John during my childhood was a very special time. Because it was a very holy day, everyone saw it as a time for renewal, and that sentiment extended to everything my family did during the Christmas season. The floors of our house had to be scrubbed, and Aunt Mam usually took on that assignment. She gathered the whitehead bush from the hill behind the house, and when these were mixed with white lime they provided the necessary ingredients to clean the floor and restore luster to the wood. Applying a varnishing finish after the floor was cleaned and dried would complete the job. We also varnished the mahogany chairs, tables, and couch. Peggy and I were charged with beautifying the exterior of the house. We pulled the weeds and covered the entire walkway with marl that we dug from one of the numerous marlholes in our neighborhood.

Mum took care of decorating the interior of the house. She sewed new blinds for the windows, purchased new linoleum for the floor in the front house and passage, and replaced the tablecloth in the shedroof. We decorated the front house with colorful streamers and balloons. Sometimes we gathered branches from the casurina tree and placed cotton wool on them, and pretended that we had a Christmas tree.

The week before Christmas was the time for non-stop baking. Mum baked sweet bread, pone, pudding, and great cake. Dad brought home the ham all neatly wrapped in its protective cover of hardened tar. On Christmas Eve the smell of some of the most delicious Bajan dishes imaginable was permeating the air in every room of our home. They included baked pork, fried chicken, black pudding and souse, cod fish cakes and many other familiar dishes.

I attended choir rehearsals at Society Chapel and enjoyed the plays about the birth of baby Jesus that were staged in Codrington College. We took long walks with our friends before daybreak, and we waited in anticipation for the "scrubbers" who stopped by our window at night to sing for money or food. One of the ditties they recited was "As I was crossing the Jordan River, my heart began to shiver, so please Mr. Harewood give me something to cool my liver." Dad would get up and pour a few drinks for the traveling minstrels.

I went to Watch Night Service at Society Chapel and the communion service on Christmas morning. My Christmas gifts were few and very simple. I often received a plastic flute, a plastic windmill, a matchbox car, and some other plastic toy made in Japan.

Christmas Day was a day of perpetual eating and drinking. The day began with Mum allowing my siblings and me to sample many of the goodies that she prepared. I ate to my heart's delight, being fully aware that later in the day I would sit down with my entire family to eat Christmas dinner. I drank sorrel, a red, fermented drink that at that time was traditionally served during the Christmas season. Occasionally, when my Uncle Lionel was alive I would coax him into letting me have a sip of the Gilbey's Gin or Mount Gay Rum that he and his buddies were drinking. During the course of the day, it was not unusual for many of my parents' friends to stop by to pay a brief visit.

Christmas in Barbados was not a single day but a season, and most families took full advantage of that tradition. I always got a chance to visit Broad Street in the capital city of Bridgetown to see the lights! The major department stores, Harrison's, Fogarty, DaCosta's, and Cave Shepherd would string colored lights up on their facades, and these lights attracted numerous sightseers to the city during the Christmas holidays. Then, I looked forward to the car trips across the island that Mum and Dad arranged to visit family members and friends that I rarely saw during the year.

On many occasions during the year, Kid and I went into Codrington College with our local friends to catch crawfish in the lake. Crawfish and eels were plentiful in the lake. Several of the boys knew that the stream at the back of the College was fed by water from College Spring. Spring water cascaded down from a six-inch pipe that protruded from the rocky bank on the southern edge of the campus. No one could tell me who installed that pipe, but one thing I was certain of was the fact that it provided an uninterrupted supply of fresh water to the residents living around Codrington College. A second source of potable water was also available at College Spring. It was provided by a small standpipe that was a part of the public water supply system.

The spring was the place where many of the women from the immediate neighborhood, as well as from College Park, College Tenantry, and even from as far away as Sargent Street and College Land would meet weekly to do their laundry.

As a youngster, my friends and I would follow that stream, overturning rocks and coaxing crawfish out of their numerous hiding places. Afterwards, we would start a fire using sugarcane peelings and roast our catch of the day. On the west side of College Spring, there was a tenantry road that gently sloped down to the bottom of a valley that led to Conset Bay. That community was called College Bottom. Mum told me that her friend, a lady called Iris Hunt, lived at the top of that road. She said that the Pinder, Inniss, Clarke, Bradshaw, and Beckles families lived further down that road. She recalled that a woman named Damsel Harewood lived in a house that was situated down below the Clark's home. From the bottom of the valley, the land sloped upwards towards College Savannah. Mum would also talk about Oscar Barker and Ma Sue who lived in the only two houses on the south side of the valley.

My generation referred to this hill as Burn Hill, but to the elders in my family, it was also called Rice Hill, and more properly Bryan Hill. I learned of this correct name from my Great Uncle James Firebrace (Uncle James) who left Barbados at the turn of the twentieth century for Panama. He later moved to the United States where he lived in Montclair, New Jersey. He grew up in Bryan Hill and shared many stories about his childhood experiences with me every time I visited his New Jersey home.

My familiarity with College Bottom was quite different from that of Uncle James. It was obvious to me that over the years, the neighborhood had transitioned to modernity, as the children of the early residents became better educated and joined the workforce. The first time that I remember going into that community was with Aunt Mam when I was a little boy. She knew all of the residents there. She also knew that the land besides the Inniss' house was used as a burial ground for victims of the cholera epidemic that struck Barbados in the 1800's. As the story goes, so many people died from cholera that it was impossible to follow the normal procedure for burial. Instead, the victims were placed in mass graves and those graves were filled in with the shale-like gray colored clay soil that is abundant at that location. Mum also told me of several sightings of human bones in the backyard of the Brathwaite home. This was a frightening tale to me as a youngster. I wondered whether the cholera organism that was so contagious could ever be re-awakened. And equally scary, was the thought that the ghosts from all of the hapless victims of the "plague" would forever haunt that community. When I was growing up, I only heard about the cholera epidemic from the members of my family. It was never mentioned in any of my classes when I attended primary or secondary school. I always felt that there were others in my community who knew about the story of Bryan Hill, and I would wonder why they were so reluctant to talk about what happened there.

Much later, when I was a teenager, a tropical wave hit Barbados and it rained and thundered all day. There were sharp strikes of forked lightening, considered the most dangerous of all lightening strikes. I remember that very gray and rainy day when I sat in our house looking out of the window that faced our neighbor Mrs. Bancroft's house. I heard that Mrs. Bradshaw had been struck by lightening down in Bryan Hill. Apparently, during the rainstorm she tried to walk up Goodman Hill towards College Savannah and a bolt of lightening took her life. People from all communities in the region descended on Bryan Hill to view her lifeless body. It is amazing how swiftly news traveled at a time when there were no cell phones.

I continue to be impressed by the access I had as a child to good medical care, and by the quality of service that was rendered by community physicians. The doctor serving our parish when I was growing up was Dr. Carter. He lived in a large plantation house called Villa Nova in Mount Tabor, St. John. The image of Dr. Carter that is imprinted in my mind is one of a rotund, white man, just over five feet tall, in his early fifties, with a cherubic, round face, balding, with scraggly strands of hair combed neatly across his forehead, and with a very pleasant disposition. He was a general practitioner, obstetrician, pediatrician, and dentist, all rolled into one person! He routinely made house calls, and was a valuable resource to the many families living in St. John.

The St. John Almshouse, located close to the St. John Boys' School, was a second, vital part of the health care service available in our parish. It was primarily a nursing home for the elderly and the indigent, but through an outpatient clinic, it provided emergency service to residents on days when the clinic was opened. A dispensary or pharmacy operated by Mr. Cave, the neighborhood pharmacist, was located across the street from the Almshouse. It stocked a variety of medical supplies that was available over-the-counter or by doctor's prescription. If the emergency clinic was closed, then individuals in need of medical assistance had two choices. They could get someone who owned a bicycle to take them to see Dr. Carter at

Villa Nova, or they needed to hire a car to take them to the casualty at the Barbados General Hospital in Bridgetown.

Many a night, Dad or Mr. Oscar Wilkerson, or Mr. Sinclair Bradshaw would be awakened from a deep sleep with an urgent request for help from a local resident. Help meant that they needed to be driven to the General Hospital in Bridgetown. For Dad, that involved a harrowing trip in the dark of night in an old Model-A Ford that had a weak battery and very dim headlamps. It also meant that he would have to wait for hours until a doctor was available to see the patient. The casualty's rules of first-come-first-served were always rigorously enforced.

When I was a teenager, access to health care was significantly improved for residents of College Land. A small clinic was built in Sealy Hall close to Mr. Bradshaw's shop. It provided the families in that area with an attractive option for medical care. It was managed by a single nurse who was a most delightful person. She treated minor cuts and bruises, and provided advice and guidance to residents on health related matters at no cost to the patient!

Chapter 6

Seasonal Change

The Crop Season usually began in January or February and ended in March. That was a most exciting time for children growing up in St. John. The crop to be harvested was sugarcane, and I couldn't wait to get my hands on as many of the tall, jointed, plump stalks as possible. I stripped the hard outer cover off the stalks with my bare teeth. I discarded the peelings, and sucked every ounce of the sugary, juicy fluid from the soft, spongy piths that remained. Sugarcane was the primary crop grown in the rich, dark St. John soil. Almost every acre of arable agricultural land was dedicated to its production. It was a central part of community life, and remained the lifeblood of the local economy through the 1950s. Local families sold their crops for cash to the many factories that served our tiny community.

Most of the labor force was employed to harvest the sugarcanes and load them onto donkey, mule, horse, and zebu drawn freight carts. Animal drawn carts were later replaced by lorries (trucks). During those decades, sugar was the primary foreign currency earner for Barbados. The calendar year was divided into two seasons. The crop season when lots of money was circulating throughout communities all across the island, and the hard season when folks had to "cut and contrive" to make ends meet.

The parish of St. John was a major center for sugarcane production during the 1940s and 1950s. There were plantations everywhere. The list included Ashford, Bath, Bowmanston, Cliff, Clifton Hall, Colleton, Guinea, Haynes Hill, Henley, Hothersal, Foster Hall, Kendal, Lemon Arbor, Malvern, Mount Pleasant, Moncriefe, Palmers, Pool, Society, Todds, and Wakefield. With the exception of Ashford, Henley, Hothersal, Mount Pleasant, and Todds, I believe that the rest of those plantations had their own factories. They hired pan boilers, scale beam and crane lift operators, chemists, raw and crack liquor crews, syrup and molasses workers, coopers, and a host of other laborers.

I have always been told that the rich, fertile Barbadian topsoil, especially on the Atlantic side of the island where the Parish of St. John is located, resulted from years and years of atmospheric transport of dust from northwest Africa to the Caribbean Basin. Studies of satellite images suggest that hundreds of millions of tons of dust are transported annually at relatively low altitudes, and airline pilots continue to report seeing the African dust events from their cockpits during trans-Atlantic flights. Whatever the source, the thick, dark St. John topsoil has been a major reason for the high density of plantations established in that parish.

After the donkey, mule, horse, and zebu cattle gave way to trucks, a favorite pastime for the boys in my neighborhood was to wait patiently at those points along the route where we knew the driver would have to slow down. As the speed of the truck decreased, the boys would launch an all out attack on those sugarcane stalks that could be conveniently pulled from the back of the truck. Some of the bigger boys would display their acrobatic skills by leaping high into the air from the side of the roadway to snag one or more sugarcane stalks, while the truck was still traveling at full speed.

I knew the license plates of all of the trucks, and I also knew the names of the drivers. They were dedicated workers who really earned every penny they received. Often, the Bedford trucks laden with sugarcanes would get stuck in the field when it rained. When that happened, the trucks either had to be towed from the field, or the workers had to unload the sugarcane, push the trucks out of the muddy field, and then reload every single stalk! Pay was determined by tonnage delivered to the factory, so every minute counted.

Then there was the hazard of sugarcane fires. To my knowledge, no one was ever caught setting fire to a sugarcane field. Yet every year, acres and acres of ripe sugarcanes would go up in flames. I have never ever seen a fire truck trying to extinguish a sugarcane fire during my entire childhood. After the fire subsided, it was always very distressing to see the sugarcane workers with their cutlasses slashing away at the blackened stalks, and loading them onto the trucks for delivery to the factory.

When the crop season ended, my friends and I enjoyed “mashing trash " in search of mature cane stalks that somehow managed to miss detection during the initial harvest. For some reason, those stalks always seemed to be sweeter than the ones obtained during the height of the crop season.

With their pockets filled with money, the laborers wanted nothing more than to find a venue to spend it. The local rum shops helped to relieve them of the money that was literally “burning holes in their pockets.” Sinclair Bradshaw’s shop in College Park was a very popular watering hole that served our neighborhood for many years. He was a prominent member of the community, and owned an Opel Kapitan, one of the few cars in our district. Gerald Ward owned a rum shop in Sargent Street. His shop was smaller than Mr. Bradshaw’s but more strategically located, and it attracted a large clientele of professional rum drinkers.

The casino business also flourished during the crop season. These were not real casinos, they were dance halls, and almost every weekend someone would be sponsoring a dance at which one of the popular bands provided the music. Percy Green, Syl Duncan, Clive Gittens, and Maggie Goodridge were the big bands with national reputations. Suggs Bradshaw had a local band that usually played at the Sealy Hall and Gall Hill dance halls. The casino at Sealy Hall was closest to our neighborhood. Then there was the notorious dance hall at Gall Hill where dances attracted larger, noisier crowds. Pork chops and pudding and souse were staples on the menu at those dances, along with the traditional Mount Gay rum, imported Tennents stout and beer, and Gilbey’s Dry Gin.

“Singings” and “Service of Songs” were smaller, less boisterous venues for socializing within my community. They were held in private homes all across the neighborhood. As the names imply, the primary attraction at those events was music. There was plenty of singing and harmonizing. The sponsors always charged an admission fee, and the patrons got to spend their money on pork chops, black pudding and souse, and considerable amounts of Mount Gay rum.

During my entire childhood, black businessmen controlled the public transportation system in St. John. Two bus companies served my community–the Simpson Bus Company and the Hinds Bus Company. Mr. George Simpson, a black man who lived in Cliff Cottage, St. John owned the Simpson Bus Company. These were the Route-7 buses that were painted light blue with yellow trim. Their bodies were constructed locally and the engines were imported. The typical bus held thirty seated passengers. There were approximately seven bench type upholstered seats, each capable of accommodating at least five passengers. Canvas tarpaulins were installed on both sides of the bus to protect the passengers when it rained. They were held in place by canvas straps. I loved to travel on the bus when the tarpaulins were rolled down on rainy days. The drivers and conductors on the Route-7 buses included names like Tippy, Seibert, Newton, Corbin, Barrow, Lashley, Linseed, Wesley, Pointer, and Kenneth.

The other bus company was owned by Mr. Edward Hinds, a black businessman who lived in Massiah Street. His buses were assigned to Route-9, a route that included Church Village, Massiah Street, College and College Savannah. These buses were painted red and were of similar design to the Route-7 buses. We used the Route-7 buses to travel to Bridgetown through Small Town, Four Roads, Gun Hill, Charles Row Bridge, and on into St. Michael. The Route-9 buses traveled to Bridgetown via the Parish of St. Philip. The Hinds Bus Company was smaller than Simpson's and as a consequence had fewer employees. I can only remember Diamond, Bunny, Sidney, and Pedal.

Dad was a genuine resource when it came to talking about the bus service in Barbados. He always reminded me that he was one of the popular drivers during the early days of private ownership of buses. He plied the St. Philip route, and was always called on to run errands for families who needed to make purchases from Bridgetown. Bus drivers were all male then, they wore neat uniforms, and they were usually very respectful of the law.

During the 1940s and 1950s bus drivers and conductors were terrorized by a police officer called Cyrus. Everyone would freeze when the name Cyrus was mentioned. He would conceal his motorcycle at the side of the road, especially along Constant Road. Anytime Cyrus stopped the bus he would invariably issue the driver or conductor with a summons. The worse case scenario involved removal of those passengers from the bus that exceeded the legal limit, leaving them by the roadside until the next bus arrived. Bus schedules during that period ran from six o'clock in the morning to six o'clock in the evening during the week, and much later on Saturdays, with the last bus leaving the city around midnight.

The rainy season in Barbados generally began in September and lasted through November, the end of the hurricane season. Rainy days in St. John brought out the gullies, and when it poured, the gully on the northern side of our home would be converted into a raging current of water, cascading down from Howard Hill and spilling its contents right onto Highway-3. When the rushing waters subsided after a sustained heavy downpour, the road would be filled with thick black dirt, lots of silt, and stones of all sizes and descriptions, all dislodged from the hills in the back of our home.

One day in 1947, in the middle of the rainy season, when I was spending time at our home in Church Village, it rained and rained all day. I was forced to stay indoors, and I did not enjoy being confined to the indoors on rainy days in Church Village. Aunt Mam and Kid were the only family members at home in St. John. Kid recalls that he was lying on the large storage trunk in the shedroof while the rain was pouring outside. It was early afternoon, and for some unexplained reason, he said that he felt an urge to get up and leave the house. So he got up, donned one of Uncle Lionel's old jackets, and walked out the road towards the Brooks' house. Aunt Mam was left at home alone.

According to her, she saw a sharp flash of lightening, followed by what she thought to be a distant rumble of thunder. Like most older Barbadians, she covered all of the mirrors with bed sheets to protect the house from lightening strikes, and sought refuge under the bed. As she waited, the thunder seemed to get louder and louder. This time, however, it was not thunder that was making the noise, but it was a large boulder that was rolling down the hill behind our house. The heavy rain had dislodged it from where it had been anchored, and as it careened down the hill it gained momentum. When it made contact with the galvanized paling at the back of the house, it crushed it as if it had been made of paper. Then it completely destroyed the back of the house, entering the shedroof where it punched through the wooden floor. Thank God that the cellar was deep enough to stop it dead in its tracks. That boulder finally came to rest in the shedroof where it resembled an iceberg with its base submerged, and its jagged edge protruding several feet above what was left of the floor. I don't remember how we got word in Church Village of that devastating event, but when I made it home to St. John, I was horrified by the size of that gigantic boulder sitting in the middle of our dining room.

That was a very difficult time for the family. First, there was the embarrassment of having the privacy of the home violated by such an unwelcomed intruder. Then, there was the inconvenience of having to negotiate our way around that massive obstruction that had become a part of our daily existence. Finally, there was the challenge of deciding what we needed to do to get rid of the boulder and restore our home to a state of normalcy. In 1947, that was a monumental task, and Mum and Dad quickly realized that the projected cost for labor and materials far exceeded their limited resources. They were advised by the church and the political leaders in the parish to appeal to the plantation owners and other well-to-do St. John families for help. The official instrument used by Barbadians at that time was called a Brief. I had never heard of such a thing, but Mum was soon on her way to the District-C police station to formally apply for a Brief that would permit her to legally solicit funds from potential donors.

Armed with her Brief, and accompanied by her longtime friend Mrs. Ford from Massiah St., Mum began the painful and embarrassing task of asking some of the most highfaluting plantation managers and big shot white people in St. John for help. It turned out that the majority of them had little or no empathy for her desperate situation. She got little help, and to make matters worse, one of them even had the gall to tell her that she had no right to build her house under a hill and right in the path of a boulder!

With little support from the landed gentry and plantation managers, the family had to depend on its own resourcefulness to get the problem resolved. Equipped with a steel drill of the type used in coral stone quarries, and an ax, Dad worked for several months whittling away the top of the stone. My siblings and I helped as best we could, and so did some of the other men in the neighborhood. Eventually, the top of the boulder was reduced to the level of the floor. Drawing on his masonry skills, Dad then cemented the entire shedroof floor restoring it to its previous functional state. I am sure that the boulder is still in the cellar beneath the shedroof where it came to rest over sixty-two years ago!

In September, 1955 one of the most powerful hurricanes hit Barbados causing considerable damage in the southern parishes. It organized in the Atlantic Ocean east of Barbados. What began as a weak tropical wave later picked up enough energy to become a category three hurricane called Janet. When Hurricane Janet hit the south coast of Barbados, maximum winds were estimated to be about one hundred ten to one hundred twenty miles per hour. Officials on the island were aware of the gathering storm and had warned communities all across the country. Our warning was delivered from the District-C police station located at the top of Station Hill, St. Philip. As was customary, we filled the large wooden barrel in the kitchen with drinking water. The sheep and goats were kept in their pens, and our larder had a plentiful supply of canned sardines, pilchards, corned beef, and salmon.

I remember the morning of September twenty-second very well. The sky was dark and ominous, and I could hear the District-C sirens whaling in the distance. The hurricane warning was as scary as the thick, dark clouds that started to gather over the horizon. Soon, there were flashes of lightening visible in the distance, followed by the muffled rumble of thunder. As I helped Mum and Dad batten down the hatches, I could hear voices in the street as the neighbors began their trek into Codrington College, the designated shelter for our community. My family decided to remain at home, so there we were, in our familiar setting huddled into the corner of the front house preparing for the worst.

We did not have to wait long before the wind began to pick up, and the full force of the storm was soon upon us. Two horrific claps of thunder sent us scurrying for shelter into the bedroom where we all appealed to God by reciting the familiar prayer, "Lord have mercy, Christ have mercy." We always thought of the bedroom as a place of refuge, and we knew that we could crawl under the bed if the hurricane got worse. The wind was howling outside, and the rain was pummeling the shingled roof of the house as it attacked in waves. I believed that if Janet had made a direct hit on St. John, our home could not have withstood its force.

As wind speeds increased, I could feel the entire frame of the house shake as if it was about to come apart. I was scared stiff, although I must admit that a certain part of me was fascinated by the thought of riding out the storm. I remember hearing Granny Kidney and Aunt Mam talk about their experiences in the big storm of 1898. They were children then, and the old family house was still standing after that storm passed. That thought was comforting, and my desire to experience the fury of Hurricane Janet grew in intensity.

As Janet raged on, what I feared most was the possibility of the wind lifting the roof from the frame of the house leaving us completely exposed to the full force of the elements. Anyone familiar with rain in the Caribbean knows that it falls in torrents. The local expression is that the rain normally fell "bucket-a-drop." I couldn't imagine what it would have been like to be left open to the elements during such a hurricane.

As I look back on that day in September 1955, I am convinced that our guardian angels were looking over all of us. We learned later that as Janet approached Barbados, the eye of the hurricane wobbled to the south of the island causing major damage to the residents of St. Philip, Christ Church and St. Michael. Although we were not completely spared, our homes remained intact. Our windows did not shatter, and we did not lose any of the wooden shutters. No shingles were blown off the roof and there was no damage caused by any trees or objects blown around by the hurricane force winds. In typical fashion, there was a lull in the wind and rain, and then they returned in full force, reminding all of us of the awesome power of nature. Soon, the thunder and lightening subsided and we mustered enough courage to walk back into the front house where we could peek through the window to get a glimpse of our surroundings.

The next day, as Janet moved away from the battered island of Barbados, the wind and rain subsided. It was obvious that the worst was over. I ventured out of the house to survey the damage and could not believe my eyes. The road was almost impassible. It was completely blocked by rocks and mud and everything the gully was able to dislodge from the hill behind our home. An eerie calm had descended on our neighborhood. Urged on by courage or curiosity, a few of my friends and I decided to walk the mile or so over to Codrington College to survey the situation. With much trepidation, we passed the homes of the Maynards, the Marshalls, the Cooks, the Wiltshires, and the Jordans before reaching the perimeter of College Woods. I could never forget what I saw. Several of the towering mahogany trees had succumbed to the swirling winds of Janet. There was devastation everywhere, with tree trunks and large branches scattered all across the road. In spite of it all, I was not deterred. Climbing stealthily across all sorts of obstacles that blocked my way, I made it to the Cabbage Walk, and then to the imposing building of the College that loomed ahead of me like a gigantic fortress. As expected, all of the families that had retreated to the College before the hurricane hit had spent an uneventful night.

I later learned that Janet had devastated the south coast of Barbados. The Cadet Corps from Lodge School was mobilized and I was taken to the Christ Church Lighthouse to assist with the distribution of food and clothing. Most of the residents we helped had lost their homes and all of their belongings. I could never forget that day. Cadets from Lodge, Harrison College, and Combermere came together for a very worthy cause. I felt that our presence there meant so much to so many. As I left the lighthouse that evening, I thought about how lucky we were in St. John to have escaped the full fury of Janet. The hurricane had claimed the lives of thirty-three Barbadians. An additional one hundred fifty people were reported to have been treated at the Barbados General Hospital for injuries sustained in the hurricane. It was reported that more than eight thousand homes were destroyed and over twenty thousand Barbadians left homeless.

It was not surprising that the Anglican religion was the dominant religion in our community. St. John's Church that loomed majestically at the top of Church Hill was the major venue for Anglican worship. It was also considered to be one of the popular tourist attractions in the parish. The famous grave of Ferdinand Paleologus, descendent of Constantine VIII, the Christian Emperor of Constantinople (Istanbul) is located there.

Then there was Codrington College, a dominant force within the Anglican Church. As stated earlier, Codrington College was supported by the largess of Christopher Codrington's two plantations. It trained almost all of the Anglican priests in the island of Barbados and the entire Caribbean region. The succession of Principals Rawle, 1847 to 1864; Anstey, 1910 to 1918; Whippell, 1918 to1945; Sayer, 1945 to1955; Graham, 1955 to 1957; and Genders, 1957 to 1965, had a profound influence on religious life in St. John. These were extraordinarily powerful men. They baptized, confirmed, and married almost everyone in our community. They wrote the testimonials that got students accepted into schools and colleges, and helped their worshippers obtain jobs in Bridgetown. They also made decisions about where, when, and how to bury the dead!

Society Chapel, now Holy Cross Church added muscle to the college's clout within our community. It was the place where students at the college received their practical training. Those trainees would fan out across the district visiting the sick and shut-in and socializing with the families in ways that strengthened the bonds between community and church. None of the other churches in St. John had the organization, resources, or reach that the Anglican Church had. There were the Methodists, the Seventh-Day Adventists, the Catholics, the Moravians, the Pilgrim Holiness and other denominations scattered across the parish.

The Kidneys were Anglican, and consistent with that tradition, Mum did everything in her power to ensure that my siblings and I modeled good Christian behavior at all times. We were all expected to observe the Sabbath, so every Sunday, Mum would get us up early, and after breakfast, we all dressed up in our finest Sunday outfits and set out on foot for morning service at Society Chapel. In the afternoon around three o'clock it was back up to Chapel Hill to attend Sunday school. Then at six pm we went back to church for evensong. I joined the choir when I was just a youngster, and with that came the requirement to attend choir practice on Wednesday nights, and sing in the choir for morning and evensong. I enjoyed the routine, and looked forward to seeing my friends at church every Sunday. After a while, I could recite the entire Communion service without even pausing, and I was able to memorize many of the hymns and responsive readings.

Weekdays in our home were all about work. When school was in session, I strictly adhered to a schedule that enabled me to arrive on time for classes, and reach home in the evening at a reasonable time. Mum's routine was even more predictable. She was such a multi-tasker, switching roles from mother, to housewife, to cook, and cleaner, without even missing a beat. She washed the clothes on Monday, bleached them on Tuesday, starched on Wednesday, and ironed on Thursday. She repeated that practice every week. Then she was our nurse, our coach, our teacher, our mentor, and our friend. She made dresses and pillowcases, and she taught us the value of family, constantly reminding us of our many cousins and other relatives that were scattered all across the island of Barbados. She was such a warm and loving person, that I always felt so blessed to have her as my mother.

Dad was the consummate breadwinner. During the week, he would get up early in the morning, and be on his way to work before I was fully awake. I remember, as a little boy, I would watch out for his bicycle as he approached Cox Hill in the evening, and I would drop everything and run straight into his welcoming arms for the short ride home on his bike. On weekends, Dad would work around the house building a wall, fixing the car, or planting an exotic tree that he obtained from the Government Agricultural Station. Dad was a physical fitness guru who always reminded us of the importance of striving to keep the physical and spiritual parts of our being in perfect balance. He was a positive thinker, and he found a way to shower us with praise even for the most modest accomplishment.

I was a wartime baby, born a few months before Germany invaded Poland. As I grew older, I couldn't understand why the war would have reached our tiny island, but it did. I have childhood memories of survivors of German ships torpedoed at sea washing up at Bath Beach and being transported by the authorities through our neighborhood. I also remember the fear I experienced every time I saw one of the German Zeppelin-type airships fly over Barbados. The torpedoing of the Cornwallis in Carlisle Bay on the eleventh of December, 1942 by a German U-Boat was a major reminder to all Barbadians about how dangerous the war was.

For years, Dad wondered whether the Germans had any help in planning and executing that dastardly act right in the Barbados careenage. He would be very surprised to learn that two of the athletes he spoke highly of–Whiskers Blake and Joe Gotch–were implicated as the spies who allegedly provided the Germans with the information needed to sink the Cornwallis. Dad thought that the two men came to Barbados to showcase their skills as wrestlers, and he and many other Barbadians admired them for their talent. In fact, Dad had their photographs prominently displayed in our living room along with pictures of the likes of Joe Louis and Jersey Joe Walcott. Dad never would have suspected them to be German spies!

I overheard Dad tell of the time during the blackout when he was riding home at night, and he did not have the light on his bicycle properly covered. As he approached the cut-wall by Thickets Plantation, a bright light illuminated the entire area, a very scary reminder to him that someone, friend or foe, was watching his movements. Then there was the time when Mum was in the living room of our home sewing. She routinely worked on her projects in the evening. That evening I was by her side watching as she meticulously assembled a dress from the patterns she had cut the night before. The window was open and the kerosene lamp was flickering with the dull light helping her to lay down her stitches on the Singer sewing machine with the usual precision. All of a sudden, a bright light flashed from the darkness of the Atlantic Ocean illuminating the entire living room. We couldn't believe what had happened. Mum quickly closed the shutters to the window, put out the light and retreated to the safety of the bedroom. She never sewed at night again until the blackout was lifted.

There was one other event from my childhood that is still permanently etched in my mind. It was the incident involving my friend Nippon, and how he violated the trust that Dad had placed in him. Dad was always a person who trusted people unconditionally, so when Dad befriended Nippon, he treated him as if he was one of his own children. Nippon was a youngster, about my age, who lived in Church Village. We played together, and he helped Dad on occasion with the cow as well as with running errands. In exchange, Nippon was a constant visitor to our home in Church Village and we all trusted him.

Our shop in Church Village was by no means a successful business. There was considerable competition all around us for a limited clientele. The Greaves, Holder, Manifold, and Garner families all had shops. Then there was the fact that Mum and Dad never really tracked revenue or expenses. I believe that they simply looked to see if there was money in the cash box, and if there was any money there, they used it to meet whatever was their most pressing need at the time. So with that as their *modus operandi*, they became very concerned during that particular period to find that the cash box was always almost out of money.

Mum later told me that she thought Dad was taking the money, and Dad thought that it was Mum who was the culprit. I don't know what was the trigger, but it soon became apparent to them that the reason that the cash box was always low had nothing to do with either of them. It seemed that someone else was raiding the cash box, and Dad was determined to catch the thief. One day, Dad decided that he would let everyone in the neighborhood think that he would be away from home. So he told all of the men in the neighborhood that the shop would be closed. He also told Nippon his friend and confidante that he would be away on business. Then, he positioned himself strategically inside the shop and waited and waited to see what would happen.

I was flabbergasted when Dad told me that about mid-morning, he was huddled down in a corner in the darkened shop when he heard a noise that sounded like an intruder. He remained as quiet as he possibly could, and before long he saw the window over the door that connected the house to the shop open ever so slightly. Then the shadowy form of a person's hand appeared through the window. As the intruder tried desperately to disengage the bolt to the door, Dad grabbed the person's hand and warned him not to move. What happened next was something that Dad could not have imagined. The person whose hand he had gripped so firmly was Nippon, the family's trusted friend! I can only imagine the flood of emotions that raged through Dad's very being in those desperate moments. Here was a person who was taking food out of his children's mouths. Here was a person whom he trusted. An uneasy calm prevailed over Dad as he held the trembling frame of that young man from the neighborhood. After alerting the men on the bridge outside of the shop, Dad took Nippon to the police station at District-C and, after conviction, the young man was sent to the Boy's Industrial School at Dodds, St. Philip where he was incarcerated for several years. I have not seen Nippon since that time.

Much of the crime in Barbados during my youth involved larceny in one form or another. A lot of people were really very poor, and it was therefore not unusual to read about some youngster being arrested for stealing potatoes or corn, or even the neighbor's chicken. Usually no one was physically hurt, only their reputations were tarnished, and often, many of the wayward boys wound up serving time in the Boys Industrial School at Dodds, St. Philip. The girls had their own facility at Summerville.

The only major criminal activity that I can recall, involved two gruesome murders in St. Philip that had the elders in our neighborhood and all across the island shaking in their proverbial boots. The first, occurred near Thicket Plantation and involved the stabbing of a bus driver by his own conductor; and the second took place in Brereton Village and was allegedly committed by a man called Lloyd Linton. Babsey Beckles from College Hill was found guilty of murdering his bus driver and was hanged for that crime. Lloyd Linton was accused of the Brereton murder and he went into hiding and to my knowledge, was never found. Then there were rumors about outlaws in the sugarcane fields in St. John and St. Philip, a heartman in the caves in St. Lucy, and the old story about the plantation manager at Warrens, St. Michael, who allegedly shot a boy and claimed that he mistook him for a rabbit.

Chapter 7

The Lodge School

In 1948, after considerable prompting from Mr. Freddie Gittens, my teacher at Society Mixed School, Mum and Dad decided to have me take the entrance exam for the Lodge School. Lodge was an old English boarding school in St. John with an excellent reputation for academic excellence. At that time, I was in the fourth standard at Society Mixed School. Mr. Gittens had recommended my promotion to fourth standard because of my ability to handle some of the more difficult and complex mathematics problems. Fourth standard was on the second floor of the building. I was very proud of the fact that I had finally made it upstairs where the classes for the big boys and girls were located.

Mr. Gittens' recognition of my latent scholastic abilities profoundly changed my life. It opened more doors for me than I could have ever imagined. I now believe that my passionate commitment to giving back, especially in the sciences, stems directly from my desire to repay Mr. Gittens for the unsolicited support he provided me at that critical juncture of my life. Unquestionably, Mr. Freddie Gittens was among my most influential mentors.

Established in 1745 through a bequest made by Christopher Codrington, Lodge School became one of the oldest and best recognized secondary schools in Barbados. It occupied a sprawling campus whose grounds were contiguous with the sugarcane fields of Society Plantation. At its inception, the school's original purpose was to educate boys who could be trained for the Holy Orders at Codrington College and other seminaries in the region. However, in the nineteenth century, Lodge became a traditional boys school and operated in a manner similar to British grammar schools. The school's motto "Possunt Quia Posse Videntur" (They Can Because They Know They Can) is identical to the motto for Christ College, Whales that was founded by King Henry VIII in 1541.

Preparing for the Lodge School entrance examination was a challenge that I took very seriously. Joyce was my tutor, and what a tutor she was. She got all of her notes from St. Michael's Girl's School where she was a student, and insisted that I memorize everything on those pages. By the time she was through with me, I knew all that I needed to know about peninsulas, deltas, islands, and a wealth of other general knowledge questions. I remember staying up late the night before the exam working diligently on my math and general knowledge skills.

That Saturday morning of the exam, Joyce and I got up very early, and after I had my bath and ate breakfast, I put on my starched white shirt, short khaki pants, black shoes and socks, and began my walk up to the Lodge School with Joyce at my side. As I approached the entrance to the campus, I felt a sudden rush of adrenaline. My heart was pounding uncontrollably as if it wanted to jump right out of my chest, and my hands and feet were sweating profusely. That was the first time I was entering the hallowed halls of that prestigious boarding school, and my entire being was sensing the weight of the occasion.

The venue for the exam was the school's auditorium. I remember Joyce wishing me good luck as I was ushered into a very large hall that was filled with rows of wooden desks separated by wide aisles. I don't remember talking to any of the students who took the exam with me that day. It was a very intimidating experience for someone like me coming from the simple settings of Society Mixed School. Complete silence had engulfed the room, and as I sat quietly at my desk, I could feel my teeth chattering and my knees knocking. The invigilator was a fair-skinned Bajan who looked like a government official of some sort. He remained seated quietly at a large wooden desk surrounded by several packages of paper. Then, as if by cue, he rose to his feet, instructed us to remove everything from the top of our desks, warned us against talking to anyone, and proceeded to break the seals to each of the packages that were stacked on the top of his desk. He then walked down each aisle handing out sheets of foolscap paper along with the dreaded exam forms. I had to hold the test with both hands to minimize the shaking.

When I looked at the questions, it was obvious to me that Joyce had guessed right. Everything she had reviewed with me the night before was on the exam. I realized that I knew the answers to almost all of the questions. My palms were no longer sweating. I could sense that my confidence was increasing; and I knew for sure that I could ace that entrance exam.

On several occasions since that day, I have tried to re-live that experience, and I am still not able to remember with any specificity what I did after I left the auditorium. What I know for certain is that I thanked Joyce profusely for preparing me as well as she had done. I don't remember anyone else who took the exam with me, and I don't have the slightest recollection of talking with anyone on that day besides Joyce. I would soon learn that I did outstandingly well on the exam. My mentor and teacher Mr. Fred Gittens was right. I had proven to him and to my parents that I could compete effectively in any setting as long as I was willing to invest the time and energy; and I began to develop the self confidence that would serve me well at the Lodge School and beyond.

I entered the Lodge School in the fall of 1948 and was placed in Prep Form. Compared to Society Mixed School, Lodge was a sprawling campus with several two-story buildings and two large, well-manicured playing fields–the first eleven on the north side of the complex, and the second eleven on the south side. Classroom space for prep formers was on the ground floor of a very old building that bordered the second eleven field. My classmates included Phillip Goddard, Bancroft, Patrick Frost, Robin Green, Louis Thorne, Chesterfield Vaughan, Martin Barnard, Masson, Barnardo, Abbot, Agard, Beattie, Hopkins, Stanley, DeLabastide and many other students whose last names I can still remember. Our teachers were Mrs. Greaves, Miss Bolger, and Mrs. Ince. This was the same Mrs. Ince from Hopewell that Dad chauffeured when he worked for Mr. Garner.

Classes at Lodge were very structured, and on a typical day I spent most of my classroom time honing my skills in

English and mathematics. Spelling, verb conjugation, penmanship, and poetry were high priorities for my classmates and me. Homework regularly included memorizing the work of some of the most famous poets. I had to memorize and recite poems such as *The Daffodils*, by William Wordsworth; *The Charge of the Light Brigade*, by Alfred Lord Tennyson; and *The Moon*, by Henry Wadsworth Longfellow. From my copybooks I learned all about England, Newcastle on Tyne, and other far away places.

Lodge School was an exciting experience for me and other students like me who came from simple rural settings. It provided me with firsthand exposure to a truly international and diverse community of students. I had classmates from England, America, Dominica, St. Kitts, St. Lucia, the Dominican Republic, Venezuela, Trinidad, and other Caribbean states.

As one of the smallest boys on that campus, I had to be extremely careful not to project an image of weakness to any of my classmates. That would have been a clear invitation for the bullies to slap me around the head or humiliate me everytime they had the opportunity to do so. Despite my size, I was in great shape physically. I also had a number of friends who looked out for my interest, and that shielded me from the "slings and arrows" that some Lodge School students had to deal with on a daily basis.

During my early years at Lodge, lunchtime provided me with the opportunity to socialize with my classmates in the schoolyard. This was not a typical quadrangle with neatly manicured lawns and imposing buildings. Instead, it was a surface that was largely unpaved, with some areas covered with loose marl and gravel. On the south side of the quadrangle there was the two-story science building that housed the Biology, Chemistry and Physics Departments, along with the fifth form classroom. To the west was the sixth form building. In those days, that building also housed modern studies, classics, mathematics, the library, and the school's only bookstore. The bicycle shed was attached to the sixth form building, and across from its entrance there was a very large lavatory.

On the north side of the schoolyard there was a small garage where the masters parked their cars. The Tuck Shop was located to the right of the masters' parking lot. This was the place where I could buy ham cutters and sweet drinks from Barnett, and his cousin Francis. Next to the Tuck Shop was one of the buildings belonging to the boarding establishment. It also housed the sanitarium and the school nurse's office. Across from that facility was the headmaster's office with the old school bell situated at its entrance. To the east was a cluster of buildings where prep, first, second, and third form classes were held. A large room situated just above the third form classroom served as the masters' quarters. A cluster of old mahogany trees was strategically placed in the center of the yard.

One of the lunchtime activities that I really enjoyed was pitching marbles. The site for pitching marbles was the schoolyard on the south side of campus, proximal to the science building. Boys like Challenor Jones (who went on to become one of the greatest jockeys of all time), his brother Rodney, Arthur Bethel, "Cockeye" Wilkie; Martin Barnard, Barnardo and I met daily to do battle. I was an experienced pitcher having honed my skills with the likes of Earl McIntosh, Woogie, Malec, and Edwin Green, all guys from my neighborhood. I pitched for buttons in my neighborhood. At Lodge School I was pitching for marbles. And some days I went home with both of my pockets bulging and rattling with my lunch time winnings of shiny, new marbles.

I disliked the end of the school year with a passion. It was the time when the school's much dreaded funeral was held. That was a ritual that must have endured throughout the years of Lodge School's existence. The service was presided over by a group of no-nonsense senior boys, all of whom were prefects. During my years at Lodge, Burleigh Sealy usually played the role of priest and he was surrounded by many of his contemporaries from St. John and St. Philip.

The event began with the identification of one of the smallest boys on campus. There were several of us to choose from, and the first to be caught was placed in the casket to become the subject of that year's burial service. Once in the casket, the procession of "clergymen" and a band of the curious would wind its way across the campus in a simulated burial ceremony.

I never witnessed the entire ceremony, because as one of the smallest boys on campus I knew that the burial committee would target me, and I was always on the alert to avoid being the victim of that bizarre practice. I am proud to say that I was never placed in that casket, and have always been curious to speak with any Lodge boy who succumbed to such a fate.

When I attended Lodge, the classrooms and playing fields were comfortably integrated. The boarding establishment however, was not. All of the groundsmen and support staff were black. With a diverse student body, I never felt any sense of racial oppression. What was evident to me, however, was the existence of two Barbadian societies, one white and privileged, and the other black and filled with ambition and aspiration. Black students knew they needed an education to lift themselves and their families out of poverty. White students knew that their families had a firm grip on business and commerce and that was reflected in the way they were treated by everyone.

Our school was therefore not racially polarized as such, but everyone knew and understood what the unwritten rules were and quietly accepted them. For example, white and black students interacted completely while at school, but rarely socialized once they left the perimeter of the campus. I never visited the homes of my white school friends, and never invited them to my home. My fellow students and I, like most Barbadians, were acutely aware of what was happening in our society, but both blacks and whites accepted it as a part of our way of life.

Almost all of the masters, with the exception of Mr. Val McComie, were white. My first headmaster Mr. Tommy Evans was an Englishman and so was Mr. Dowsey (physics), Mr. Jarvis (mathematics), and Mr. Wilkes (geography). I believe that my chemistry teacher Mr. Sumpter was from New Zealand. My other teachers, Messrs. Massiah (English), Walcott (classics), Chritchlow (classics), Gooding (biology), and Mallaliew (scripture knowledge) were all Barbadian.

I was also taught by a contingent of white female teachers that included Mrs. Bolger (English), Mrs. Greaves (English), Miss Muir (French), Miss Moore (Earth science), and Mrs. Ince (French). During the ten years I spent at Lodge, leadership was transferred from Mr. Evans to Mr. Farmer and then to Mr. Newsome. Mr. Val McComie, a role model of mine for my entire time at Lodge, was the only black teacher until Mr. Glasgow, a former student, and Reverend Jones (Snow Ball) joined the staff.

As a student during those early years, I excelled in class but did not consider my performance to be extraordinary. My report cards were usually impressive, and I was promoted at the end of every academic year. I have vivid memories of teachers such as Mr. Graham Wilkes who was my geography teacher (he would later become a major force in my development as a soccer star). I absolutely enjoyed drawing those contour maps along with Wendell Kellman, one of my classmates.

Then there was Mr. Farmer my second headmaster who taught me mathematics in third form. He would terrorize the class, punishing students who failed to answer his questions correctly by forcing them to do laps around the second-eleven field. There was another teacher who the students referred to as "Young Man." He was an elderly member of the Pilgrim family from Mount Tabor, St. John. He got the name because he addressed every student as "Young Man" before reading him the riot act!

Students from Codrington High School could attend our speech day but only Lodge School students with relatives at Codrington High School could attend theirs. We had a racially mixed student body and that was good, but our boarding establishment was completely white. Day-boys were not permitted to walk through the boarding establishment to access the north side of campus.

Seats in the front of our church at Holy Cross were set aside for boarders from Lodge and Codrington High School. The tennis courts were reserved for boarders (white boys) until my friends Oscar Jordan and Frank Farnum integrated that facility. In spite of those blatantly racist practices, there were few instances of racial tension during the ten years that I attended Lodge. One incident stands out in my mind. I am not fully aware of what triggered the conflict between Holder a black student from St. John and a white boy named Mayhew. On that day, a large crowd had surrounded those two students who were obviously ready to do battle. The white boys were cheering for Mayhew and the black boys for Holder. The angry crowd moved to the far side of the first eleven field to avoid interference from any masters. The tension was palpable. And then it happened. One short right uppercut delivered by Holder to the chin of Mayhew sent him sprawling on the ground! I couldn't believe what I had seen. We were all frozen for a moment, and then, apprehensive about what might happen next. Nothing happened! Mayhew got up off the ground, dusted himself off and the crowd dispersed. That was the closest I came to racial conflict during my entire time at Lodge.

Marshall was the head Porter. He was a major figure at the Lodge School during the decade of the 1950's while I was a student there. He rang the bell to begin and end classes, and he brought the attendance and detention records to the masters in their respective classrooms. Other notable individuals included Bill Ford the head groundsman, Mr. Blackman the science laboratory technician, and Iris Jones the lady to whom most Lodge boys owe a debt of gratitude. On days when the day-boys had no lunch money, several of them consumed her ham and fish cutters without providing her with proper compensation.

In 1955, I took the much-feared Oxford and Cambridge O Level Exams. I was a fifth former then and all fifth formers were required to register for and take that dreaded exam. Performance in O Levels would determine one's academic fate. Passes in biology, chemistry, and physics made a student eligible for a career in the sciences. Students who excelled in mathematics and additional math could pursue engineering careers. Outstanding performers in English usually chose modern studies, while the top students in Latin and Greek became scholars of the classics.

Studying for the O Levels reminded me of my earlier experience with preparing for the Lodge School entrance exam. There was a major difference however. It took me just a couple of days to prepare for the Lodge School entrance exam, while my preparation for the O Levels would take an entire year!

At the beginning of the year, I elected to compete for eight subjects: English literature, English language, mathematics, biology, chemistry, physics, Latin, and scripture knowledge. Mr. Massiah taught me English literature. My class was assigned The Nun's Priest's Tale by Geoffrey Chaucer. It reminded me of some of the tales I read in Aesop's Fables. The story was about a proud rooster called Chauntecleer and his favorite wife Pertelote. Like Aesop's Fables its intent was to use the experiences of those animals to teach students lessons about life. The Nun's Priest's Tale was a difficult read for all of the members of my class because it was written in old English.

My second book assignment for English literature was Shakespeare's King Henry V. In contrast to Chaucer, I thoroughly enjoyed having to study that book of Shakespeare in the detail that was required for O Level. I was familiar with Hamlet and Julius Caesar and had even seen the movie versions of those great works while at Lodge. However, I found Henry V to be a literary masterpiece, and there are passages from that book that still resonate with me even after all of these years. I particularly like Act four Scene two when King Henry says: "Upon the King! Let us our lives, our souls, our debts, our careful wives, our children and our sins lay on the King! We must bear all. O hard condition, twin-born with greatness, subject to the breath of every fool, whose sense no more can feel but his own wringing! What infinite heart's ease must Kings neglect that private men enjoy! And what have Kings, that privates have not too, save ceremony, save general ceremony? And what art thou, thou idle ceremony? ... Can'st thou, when thou command'st the beggar's knee, command the health of it?"

For Latin, my class was assigned The Gallic Wars (Book One) by Julius Caesar and Virgil's Aeneid, Book Two, a treatise that details Aeneas' account of the destruction of Troy. In retrospect, I find those to be brilliant choices of the classics that my classmates and I benefited from immensely. Mr. Chritchlow who taught that class was the consummate classical scholar. His conservative manner and remarkable knowledge of the principal characters and events covered in those ancient texts suggested that he had benefited from the high quality of education that was available in Barbados to the children of privileged families. He was small in stature, with a neatly trimmed mustache and salt and pepper hair, and always wore an off-white suit with his three-button jacket neatly buttoned at all times.

An Englishman, Mr. Jarvis prepared me for the mathematics exam. He was one of my most inspiring teachers. He knew how to simplify the most complicated mathematical problem, and he taught us rules that I still employ today. I can remember him saying, "when in doubt whether to cancel or not, don't cancel!" That was the rule for dealing with situations in mathematics when I was not sure if I should continue with my effort to further simplify the answer to a mathematics problem. He made math fun, and as a result of his effective teaching style, I was able to ace the O Levels in mathematics, scoring one hundred percent in the first exam and ninety-six percent in the second! An unbelievable accomplishment for a student who was performing in the forty-percentile range when Mr. Farmer was my teacher.

My biology teacher was Mr. Herbert Gooding. Everyone called him Wox. He was a Barbadian who was educated in Canada. I saw in him a genuine devotee to the entire field of science. He had preserved his lecture notes from the time he was a student at McGill University, and he invariably used them to supplement the material in the text book that was assigned to our fifth form class.

Mr. Fab Hoyos taught me history. He was a gentleman with a unique ability to empathize with his students. He was caring and compassionate, and those qualities were reflected in the way he taught history and graded his exams. The reverend Mallalieu had the difficult assignment of teaching scripture. My reading assignments for that course were the Book of Matthew and the Acts of the Apostles both from the New Testament of the Bible. I am still amazed that I was able to write an exam on the material I covered in those Holy Books.

As I prepared for the examination of my life, the routine was disciplined and comprehensive. Some teachers tested the class on a weekly basis using questions taken from previous O Level exams. I was routinely memorizing passages from Chaucer and Shakespeare, and Virgil, as I learned how to deal with the unexpected. Upon reaching home in the evening after school, I had only two assignments–eat dinner, and study. My constant study-mate was my trusted friend Sam Hall. He moved from Bayfield, St. Philip, to our neighborhood to board with his aunt Mrs. Pinder who lived at the bottom of Cox Hill. Sam was a member of the Lodge School Cadet Corps and the Barbados Regiment and he was a strict disciplinarian. Although Sam was older than me, he and I became very good friends, and we would study for hours and hours as we prepared for the O Levels. I remember memorizing Virgil in both Latin and English. I also committed to memory lengthy passages from Shakespeare, Chaucer, the Book of Matthew, and the Acts of the Apostles.

The day of reckoning would inevitably arrive. I remember going up to Lodge, entering the same room that was used for the entrance exams seven years earlier, and waiting for the invigilator to instruct me to take my seat at one of those hard wooden desks spaced three feet apart on all sides. Foolscap paper and exam books were distributed to each student. Then the invigilator read the rules of engagement–no talking, no cheating. He instructed the class on the correct way to sign our names on the exam papers, and how to exit the room when we were finished. I was numb from the first to the last day of that very nerve-wracking experience. Finally, the ordeal was over, and I could go home to wait all summer before I would know how I did in the O Levels.

That summer, I reached the legal age to drive an automobile in Barbados, and that provided me with the perfect distraction from having to think about my O Level results. With Dad's help, I went to the Central Police Station in Bridgetown and applied for a learner's permit. The officer in charge approved my application, and I left there with two metal plates that I was told needed to be visibly displayed on the front and rear of the car during periods of driver instruction. The letter "L" was emblazoned in bright red in the center of each metal plate against a white background.

Our car at that time was a dark blue 1939 Ford. That car was built like a tank. It was outfitted with the sturdiest chrome bumpers I have ever seen. The headlamps were built into the curvature at the top of the two front fenders. An attractive chrome grille composed of closely spaced vertical bars was situated below the bonnet filling much of the space between the two headlights. The windscreen had numerous cracks, several of which had turned yellow from prolonged exposure to the hot tropical sun. The odometer and gas gauge had stopped working a long time ago, and the leather covered bench seats were also showing significant signs of wear and tear. The rubber pads on the clutch and break pedals were extensively worn, and all that was left was a black rubber perimeter surrounding the shiny metal in the center of each pedal.

In spite of all of those shortcomings, I liked Dad's 1939 Ford simply because it provided me with a source of transportation that I desperately needed. I thought that it was a whole lot better than the Model-T Ford that it replaced. Dad bought the Model-T from the Reverend Gay Lisle Griffith Mandeville who was Rector at St. Philip's Church and later became Bishop of Barbados. It had a convertible top. The choke and acceleration controls were built into the side of the steering column, and the side windows were made from mica. I liked the job of having to snap those windows to the frame of the door every time it rained. One thing I disliked about that car was its horn. The horn was mounted at the side of the body, and every time Dad pressed it, there was this loud *aaa-wooo-gaahh* sound, that alerted everyone within earshot that Dad's car was in the neighborhood.

Although the 1939 Ford represented a step-up from the Model-T, it had a history of breaking down all over the countryside. Sometimes it would run out of gas; other times it was due to overheating or some other mechanical or electrical problem. None of this ever bothered me, because I knew that Dad was able to get that car to run again regardless of what had gone wrong.

Dad taught me how to keep my eye on the curb as I passed vehicles with blinding headlights at night. He showed me how to engage that long clutch pedal, and use the handbrakes when attempting to move from a stationary position in a hill. He even taught me how to reverse uphill whenever I was low on gas.

On the day of my road test, Dad was unable to go with me to Central Police Station so he asked our neighbor Kenneth Mayers to fill in for him. Everything went well for the hour that the officer tested me through the streets of Bridgetown and its environs. When I returned to the station, the last challenge I was presented with was to back the car into a space between two parked vehicles. I was flawless in executing that task, and upon completion, the officer motioned me to follow him into the building. I waited for over thirty minutes before learning that I had passed my driver's test. It took them another ten minutes before they issued me my driver's license.

I cannot ever forget the feeling of euphoria that I experienced as I walked out of the Central Police Station that day. I had passed one of the most important tests that any Barbadian teenager had to take in the 1950s. I was now officially licensed to drive a car in Barbados, and the little rectangular book that I had in my possession was proof positive of my singular achievement. The book was light brown in color and I remember it had a hardcover. The official stamp of the Traffic Branch of the Barbados Police Department and the date of issue were prominently displayed on the inside of the front cover. My signature appeared immediately below. There were ten blank pages in the front of the book where renewal receipts would be attached. Pages eleven through thirty-two listed in considerable detail the six cardinal rules of driving that Clive Smith, Commissioner of Police at that time, wanted every licensed driver in Barbados to observe. Those pages even included illustrations in which police officers in full regalia were used to demonstrate to new drivers the correct signals that would be used by traffic constables. There were also illustrations of signals to be used by drivers as they negotiated the network of paved streets and highways across the island. On page twenty-one there was a complete narrative on the use of traffic light signals. My recollection is that there were perhaps only two traffic light signals in Bridgetown when I was issued my drivers license.

As I exited the station and approached Kenneth who was standing beside the parked car, I remember how difficult it was for me to control my emotions. I was so elated by my accomplishment. After I was finished celebrating, Kenneth told me that it was only fitting for me to drive home. I remember getting behind the wheel, turning on the ignition and pressing the starter. The engine turned over slowly and then stopped. I felt that the battery might have died from the rigors of the road test, so I pulled out the crank handle and proceeded to crank, and crank, and crank, to no avail. I couldn't believe it, but I had to leave the car exactly where I had parked it, walk to the bus stand, and take the next bus back to St. John.

September brought very good news. I had done exceedingly well in the O Level exam, passing all eight subjects.

For the first time I saw myself as someone in good academic standing. Previously, most of those who knew me saw me first as an outstanding athlete, blessed with exceptional skills at playing soccer. Now, I thought, they should also see me as a person capable of significant academic accomplishment.

When I returned to Lodge at the end of the summer vacation (that was prior to receiving the O Level results), the headmaster had already decided who should be placed in sixth form and who should remain in fifth. Much to my horror, all of the black boys were left in fifth, and all of the white boys were advanced to sixth. My friends Frank Daniel, and Vernon Dean commiserated with me about the decision, and we were vindicated when the results were announced. We would all have to be promoted based on our outstanding performances in the O Level Exam.

The news that I would be promoted to sixth form came approximately two weeks into the September term, and I had very little time to decide what academic direction would be most appropriate for me. The choices available were: modern studies; classics; mathematics; or basic science. I was unable to make an intelligent decision. One day as I was agonizing about the choice I should make, I sought Dad's advice. "Dad," I said, "I have to decide what academic program I should pursue in the sixth form, and I am not sure what to do, what do you think?" Dad, in his inimitable fashion responded by making a statement and then asking me a question. "Those Russians are really smart," he stated. "Can you imaging how smart they had to be in order to launch that Sputnik Satellite into space." Then he asked the rhetorical question "Who do you think helped them to place Sputnik into space?" After asking the question there was this well-calculated pause, and then he provided me with the answer to that leading question. "Scientists," he said, "science is going to be the wave of the future. I think you should seriously consider becoming a scientist." That did it for me, I had made my decision, I enrolled in science sixth, taking biology and chemistry at A Level.

Being a member of the sixth form had its benefits. Some of my classmates and I were all elevated to the rank of Prefect. I am still not sure of the origin of the title Prefect, but if I were to guess, I would assume that it was extracted from Roman governance. Anyway, as a Prefect, I got to maintain law and order in the classrooms to which I was assigned. Prefects were required to stand guard in classrooms to ensure that when the bell rang for classes to begin, each student would take his seat in an orderly fashion, and remain there quietly until the teacher arrived. In the interval between the ringing of the bell and the arrival of the teacher from the Masters' Quarters (approximately five minutes), Prefects were expected to maintain proper discipline. If students were late in assuming their seats or disruptive in any way, we were authorized to issue "lines" or "detentions." I was known to assign many a belligerent student one hundred lines to be completed overnight. Students receiving such an assignment were required to write one hundred lines of text from any textbook as neatly as possible and present them to the Prefect in satisfaction of the punishment. "Detention" assignments were rarely issued by Prefects, but when a student was particularly disruptive, the punishment was detention in a supervised setting for a specified period of time. Usually, detentions at Lodge were an after-school activity, and the assignment was usually "lines."

My studies as a member of the science-sixth proceeded on track. A Level was very different from O Level. There was no English or mathematics to worry about. Neither did I have to worry about history or Latin. All of my time would be devoted to studying biology and chemistry. My biology teacher was again Wox Gooding. He was an expert in botany and zoology. His sessions began with a lecture during which the class was required to copy copious notes. Organs and systems had to be well-illustrated with careful drawings that Wox scrutinized for accuracy. Everything had to be properly labeled. These were masterpieces that the students were very proud to display. After we completed those tasks, we would then begin our hands-on sessions. They included dissections of frogs, earthworms, and dogfish. We each had a partner, or sometimes we were divided into small groups. Those sessions provided valuable opportunities for me to get to know the members of the group, and we tried to learn from each other. I had so much fun dissecting frogs and identifying organs, arteries, and veins. The memories of my days in Wox's class are still fresh in my mind. I was being introduced to some fundamental concepts of anatomy and physiology that have served me well and provided me with a competitive advantage when I became a university student.

My A Level chemistry teacher was from New Zealand. He was the opposite to Wox. He was disorganized, unable to teach simple concepts in chemistry, and seemed to me to be generally confused. That confusion was even reflected in his body language. Very often he would have a puzzled look on his face and would stare aimlessly into space. Basically, he had no notes of his own, and as a student I felt that even if he knew chemistry he was unable to teach it effectively.

After two years, it was time to take the A Level exams. I found that to be a logistical nightmare. The exam venue was Harrison College in Bridgetown. Lodge boys had to wake up early, travel to Bridgetown, and then make their way on foot over to Harrison College. There were no clear directions informing us which building would house the exam room. I remember that I disliked the process and felt that it gave the Harrison College boys an unfair advantage. There is no way that they could have been as stressed out by that experience as the Lodge boys. After all, we had to travel from the country to the city, and then we had to prepare to take an important examination in a completely unfamiliar setting!

In spite of all of those issues, I was able to get a distinction in Biology in my first try at A Levels. Wox was so pleased with my performance that he encouraged me to prepare for a possible shot at the Barbados scholarship next time around. He felt that I had a reasonable chance at winning a scholarship if I took botany and zoology instead of biology. My third course would be chemistry. Very few of Wox's students had taken botany and zoology in the entire history of his tenure at Lodge. As expected, he had preserved his McGill University notes, and was willing to devote all the time necessary to prepare me for the task ahead. In 1958, I was the only member of the Lodge School science sixth that took the A Level in botany, zoology and chemistry.

As in the previous year, the venue for the exam was Harrison College. I was up early in the morning and traveled to Bridgetown by bus. When I arrived in the city, I took a brisk walk to Harrison College. I remember waiting on the campus to gain access to the building. The previous year, a number of Lodge, Harrison College, and other students joined me as I waited. This time, there were no students congregating for the botany exam. That worried me deeply. Was I waiting at the wrong building, or did I misread the time for the start of the exam? I kept asking myself.

Eventually, a young lady in a Modern High School uniform joined me. She introduced herself as Ester Archer and asked if I was waiting to take the botany A Level exam. I was thrilled to learn that I had not misunderstood the instructions about location and time of the exam. It turned out that in 1958, Ester Archer and I were the only two students in Barbados registered to take the botany and zoology A Level exam. It was an eerie experience being in a large classroom with only one other student. Ester and I were able to survive that stressful exam. She went on to pursue a very successful career in medicine, and every time we met it was impossible for us to avoid reflecting on that unique experience we both shared back in 1958.

The Lodge School provided me with such a strong academic foundation that I did not pay much attention to my budding talents in athletics. It was not long before I was thrust into athletic competition as a representative of the Laborde House. First, it was track and field. I remember competing in the fifty-yard dash as well as in the one hundred fifty-yard sprint in my first Speech Day as a student in prep form. Mum was in the Pavilion along with several of her friends who also had sons attending Lodge. I wish there was a videotape of those races. From the moment the gun sounded, I took off, never looking back. It was an easy win in the fifty-yard and one hundred fifty-yard sprints. My reward was a silver cup presented by the head boy at the conclusion of the athletics competition. Mum and Dad were so proud of my accomplishment. My win that day had some repercussions that Dad shared with the family at a later date.

At that time in 1949, Dad was employed at River Plantation. River was located approximately six or seven miles to the southeast of our home in St. John. It was a small plantation situated in the lowlands of the Parish of St. Philip. I never knew how the plantation got its name, but based on the flooding that occurred there after even the slightest rain event, I always assumed that it got its name from the artificial lakes that would form in that region after a heavy downpour of rain.

Dad's job at River was Yard Manager. As Yard Manager he supervised the employees who maintained the tractors and other motorized vehicles, and he provided equipment and supplies essential to meet the operational needs of that medium-sized plantation. River owned and cultivated several acres of lush sugarcane fields. The plantation also planted potatoes, corn, and yams, and employed a number of laborers to maintain and harvest those very important crops. As Yard Manager Dad also got to drive the tractors used to plough the sugarcane fields.

I was particularly intrigued by the skill he displayed in maneuvering the massive Massey Harris vehicles with their heavy, cast iron ploughs through the recently harvested sugarcane fields. Those tractors were painted yellow and their extremely noisy engines caused the entire vehicle to vibrate as it spewed copious clouds of dark smoke out of its vertical exhaust pipe. I truly loved the power that was generated from those seemingly indestructible machines.

During summer holidays from school, Mum would prepare Dad's lunch, and I was the one assigned the task of taking it over to River. Mum packed the food in a three-tiered carrier. She placed the carrier in a cabbage basket (a rectangular basket made from the fronds of the Royal Palm), and secured the cover with a wooden stick. I hung the basket over the bicycle handle before setting out on my journey to River. The trip took me through Sealy Hall, across by Palmers Plantation and out to Thickets. At Thickets, I made a left and proceeded down the hill towards Three Houses Plantation where I followed the main road towards Mapps Plantation. At Mapps, I took a left and follow the unpaved road straight down to River Plantation.

When I arrived in the yard, I sought out Mr. Butcher to inquire about Dad's location. If Dad was plowing a field, Mr. Butcher would give me directions to that field. I always breathed a sigh of relief when I was able to locate the tractor. After I found Dad, I would leave the bike at the edge of the field, and make my way over to him, clutching the basket carefully to avoid spilling any of the gravy in the carrier. As Dad ate, I sat beside him and played with the controls of the tractor. Occasionally, when Dad finished his meal, he let me operate the tractor.

I remember one summer, my friend Kingsley Maynard accompanied me to River to deliver Dad's lunch. When we arrived in the plantation yard we inquired about Dad's location and set out to find him. On that occasion, we simply could not locate the field where Dad was plowing. We searched and searched and could not find him. Then Kingsley had a brilliant idea. With a straight face he said to me, "Ken, why don't we just sit down under this tree and eat this food!" It was indeed a funny line that we could laugh at loudly every time we talked about our experiences growing up in St. John.

Dad's boss at River was the manager of the plantation. He had two sons who were also students at Lodge. Apparently, he was present at Speech Day and witnessed my performance when I won the two races in my division. That night at dinner, the maid told Dad that she overheard the manager asking his sons, "who was that little black boy who ran so fast today." When they replied that the little black boy was Harewood-the-Yard-Manager's son, she said that the manager went completely silent, and his face looked like that of a man who was filled with rage. Stunned by the resentment that my win at Speech Day seemed to be causing, the maid felt a need to warn Dad about possible repercussions from his boss. It did not take long before Dad noticed a significant difference in his boss' attitude towards him. The bad treatment meted out to him would gradually get worse, making it almost impossible for Dad to function effectively as Yard Manager. One day when Dad came home from work, I could tell from the look on his face that something was wrong. He and Mum sat quietly talking in the living room after we had gone to bed. The following morning I learned that Dad would not be going back to River Plantation. The reason–his boss was unable to get over the jealousy he felt after learning that his black Yard Manager's son had distinguished himself at the Lodge School Speech Day in a manner that his own sons had not.

Chapter 8

Soccer Star

Soccer or Football as it is called in Barbados is a sport that I enjoyed playing. When I was in elementary school, I developed my skills by kicking tennis balls or young breadfruits with my friends in the neighborhood. I was quick, possessed innate abilities to elude my competitors, and had the sort of endurance that permitted me to play for hours without interruption. In the neighborhood, friends like Woogie and Jallion, Karl Mapp and others tried to imitate Sleepy Smith and Boogles Williams, two outstanding players on the Codrington College Soccer Team. Every time Codrington College hosted a rival team on their field, I would position myself strategically behind the goal post to recover the ball when a player took an errant kick. When I got control of an out-of-bounds ball, the challenge was to kick the ball into the air as high as possible to demonstrate the power of my kick.

Equipped with the skills that I acquired from playing the game in my neighborhood with makeshift soccer balls, I found it much easier to control the larger, official soccer ball that was available at Lodge. For example, at Lodge during the lunch hour, I would go to the first eleven field where the boys would line up to get a soccer ball from one of the groundsmen. Whoever was lucky enough to get a ball would have an opportunity to lift it into the air and kick it skywards as high as possible.

Some of us, and I was among that group, sought to monopolize the ball by dribbling it on the ground for as long as we could elude our pursuers. I liked to take control of the ball during such sessions, and found it remarkably easy to keep it away from the boys, sometimes for the entire lunch break! I remember there would be times that I would have the ball for so long that I would voluntarily give it up through exhaustion! That was a training ground that helped me to perfect my dribbling skills. I knew that my classmates respected, and in some cases envied my abilities.

It was not long before word got around campus about my exploits with the soccer ball, so I was not at all surprised when Mr. Critchlow, my Latin teacher recruited me to play competitive soccer for Laborde House. Playing on the frontlines of the junior team initially, and then as captain of the senior team, was the thrill of my life. I scored more goals than I could keep track of. Critchie or "Scratchgrain" as we called him, was always thrilled by my performances. During a House Match, he would run back and forth on the sidelines cheering for our team. And during our conversation at halftime, I noticed that he treated me as though I was a colleague and not a student.

I later learned that our games master Mr. Graham Wilkes was also paying much attention to my exploits on the soccer field. He was a no-nonsense type of guy, and a brilliant soccer player. I was told that he had played professional soccer for one of the British clubs prior to coming to Barbados. Before I knew it, I would have Mr. Graham Wilkes as my soccer trainer and mentor. My career as a schoolboy soccer phenom and a member of the Barbados Soccer Team was underway.

It began one day when I was walking across the schoolyard. I could hear footsteps behind me and before I could check on who was so eager to catch up to me, Mr. Wilkes was at my side. He told me that he was very impressed by my abilities as a soccer player. He said that while he was aware that I was much younger and smaller than the average soccer team member, he was confident that I could compete at that level, and he was prepared to give me a try on the Lodge School Team! I really do not remember how I responded, but I know that the real implications of that brief conversation only hit me later that evening while I was on my way home. That brief encounter with Mr. Wilkes catapulted me into the spotlight as a member of the Lodge School, Barbados School Boys, and Barbados National Soccer Team.

My exploits on the soccer field were legendary. I had the ability to outrun anyone to the ball, stop on a dime, fake to any side to throw my opponent off stride, and shoot with either foot.

My teammate Ronnie Hall and I would run circles around the competition, whether it was a schoolboy team from Harrison College or Combermere, or a team of adults from Police, Carlton, or Cable and Wireless. After Ronnie graduated, I was named captain of the Lodge School Soccer Team. All of my teammates knew me and respected my skills and leadership abilities. The referees also knew me, and they had the pleasure of recording all of the goals I scored during that action-packed period of five to six years when the Lodge School players were literally tearing up the nets.

During the years of “Hall and Harewood,” Lodge School became the team that instilled fear into all opponents. We racked up many championships, and were so revered by the Barbadian soccer fans that to this day I still hear stories from guys who have vivid recollections of my exploits on the soccer field. When I am in Barbados, it is not unusual for former fans to tell me how much they admired my skills and talent when I played for Lodge and the National Team. To be honest, it is only now that I fully appreciate how fortunate I was to have played on teams with soccer stars like Graham Wilkes, Earl Glasgow, Ronnie Hall at Lodge School; Emerson Whittington, Algie Symmonds, Winston Grant and others at Empire; and Passion Drayton, Rodney Norville, Dudley Downes, Tosh Gittens, Winston Grant, and Reggie Haynes on the Barbados Soccer Team. Most Barbadian soccer fans still consider the combination of Hall and Harewood to be one of the best forward lines that ever played at Kensington Oval.

My first tour as a soccer player came when the Lodge School Team traveled to St Lucia in 1955 to play against a team from St. Mary’s College. That was my first trip out of Barbados. I remember the excitement in everyone’s eyes as the day of departure for St. Lucia arrived. We were all instructed to meet at the careenage in Bridgetown in the early afternoon. Parents and other family members accompanied the team. After posing for photographs with the Barbados Advocate photographer, we were ushered onto the Daerwood, a small diesel powered schooner anchored in the careenage. Sometime in the late evening, the captain lifted anchor and away we went into the vast Caribbean Sea. I could see the coast of Bridgetown recede into the background. At nightfall, the lights of Barbados flickered against the dark grey ocean, and eventually disappeared. It seemed like we were in the middle of a very large bowl, completely surrounded by darkness. It was such an eerie experience!

Approximately two hours after our schooner left the careenage, my teammates and I began to feel the effects of breathing the diesel fumes and the constant tossing and turning of the Daerwood. We each took turns hanging over the rail on the upper deck and emptying our stomachs of any food we had consumed prior to departure. The trip to St. Lucia seemed to take an eternity. Around midnight, I heard the vessel's engines sputter and stop. All was quiet for several hours as we drifted on this vast expanse of ocean. I had no idea whether the captain shutdown the engines intentionally, or if we were experiencing a genuine engine failure. I think that it was about five o'clock in the morning of the next day that I heard a reassuring chug, chug, followed by the steady rumble of the Daerwood's engines starting up. To my relief, we were on our way again. Two hours later, at sunrise, I could see the mountains of St. Lucia appearing in the distance, and soon after, we were cruising into the most beautiful harbor I had ever seen. On the right side were the Pitons, like sentinels watching over that picturesque scene. Over the left side of the vessel, we could see the tiny heads of boys bobbing in the crystal clear water and diving to recover coins thrown overboard by my teammates.

It was not long before the Daerwood docked at the harbor in Castries, and after completing the formalities with the immigration and customs officials, we were on our way to our hotel in Vigie. It was a small bed and breakfast that was nestled in the hills overlooking the city. Approximately one hour after checking in, and receiving our room assignments, I joined a small group of my closest friends on an exploratory trip through the city. We hardly walked more than six blocks through what seemed to be a mixed-use neighborhood before we heard a hissing sound. We identified the source to be a lady sitting at a first floor window of one of the residences.

After attracting our attention, she asked if we were members of the Barbados Schoolboy Team that was touring St. Lucia. She was such a friendly lady that we stopped to say hello. It turned out that she had strong ties to Barbados. She was Barbadian, and her mother was still residing in the parish of St. Michael. She had married a St. Lucian who was a senior official in the government, and the family had settled in Castries. She really did make us all feel at home, and the friendships we made with her children Clevedon, Myrna, Angela, and Dudley have withstood the test of time.

Our trip to St. Lucia was memorable in many other ways. Our team defeated St. Mary's at soccer, and their cricket team was no match for the Lodge School boys. We toured the dormant volcano at Soufrier, and we sailed around the coast of the island on boats that seemed to be the primary mode of transport for most St. Lucians. One of our team members Tony Cozier was St. Lucian, and we got to spend an enjoyable day at his family home where we met his father, a prominent newspaper publisher on the island.

My second tour was in 1958 when the Barbados Soccer Team traveled to Trinidad to play against the Southern Amateur Football League. Our team included two schoolboys, Tony Best and me, representing Harrison College and Lodge School, respectively. The leader of our squad, Winston Grant, later became my team captain at the Empire Soccer Club. The team manager was Keith Walcott, brother of the famous Clyde Walcott of the West Indies cricket fame. Rodney Norville, Passion Drayton, Michael Evelyn, Martin Haynes, Tosh Gittens, Ivor Alleyne, and others were my teammates.

We boarded a regional plane at the old Seawell Airport around dusk, and took off on time for the short flight to Piarco Airport in Trinidad. I was home sick approximately fifteen minutes into the flight, and wrote my Mum and Dad a post card while I was still in the air. We arrived in Trinidad after what seemed like a very long flight, and then we had to travel from Port of Spain to San Fernando by car. The trip was awesome. I recall traveling at high speeds along wide expressways that I did not know existed anywhere in the Caribbean. When we reached San Fernando, we checked into a bed and breakfast on Lower Hillside Street.

San Fernando was the city where we were scheduled to play a series of matches against the Southern Amateur Football League, a major soccer team representing that city. Although we lost the series, that tour to Trinidad was an enriching experience, and my teammates and I were gratified by the positive reports that appeared in the Trinidadian and Barbadian daily newspapers. Aside from the competition, I got to meet mayors, and community leaders in San Fernando as well as in Port of Spain. I also toured attractions such as the Pitch Lake and the Texaco Refinery. One of the most intriguing experiences I had during that trip was to stand at the Coconut Creek resort at the southern tip of Trinidad and look at the mountains of Northern Venezuela in the distance.

Tony Best and I spent a lot of time exploring the city of San Fernando together. Tony knew a family that lived there, and I accompanied him on visits to their house on more than one occasion. I also made some valuable friendships with other members of my team, as well as with a few local Trinidadians. I often remember Bing Dymalley a young man from whom I learned a lot about life in the south of Trinidad. Looking back on that tour to Trinidad in 1958, I can unequivocally state that it helped me immensely in making the transition from schoolboy to adult!

While I was a student at the Lodge School, in addition to soccer, my other extracurricular activities included the Boy Scouts and the Cadets. The Lodge School Boy Scouts Troupe was small and enjoyed little visibility on campus. Few of my classmates tended to join that organization. The Troupe was led by a diminutive Englishman. He was a middle-aged man with a dour personality, who gave the impression that he was unfriendly and uncaring. I don't believe that he was a member of the Lodge School Staff. My longtime friend Frank Farnum could have influenced me to join the Troupe. Frank was a sort of pioneer at Lodge. He was the first black boy I saw with a tennis racquet. I was so curious that I asked him, "Frank, why do you have that racquet?" His response was simple and direct, "I joined the tennis club, and all club members are expected to buy their outfit and a racquet!" That was Frank, a real trailblazer. So I believe that it was Frank who first introduced me to the Boy Scouts.

The troupe met after classes right in front of the Great Hall next to the headmaster's home. I remember my semaphore lessons when I learned to communicate with my troupe members using two flags. I learned semaphore in less than one hour, and was proud to show off my talent every time we had a troupe meeting. I quickly advanced through the ranks, passing every challenge I faced. The big challenge was to prepare myself for my Second Class Badge. The scoutmaster took us to Codrington College to take the test. It included knot-tying, making a fire, and cooking a pot of porridge. I would never forget that we were required to stir the pot using motions that resembled the figure eight. The thing I liked the most about being a boy scout was the uniform. I loved the hat, the whistle, and the numerous badges I accumulated.

I joined the Cadet Corps when I was in the third form and remained long enough to be promoted to the rank of corporal. In the 1950s, the Barbados Cadet Corps was a military style organization. Similar to the U.S. ROTC, recruits to the Cadet Corps were required to participate in a rigorous program that emphasized communications skills development; map reading; military drills and formations; weapons training; marksmanship; and a variety of other youth development skills. We wore khaki uniforms immaculately starched and ironed; matching beret and stockings; a three-inch belt with brass buckle and glides; and highly polished, black boots.

Once a week, our platoon spent about one hour on the range for marksmanship practice. The range was an innocuous stretch of grass located behind the bicycle shed. The Corps used old twenty-two gauge rifles and real bullets. I remember one session when we were target practicing, one of the cadets had been sloppy in attaching his target to the board. After the second volley of bullets, his target became detached and fell to the ground. The Lieutenant, a teacher at Lodge, was in charge of the squad, and Mr. Glasgow, another master was assisting him. As soon as the target fell, the Lieutenant yelled, "put down your rifles and stand clear!" The entire squad immediately complied, and the young man ran the fifty-yards down to the board to re-attach his target. Two volleys later, the same thing happened. The target fell to the ground and the Lieutenant instructed us all to stand clear. We all stood clear, but as soon as the cadet got halfway down the range, the Lieutenant who was obviously enraged by the cadet's apparent sloppiness gave Mr. Glasgow an order that I could never forget. In a fit of rage he yelled, "puut a bullet in him Mr. Glasgooowww!"

I attended two cadet camps during my stint as a member of the Cadet Corps. My first experience was at Fortescue, St. Philip. That was a beautiful location in the flatlands of the southeasterly corner of the island. St. Philip was noted for its very rugged coast, and the lighthouse at Ragged Point was a major landmark. The legendary Sam Lord, one of the most notorious of the Caribbean pirates was alleged to have operated from his castle that was just a few miles south of Fortescue. Our campsite was mostly flat grassland with some casuarina trees bordering an open field. The grassland extended easterly toward a very rocky coast. Skeete's Bay was proximal to our elevated campsite, and to reach it we had to descend a very steep set of steps that led to a white, sandy beach some twenty to thirty feet below.

Camp Fortescue was a test of my stamina. The contingent of cadets from Lodge School did a phenomenal job of pitching the tents alongside those of our colleagues from the other secondary schools. The officers' tents were set apart from ours. Every morning at six o'clock, I would be awakened by the familiar sound of *reveiller*. The bugler was a guy called Humphrey. He was a very friendly guy who did a masterful job of getting the entire camp up and ready for the day's exercises. After breakfast we assembled in platoons as we prepared for inspection by our commandant. Then, we marched from the campsite into the adjoining fields where we were divided up into teams and taught the basics of war-fighting, under conditions that simulated an actual battlefield. I remember on one of our pitched battles, my team members and I had a group of enemy combatants pinned down in a cluster of grass and shrubs approximately one hundred fifty-yards ahead. We opened our attack with a continuous volley of fire from two Bren guns that we had positioned strategically behind a well-camouflaged barricade. As expected, the relentless assault with the Brens had immobilized the "enemy." Consistent with instructions, our line of fire was directed at a safe trajectory over their heads. In the heat of battle, however, the bipod supporting one of the Bren guns slipped, altering the trajectory of the tracer bullets. We all saw the tracer bullets moving lower and lower over the heads of our colleagues who were trapped in the grass ahead of us. Fortunately one of the officers realized what was happening and immediately called a halt to the shooting, just in time to avoid any fatalities.

At night we broke out of camp not with any particular agenda in mind, but simply because we considered it to be a part of the routine of being a cadet. I remember one night we broke out of camp and walked all the way from Fortescue to Massiah Street in St. John! We did nothing of consequence when we reached Massiah Street. We simply went there, turned around and headed back to camp. As we approached the perimeter of the campsite, I felt a rush of adrenaline because I knew the guards were on the lookout for violators of camp policy. Cadets found guilty of breaking out of camp always faced stiff penalties, including the possibility of being sent home. That night, I was with my close friends Patrick Medford and Vere Brooks and some other cadets whose names I have since forgotten. We crept stealthily through the underbrush, making sure that we did nothing that would alert the guards to our presence. Whether through skill or luck we were able to make it back into camp without any major incident!

The camp at Walkers, St. Andrew was a similar experience. Camp Walkers was even more remote than Camp Fortesque. It was desolate, and it was difficult to see any signs of civilian life without leaving the campsite. Our daily routine was comparable to that at Fortescue. When we broke out of camp at Walkers, the closest neighborhood that we wanted to visit was in the parish of St. Joseph. I remember walking with a group of my friends along the coast all the way to Horse Hill, St. Joseph. I am absolutely convinced that my colleagues and I benefited as much from the experiences we gained from breaking out of camp as we did from participating in the organized activities of the Barbados Cadet Corps.

Outside of the Lodge School setting, I was a carefree teenager. I pitched marbles, climbed trees, swam, rode my bike, and spent a great deal of time either visiting or entertaining my friends. I loved the guitar, and I invested quality time in learning to play that instrument. My interest in playing the guitar began at home. Dad always had a guitar in the house, and periodically, he would strap it across his shoulder and strum a few chords. We also had a local guitar player called Gary who inspired me.

When I entered Lodge and heard Oscar Jordan and his brothers Junie and Rex play the guitar, I knew it was time for me to get serious. I learned the basic chords and began playing songs like *Blueberry Hill*, *Home on the Range*, and *On Top of Old Smokey*. My repertoire of songs was later extended to include *Little Christmas Tree* as sung by Nat Cole, Harry Belafonte's version of *Jamaica Farewell* and *Island In the Sun*, and Judy Garland's unforgettable rendition of *Somewhere over the Rainbow*. My favorite song of all time was a country and western song called *Remember Me*. As my confidence increased, I entertained friends at home and at school, but never mustered enough courage to appear on Rediffusion, the local Barbadian radio station.

I received formal music training by attending piano lessons with Peggy. Our teacher was Ms. Lester Hall who lived in Massiah Street. Between Lester Hall and my Aunt Ene, Peggy and I learned to play a variety of songs on the piano and organ.

Stamp collecting was also a favorite hobby of mine. I traded stamps with my friends at Lodge School as actively as stocks are traded on the New York Stock Exchange. I remember negotiating a major deal that enabled me to acquire one of the most sought-after stamps in circulation at the time. My collection included some of the oldest Barbadian and British stamps, as well as stamps from many African colonies, prior to their independence from England.

Looking back at the ten years I spent at the Lodge School, I can say without hesitation, that I was fortunate to have been exposed to such a stimulating environment during that critical stage of my development. Lodge School had a rich history and an enormous reputation as an institution of uncompromising academic standards. It was at Lodge that I first learned that hard work really pays big dividends. It was there that I was exposed to individuals from different cultural and socioeconomic backgrounds. That experience was invaluable, and it has served me well, particularly when I left Barbados to continue my education in America.

Chapter 9

The Graduate

I graduated from Lodge School in 1958 with four A Level subjects: biology, botany, zoology, and chemistry. That same year, I joined the Empire Soccer Club. I must admit that I knew very little about the history of Barbadian sports clubs when I made the commitment to become a member of Empire. What little knowledge I had of the first eleven teams was drawn from personal experience as a soccer player. For example, it was obvious to me that, based on the color of teams I played against as a schoolboy, there were white clubs and black clubs. The club that seemed to me to be on the path to integration was Spartan. This was based on firsthand knowledge that I had from my friend Vere Brooks who was a member of their cricket team. I considered Empire to be one of the black clubs, and felt that I could have easily joined their soccer team, but took no action to officially sign up. It was not until I met with one of its members on a job interview that I officially decided to cast my lot with Empire.

Empire's home field was in Bank Hall. The grounds were not attractive, especially when I compared them to the large, well-maintained field I had grown accustomed to at Lodge. I loved the clubhouse and was definitely honored to have the opportunity to play alongside sports personalities like Winston Grant, Algie Simmonds, Desmond Dostie Weekes, Ivan Smith, Douglas "Dougie" Gay, Harcourt Walcott, Lance Bynoe, Colin Bynoe, Wilfred Passion Drayton, Rodney Norville, Seymour Nurse, Harold Griffith, and Emerson Whittington. Emerson was also my colleague at the Bacteriological and Pathological Laboratories of the Barbados General Hospital, so we often traveled together from work to soccer practice or to the game.

Some games were played at Empire, but most were played at Kensington Oval in the city. I remember after playing a scheduled game at Empire or Kensington Oval, I would have to walk to the bus stand to take the Route-7 bus to St. John. On more than one occasion I discovered that the six o'clock bus to College had already left, so my only recourse was to catch the seven o'clock bus to Greens, St. George. After arriving at Greens, I would have to walk all the way from St. George to College, St. John. In 1959, after we purchased a new car, I could routinely attend team practice, stay late after any game, and even attend more of the club's social events.

My days playing soccer for Empire broadened my network of contacts with an important segment of black Barbadian society. I learned quite a lot about the subtle and not so subtle class stratifications that existed in Bridgetown and its environs during the latter part of the 1950s. My teammates and I were well-respected because our club was a dominant force in Barbadian soccer circles, and we had an impeccable record of winning championships. During the two years that I played for Empire, I was fortunate to be on two championship teams. I still have a photograph of our 1959 championship team hanging on the wall of my office in Durham, North Carolina. I can never forget what it was like playing for the famous "Blues" Soccer Team.

I first played for the Barbados National Soccer Team when I was still a schoolboy at Lodge. That made it awkward for me, because most of my teammates were much older, and some of them were married men with children. The majority of them lived in the city and played for teams like Empire, Everton, Spartan, Carlton, and YMPC. In the late 1950s, the Barbados Football Association was not that well organized, and it always seemed to me to be operating on a shoestring budget. The roster of matches for the season was not effectively communicated to the players. If there was an official schedule of games to be played for any season, I never saw it, so it was very difficult for me to be mentally prepared for any of the major contests. Mr. Graham Wilkes, my games master at Lodge School, was one of the official coaches for the Barbados Soccer Team. He lived in the country then, so he would be my primary contact with the Barbados Football Association. Whether it was for team practice or a game, he would place a telephone call to the Chlorine Station, a small wooden booth situated on the north side of the

Lake at Codrington College. The watchman on duty there would then send a runner over to my house to tell me that there was a telephone call from coach Wilkes, and that he needed me to attend practice or play a game at Kensington Oval. It was my responsibility to gather my equipment, make the necessary travel arrangements, and show up at the stadium in time for practice or the start of the game. Before I got my own car, travel to practice or a game presented me with a major challenge, especially during the week, but in spite of that, I never missed a game!

Very often, I did not know anything about the team that I was about to face on any given day. There was no effort made to scout a team or to provide us with any information about the skill level of any of our opponents. I was simply asked to show up and play to the best of my ability. Most of my games were played against British teams, especially when naval vessels made calls to the Port of Bridgetown. Occasionally I played against teams from Trinidad, Grenada, Dominica, Air France, and Martinique, but I never had the opportunity to play against a team from Jamaica, or teams from any of the Central or South American countries. My great uncle Joseph Bradshaw who lived in New York never wanted to believe that anyone my size could be a member of a football team. Thinking that I played American style football he would say, "football, what kind of football can you play? In New York, if you ran onto the field, the players would mistake you for the ball!" In spite of Uncle Joe's reluctance to believe that I could hold my own on the soccer field, my career moved steadily in the right direction–up.

Prior to 1958, although I was acutely aware of the racial and social stratification of Barbadian society, I spent little time worrying about such matters. When the soccer tournament to Trinidad ended and I returned to Barbados, I was quickly reminded of the insidious role color played in determining who could gain access to the limited number of employment opportunities available in Barbados in either the public or private sector. I was now a Lodge School graduate, and in my mind, I felt a sense of entitlement. After all, I had a very impressive resume. I earned passes in eight out of eight O Level, and four out of four A Level subjects, including a distinction in Biology. I was a successful student and a national soccer star. I felt like I was on top of the world. Unfortunately, in the late 1950s, my scholastic and athletic achievements were far outweighed by the color of my skin.

I was simply trying to find a respectable job until I could figure out what I wanted to do with the rest of my life. I developed a portfolio of my most important accomplishments. It included copies of my certificates and testimonials from the headmaster at Lodge School and the principal of Codrington College. I got all dressed up and went to Bridgetown in search of employment. I started at the Ministerial Buildings on Bay Street where the government's personnel department was located. At that time, the Chief Personnel Officer was a middle-aged man, short in stature and stern in disposition. I guessed that he had worked his way up through the ranks of the Civil Service, and wanted to show me how much power and influence he had as a gatekeeper for jobs in the public sector. My conversation with him was brief, and devastating to my psyche. He simply explained how the Civil Service application process worked, and then told me that there were no positions available anywhere within the system. That is all he said without even looking at the portfolio I spent so much time preparing. He dismissed me, certificates and all! I left his office convinced that the probability of me securing a job in the civil service was slim to nil. I remember thinking that even if he wasn't impressed with my academic achievements he should have been aware of the fact that I was a soccer star whose photo appeared frequently in the Barbados Advocate newspaper.

I was so naive then that I was unable to think clearly about what was happening and how best to respond. So I left the Ministerial Buildings and walked back into the center of Bridgetown still determined to find a job. My next stop was at the BOAC (British Overseas Airways Corporation) office in Lower Broad Street. I had heard that BOAC had recently hired two secondary school graduates, and I felt that I had nothing to lose by inquiring. The outcome of that visit was predictable, courteous dismissal!

From BOAC I headed back up Broad Street walking slowly and wondering what to do next. Where should I go? What would be the best option for me to pursue? Halfway up Broad Street I ran into one of my former classmates from Lodge School. We called him Duck because he tended to waddle as he walked. I knew him to be a genuinely nice guy. As a member of the privileged white class, he never projected any images of superiority or racial insensitivity to anyone. He greeted me cordially, and seemed happy to see me. I responded to Duck's query about why I was in town by telling him that I was in the city job hunting. Without any hesitation he told me that there was a vacancy at the company where he worked. He urged me to go there right away and fill out an application. He knew how well I had done on the O Level and A Level exams and felt that I was more than qualified to fill the position at his company.

I remember leaving Duck and heading straight to the address where he worked. It was one of Bridgetown's larger commercial establishments, so as I reached the top of the stairs I realized that I was in unfamiliar territory. I pulled open the large glass door to the reception area, approached the secretary, and politely informed her of the purpose of my visit. She took my portfolio, asked me to take a seat, and disappeared down a short corridor. After waiting for about one to two minutes, she returned and instructed me to follow her. Soon we were standing in front of one of the offices. She knocked gently on the large wooden door and waited quietly with me. It was not long before a middle aged, white man opened the door, greeted me with a firm handshake, and ushered me into his modestly furnished office. I could see that he had already perused my portfolio, as the folder with my resume and certificates was visibly displayed on the top of his desk. After exchanging a few pleasantries, he turned to the business at hand and began by letting me know how impressed he was with my record of achievement. He stated, "Mr. Harewood! I can't believe that you have eight O Level and four A Level certificates. This is a remarkable achievement, and I am really proud of you. You are more than qualified to do this job. Unfortunately, however, I wish that you had come in a little bit sooner because we just filled the position!" I was devastated by the news. So many thoughts went racing through my mind as I sat there. In my naivety, I wondered what kind of job he would have offered me had I arrived a little bit sooner. I am sure that he could have sensed the disappointment that was clearly written all across my face. I remained in his office long enough to reclaim my portfolio, and then I was on my way back to reality. As I walked slowly down the stairs and approached the busy city streets below, I felt a sense of total despair. I was conscious of the fact that in less than an hour, my hopes of finding a good job had been raised and dashed. I felt that my luck had run out, and it was highly unlikely that I would find employment that day. I also began to come to grips with the stark reality that no one really seemed to care about my academic achievements, or the fact that I was a national soccer star.

The bus ride back home was more painful than ever. I reflected on all of the disappointments of that day–the government personnel officer, the BOAC receptionist, Duck, and my encounter with the manager at his company. When the Route-7 bus rounded the corner on top of Coach Hill to begin its slow descent to Welch Village overlooking Bath Plantation, I realized that I had very little awareness of what transpired on that bus during the entire trip from Bridgetown to St. John. I kept worrying whether I would ever be able to find a decent job in Barbados.

The next day I dressed, grabbed my portfolio, and boarded the bus for Bridgetown one more time. I had no appointments nor scheduled interviews. It was simply going to be a fishing expedition. I reasoned that if I spent the day in the city, I might get to meet someone who could give me some clues, or point me in the right direction for a possible job interview. If anyone had told me that one of the first people I would meet would be Duck I would have found it hard to believe. But as fate would have it, I crossed paths with Duck once again, and his first query was "Ken, I thought that you told me that you were going over to my company yesterday?" "Yes," I answered, "I went, and was told that the position was filled!" He looked at me as though he did not believe what I had just told him. Then with a quizzical expression on his face he asked, "who told you so?" Before I could respond, he stated categorically, "the position is not filled, we are still interviewing candidates!" I did not have to say anything else, I could tell that he was very much aware of how the system worked, and why I was not seriously considered for the job. His company did have a job opening, but that position was being held for someone whom they considered to be a good fit. At that time in Barbados, there was a distinct racial divide, and companies such as the one that Duck worked for were committed to the two-society concept.

In spite of an obvious lack of success, I kept up the pace of my search for a job. My luck changed when I ran into Oscar Jordan, a friend and fellow Lodge School alumnus. Oscar had won a Barbados scholarship and was scheduled to leave Barbados in September to attend medical school in Edinburgh, Scotland. Until his departure, he had secured a summer job at the Barbados Registry. Oscar was getting ready to leave his position and he strongly urged me to apply. That seemed like the opportunity I was waiting for, so I lost little time in trying to capitalize on it. I rushed over to the Registry where I was able to gain access to the Registrar who was none other than a well-known soccer player. I believe that he was one of the goalkeepers for Empire.

My conversation with him was very positive, and focused more on soccer than on the position. It went something like this, "I am glad that you have decided to play for Empire, Ken, I believe that the club will have little trouble waiving the membership dues for you this year." I politely thanked him hoping that the conversation would be shifted to the real reason for my visit. I again was too naïve to realize that my appointment to the position was a *fait accomplie*, and there was no reason for us to treat our meeting like a job interview.

I went to work as a clerk at the Registry after Oscar left for Scotland. My primary assignment was to respond to requests from ordinary citizens or attorneys-at-law for official copies of birth or marriage certificates, deeds, conveyances and other legal documents. The senior staff at the Registry included Mr. Daniel, Deputy Registrar, Mrs. Cox, Grace Jackson, and Hermese Griffith. I really enjoyed that experience. I learned so much by perusing some of Barbados' oldest records of land transactions, marriages, and births. I also got a unique opportunity to attend court sessions to get first-hand experience on how our legal system really worked.

One day, I was walking across Fairchild Street on my way to the St. John bus stand. As I passed in front of the Barbados Fire Station I met Edward (Eds) Batson. Eds had attended Harrison College, and we got to know each other well through the cadet corps and our rivalry on the soccer field. After exchanging a few pleasantries, Eds asked me what I was doing since I left school, and when he found out that I was working at the Registry after completing the science sixth at Lodge, he told me that he thought that I should consider applying for a position at the Bacteriological and Pathological Laboratories where he worked. He said that one of the senior technicians had been granted study leave and there was a vacancy at the lab. He thought that I would be the perfect candidate to fill the position. He suggested that I should make an appointment to meet with the Pathologist, Dr. J. E. Walcott.

Very soon after that conversation with Eds, I was sitting in Dr. Walcott's office seeking a position as a Clinical Laboratory Technician. Dr. Walcott was a fascinating individual. Dad later told me that he had worked as a sugarcane factory manager for years, before he decided on a career change that took him to medical school where he was trained in pathology. He apparently did all of this when he was in his forties. As a pathologist, he was the same no nonsense person that he was when he worked as a factory manager. He was high-strung, and not bashful to share his opinion with anyone. He delivered his commentary in an inimitable staccato fashion. Dr. Walcott was blatantly honest in all of his pronouncement. After he had thoroughly perused my resume and certificates he began the interview by heaping praise on me for my impressive academic record. Then he openly stated that he was biased towards Lodge School graduates. He believed that Lodge did an outstanding job with science education, and assured me that he was confident that I could hold my own when pitted against any of his technicians. I was hired on the spot–a real confidence booster, considering all of the negative things that happened just a few months earlier.

My job at the lab was so satisfying that I couldn't wait to get to work in the morning. Emerson Whittington, my friend and teammate at Empire, taught me how to analyze blood samples and other biological specimens. He taught me biochemistry, hematology, immunology, serology, and histology. Eds and Freddie Jones also shared their experiences with me, and in short order I was proficient in carrying out any test requested by the doctors.

The head porter at the lab was a man called Carrington. I am not quite sure what his role was, but he was an important member of the team. Carrington knew every nook and cranny at the hospital, and he was so resourceful that we all benefited from his presence. Then there was Eslyn Murrell a youngster who worked diligently to keep equipment and laboratory supplies clean and available to us at all times. I will always remember Ms. Sybil Jones, the Secretary to Dr. Walcott. When I first joined the lab, she was the only female member of the group. Mrs. Valerie Adeymo joined the technical team later along with Tony Best, who was my teammate on the trip to Trinidad with the Barbados Football Association. My work at the hospital lab prepared me well for the next stage of my life, which came sooner than I could have planned.

We purchased our first new car in 1959. It was a brand new Zephyr Six made by the British Ford Motor Company. I remember going into Charles McEnearny (the Ford dealership) with Dad to look at their new cars. At that time, McEnearny was in Bridgetown at the lower end of the city, close to St. Mary's Church. Dad knew the supervisor, a Mr. Butcher, and I knew the manager who had graduated from the Lodge School three to four years ahead of me.

Dad and I had settled earlier for the Ford because of its price, and reputation for speed and power. The other contenders were the Opel Kapitan, Hillman Minx, and Vauxhall Victor. I had waited several years for that day, and now the moment had finally arrived. The money that Joyce contributed served as our down payment. It met the fifty percent deposit that dealerships required for new vehicle purchases at that time. The balance due would be paid off in equal monthly installments over an approximately two-year period. I signed an agreement to pay the balance from the monthly salary that I received from my job as a technician at the lab. I was so excited that I hardly thought of the enormity of the financial commitment I was making. The choice was between a beige and a light blue vehicle. I settled for the light blue.

I picked up my new car on a Friday evening. I find it impossible to describe the feeling of pure elation that I experienced as I drove that shiny, powder blue Ford Zephyr Six with its chrome trim through Broad Street, past Queen's Park and onto Roebuck Street. All along the route, I was hoping that my friends would see me. After years of embarrassment from driving an old 1939 Model Ford with a cracked windscreen and dim lights, I was finally behind the wheel of a spanking new 1959 Ford with all of the whistles and bells.

There were so few cars in St. John at that time that the license plate issued from the Treasury was J-449. So many of my friends remember that car. I drove it to work every day and was able to take Peggy to St. Gabriel's School where she was a teacher. I could attend soccer practice, play in competitions at Empire and Kensington Oval, and even take in a movie at the Plaza or Empire theaters during the week.

One evening, I attended a gala event at the Drill Hall in Bridgetown. I believe that it was the annual dance sponsored by Spartan Athletic Club. It was one of those events when all of the guys and girls were in attendance. I took a group of my closest friends from St. John in the new Zephyr. I picked up Pat Medford, and Vere Brooks, Vere's cousin Von Bancroft, and my soccer teammate Ronnie Hall and we all went to the Drill Hall. We had a terrific time dancing and socializing with our friends.

I left the Drill Hall around two o'clock in the morning with the same group of friends that I brought to the dance. I don't know why I decided to take the route that passed by the District B police station at Boarded Hall, but I did. It was dark outside and as I drove by the police station it started to drizzle. My friends were all asleep in the car, exhausted from the night of celebration. As I approached Bentley, the plantation where Granny Harewood once worked, I saw what appeared to be an animal in the street. It was brown and much larger than any dog I had seen. I thought that it was a calf that had lost its way. When the high beam from the Zephyr illuminated the creature, it froze like a deer caught in the headlights of an oncoming vehicle.

I pumped the brakes gently to avoid skidding on the wet surface, but it was clear to me that if the animal did not move, I would have no choice but to make contact with whatever it was. When my front bumper made the initial contact, I heard a muffled sound, then a thud and a bump as the rear wheel rolled over the injured creature. There was no other sound, just the peace and quiet of the deserted country road. As I continued on the rest of the route, I kept replaying the moment of impact over and over in my mind. I wished that I could have braked sooner, and I even regretted that I had not used the bus route as Dad always advised.

When I reached Church Village, I thought I heard a slight rattle coming from the front end of the car. I was convinced that it might have been the license plate that could have come loose after the impact. I awakened Vere and asked him if he heard the rattle, and when he said he did, I immediately pulled to the curb and got out to check my front license plate. I could not believe what I saw. Instead of a loose license plate I saw a gaping hole in the grill, and the left side of the bumper literally ripped from the frame of the car. How was that possible? I was only traveling about twenty-five miles per hour, and I was feeling sorry for the animal! A heavy sadness settled over me as I dropped off my friends one by one before turning into our driveway and parking the car. Dad was awake when I opened the door, so I had to tell him what happened. His reluctance to say anything to me at that time was a clear signal that, he like me wished it was not true.

The next morning, Dad got up early and went down to the garage to inspect the car. It was only when he found animal hair stuck to the damaged bumper that he believed my story of colliding with an animal. We both dressed and left for the city to take the car to the Ford dealership. On our way there, we drove by the spot where the accident occurred, and much to my surprise there was no sign that an animal had been injured there. When we reached the Ford dealership, the service manager Mr. Butcher met us, and Dad told him of my mishap. After inspecting the damage, he told Dad that only a stone or tree could have caused so much damage. He was only convinced of my story when Dad showed him the animal hair! In spite of the collision coverage we had on the car, the cost of the repair was staggering. Joyce came to the rescue by providing the money to help defray those expenses. I still cannot believe how they were able to get the car to look like new again.

I quickly found out that it was virtually impossible to drive my new Zephyr anywhere in Barbados without someone recognizing the car. Sometimes that worked against me. For example, occasionally one of Dad's friends would tell him that they saw the car in a particular neighborhood at a specific time, all along assuming that he was the driver. In this way he was able to keep an accurate record of everywhere I went across the island, as long as I was driving the light-blue Zephyr.

Codrington College

Holy Cross Church

Robert Kidney's Wedding

Kidney Home

View of Conset Bay from Family Home

Society Mixed School

Dad

Mum, Dad, Gran, Joyce

Aunt Mam

Aunt Eude

Lodge School Track Team

Lodge School Soccer Team

Barbados Soccer Team

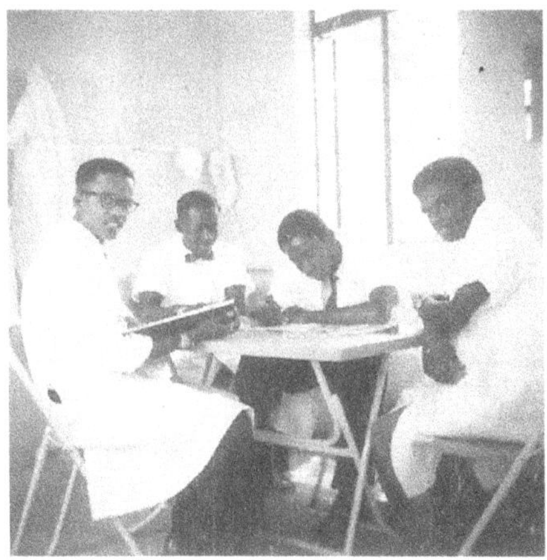

With My Coworkers at the Barbados Hospital Lab

NYU Soccer Team

Our Wedding

Kevin, Dionne, Eudine & Me

Bajan Biochemist

Project Team Meeting With Pfizer Colleagues

With Rep. Dan Blue, Surgeon General David Satcher, Chancellor Chambers, and William Smith at BBRI Dedication

At O. Max Gardner Award Ceremony

Gold Crown of Merit

Phil, Peggy, Roger, Eudine, Kevin, Me, Joyce Dionne, Ralph

Chapter 10

Bedford Stuyvesant in 1960

My good friend Jim Wedderburn was a phenomenal athlete. He had distinguished himself in distance running while he was a student with me at the Lodge School, and his reputation was such that New York University (NYU) offered him a full athletic scholarship. Jim enrolled in NYU's School of Education at Washington Square College in the late 1950s. On one of his trips to Brooklyn he visited Aunt Eudie and Joyce, and couldn't wait to write to let me know. In his letter he spoke positively about his experiences in New York, and urged me to consider NYU as a place to continue my education. Jim went as far as to even enclose an application package for NYU in one of his letters to me. I lost little time in completing the application and forwarding it to the NYU Admissions Office.

Much to my surprise I received a prompt response from NYU indicating that they were impressed with my academic record, and were prepared to offer me a place in their undergraduate program. I could not believe it, and I certainly was not ready to accept the offer. There were several reasons for my hesitation. Aunt Mam had suffered a severe stroke that paralyzed her on the right side. True to family tradition, she remained at home with Mum, Dad, and all of us chipping in to help. I had also just bought the new car and I was committed to helping with paying the note. One of my greatest concerns, however, was the fact that I had no way of raising the money to pay my expenses at NYU. So I simply informed them that I could not accept the offer of admission at that time, indicating that I would apply for the next academic year.

Early in 1960, I began to make plans to attend NYU in the Fall semester. I submitted the necessary paperwork to the university and received an updated letter of acceptance. I contacted Joyce in New York and informed her of the latest development. After a brief attempt to convince me to try to consider applying to the University of the West Indies at Jamaica, or to one of the British universities, she relented and agreed to help me in my desire to continue my education in America.

My first task was to visit the American Consulate in Bridgetown to apply for a student visa. I was stunned when I found out that I could not obtain a visa to travel to New York as a student unless I could clearly demonstrate that I was fully capable of taking care of all of my expenses. I was speechless when I learned that they expected me to have such a large amount of money on a savings account before they would consider issuing me a student visa.

I remember making an appointment to meet with the Minister of Education. He was the representative for St. John, and I had known and respected him for several years. Before getting into politics, he served as headmaster of St. John's Boys School. My brother Roger attended St. John's Boys School, and that brought me into frequent contact with the leadership of that school. Additionally, Dad knew the minister well, so I was confident that he would be sympathetic to my cause.

On the day of my appointment, I walked into his office at the shiny, new Ministerial Building on Bay Street. I was thankful that he had agreed to see me, and excited by the prospect that the minister would come to my rescue. I remember him being sympathetic to my cause but not persuaded by my pleas for help. He explained that government loans were only granted to students seeking to be educated in the United Kingdom. Because I was planning to attend an American university I was ineligible to be considered for a student loan. I remember looking at him and not hearing anything else that he said for the rest of the time I spent in his office.

All I could think of was the fact that I was asking for a loan, not a scholarship, and I was absolutely unable to comprehend why it was so difficult for the ministry to accommodate what I considered to be a very reasonable request. I left his office visibly disturbed by the policy, and by the very cavalier manner in which he handled the situation. I was determined to prove that I would not let a shortsighted government policy prevent me from pursuing my dreams.

Joyce and I worked quickly on Plan B. That plan involved raising the money from a private source. She told me that she would try her best to borrow the money in New York. I in turn assured her that I would return any funds to her as soon as the American Consulate approved my visa application. I had no idea that I would be able to put that plan into action a few weeks after it was conceived.

It began with the arrival of a letter from Joyce that contained a United States Money Order for the exact amount I needed to show to the American Consul. That January in 1960, I went to the Government Savings Bank and deposited all of the proceeds into my savings account. I then made an appointment with the American consular office. I cannot describe the feeling I had when the officer expressed complete satisfaction with my application and granted me a visa to travel to the U.S. as a student. Later that month, I was back in the Government Savings Bank to withdraw in-full the money that I deposited earlier. Just as planned, I mailed every penny back to Joyce in Brooklyn, New York, along with a note sharing the good news about receiving my student's visa.

The story about how Joyce was able to raise the money was very interesting. In 1957, while vacationing in New York at the invitation of Aunt Eude she was urged to apply for a job at St. John's Episcopal Hospital in Brooklyn. Her experience as a registered nurse in Barbados had prepared her well for employment in the U.S., and she was immediately hired. One day in 1960, while on the job, one of the nurses on her floor noticed the frustration on her face and asked her what was bothering her. Joyce told this complete stranger that she was trying to help her brother back in Barbados get a visa to enter NYU in the fall. She also told her that the American Consulate expected her brother to be financially independent and requested proof of his ability to fully support himself after arriving in the U.S. She told her that she was trying to borrow the money to send to me, but was having a difficult time finding anyone to lend her that much money. Joyce was not ready for what happened next. Without pausing, that lady said that she would loan her the money. She kept her word and the next day she presented Joyce with a check for the entire amount! I never got a chance to meet or thank that generous nurse, but every time I help a needy student, I know that I am repaying that nurse for the generosity she extended to me when I most needed it.

Reality soon set in, and I realized that I did not have a lot of time to prepare for my trip to New York to begin my freshman year at NYU. I knew that I had to let Dr. Walcott know that I would be leaving my job at the Bacteriological and Pathological Laboratories. He was so gracious when I broke the news, that I couldn't believe it. His first reaction was to congratulate me on gaining acceptance to a university with the reputation of NYU. He then told me that he was confident that I would quickly find out that the things I would experience in New York in one day, would have taken me more than a year to experience in Barbados!

I next had to come to grips with the fact that I would soon be leaving Mum, Dad, and my younger siblings whom I loved dearly. While I recognized the importance of seizing the opportunity to pursue my education in New York, I was apprehensive about leaving my job; my home; my family; my community; and the island that meant so much to me. I was particularly saddened by the thought of having to leave Aunt Mam at a time when she desperately needed my help. I tried to compensate for my sadness by devoting as much of my attention as possible to shopping for personal effects and souvenirs to take with me to New York. I remember buying a light grey straw hat and an autographed cricket bat from Cave Shepherd in Bridgetown. I searched for inexpensive souvenirs, and I bought several bottles of rum and falernum for Joyce and Aunt Eude. My friends Vere, Von, Sylvia, and others arranged for a memorable evening at a west coast nightclub called the Coconut Creek where the music and drinks set the stage for a very enjoyable time. Then it was off to the Roodals Drive-in Cinema to the movies.

I left Barbados for Brooklyn, New York in 1960. Several members of the Kidney family had made a similar trip under different circumstances since the beginning of the nineteenth century. Great uncles Joe Bradshaw and James Firebrace immigrated to the United States from Panama after the Canal Project was successfully completed. At that time, racial segregation was the order of the day, and they were forced to settle into the black communities of Harlem and New Jersey, respectively. Then in 1920, a sixteen year old, shy, black girl from College Land, St. John boarded a ship at Bridgetown and sailed to New York at the invitation of her uncle. That shy, little girl was Aunt Eude, and her uncle was my Great Uncle Joseph Bradshaw. In 1957 Joyce followed in the tradition of previous family members by making a similar journey.

Now it was my turn, as a member of the third generation of Kidneys to make the trek to North America in search of a better life. Because of the excitement of the moment, I did not stop to think about the fact that I was leaving a very warm, caring, predictable setting to travel to a big, impersonal city that would challenge me in ways I could never have imagined. I did not take a moment to reflect on the possible consequences of my decision to leave Barbados. Those consequences included leaving my devoted parents, my dear sister Peggy, and my younger brothers Roger and Philip. I did not want to think of the possibility that I might not ever see Aunt Mam again. I dared not think of my friends, the rich social life to which I had grown accustomed, or the protective umbrella afforded me as a member of the Kidney and Harewood family from College Land. I awoke early that morning filled with excitement. I kissed family members goodbye, loaded my suitcase into the car for the ride to Seawell Airport. Most of my closest friends were there to see me off. Soon I was saying goodbye to Mum and Dad and I was on my way to New York.

After a long flight with local stops at several of the small airports along the chain of islands, the twin-engine Pan American turbojet came to a stop on the tarmac in San Juan, Puerto Rico. The pilot taxied to the arrival gate and notified all of the passengers of the need to change planes. Equipment problems with the big jet that I was scheduled to take to New York delayed my flight for several hours, leaving me to roam the spacious concourse in San Juan decked out in my straw hat and carrying the Don Bradman cricket bat that I had purchased in Barbados for my brother-in-law Eldon.

Finally, I got the call to board and I was on my way to New York. The flight to New York was uneventful. After what seemed like an eternity, the captain announced that he was preparing to land. My heart raced with excitement as the jet descended into the New York airspace, and the lights of the city came into full view beneath a thin cloud cover. The display of the New York skyline was even more impressive than I had imagined.

I was soon on the ground working my way through immigration and customs. As I entered the waiting area, I could see Joyce and the entourage of friends she brought to the airport to welcome me to New York. I am sure that it was easy for her to recognize me. I was the one with the cricket bat and the straw hat. There was her best friend Aletha and her longtime classmates from nursing school Ernie and Glendine. Joyce's husband Eldon was there along with his cousin Vernon who provided the transportation.

I remember thinking that the ride from the airport along the Belt Parkway into Brooklyn was incredibly smooth. Vernon's full sized DeSoto sedan seemed to be floating along the highway. The traffic on the Belt Parkway, red lights ahead and bright headlamps approaching on the other side of the divided highway, was simply an unbelievable sight. I had never seen so much traffic flowing in a steady pattern in both directions and seemingly without end.

Vernon soon exited the highway and turned onto the local streets of Brooklyn. There were brownstones and parked cars on every block. As we drove along the dimly lit, tree-lined streets, I kept hoping that I had not arrived at Quincy Street. Finally, Vernon pulled the car over to the curb in front of a two-story building that was next to an auto repair shop at the junction of Quincy Street and Marcy Avenue. Two old aluminum garbage pails were pushed up against a low wrought iron rail. I looked up and noticed the number on the house and realized that it was Aunt Eude's address.

I was glad that Joyce could not see the disappointment in my face. I had never envisioned Quincy Street to look like what I was seeing. Is this where I would be spending the next few years of my life? I thought. Where was the America that I fantasized so much about as I was growing up in Barbados? Where was the America that I had become so familiar with from the movies I had seen at the Plaza, or Empire, or Globe cinemas? I remember Joyce telling me about the squalor she had seen during the brief time she had been in America, but I didn't want to believe her. Now I was in America, and I did not like what I was seeing. I felt then that Brooklyn was going to be a very lonely place, a concrete prison, with old, heavily fortified brownstones, filled with nameless, faceless neighbors that I could never ever trust.

Aunt Eude greeted me that night in her inimitable way. First with hugs and kisses and much affection, then with a very caustic reminder that she had done more than enough for her sister's children, and no longer felt any obligation to do anymore than she had already done. I ignored her protestations then and continued to do so during the three years that I lived with her on Quincy Street. I knew that she really never meant a word of what she was saying.

My first week in Brooklyn was a real test of my commitment to obtain a college education. I realized that meeting the day-to-day challenges of life in Brooklyn would be just as demanding as dealing with the rigors of undergraduate college. I knew that I would have to endure much pain before realizing any gain. Relief came in the form of Aletha's husband. He called during that first week to say that he was coming to get me. I had never met Keith, but when he came to pick me up, it was as if we had known each other for a very long time. We took the Gates Avenue bus and traveled to Broadway, a commercial section in Brooklyn that was not far from where I lived on Quincy Street. There were numerous stores under the elevated train tracks, and all of them were filled with lots of merchandise. I remember Keith bought me a pair of slacks. What I liked most was the sheer joy of being out of the house at Quincy Street.

When I returned that evening after an enjoyable day of shopping and sightseeing, I faced the reality of what life was like for most West Indian families in the Bedford-Stuyvesant section of Brooklyn in the 1960's. I could enter the brownstone on the ground floor level through a heavy wrought iron gate, if someone was at home to unlock the padlock from the inside. The preferred option for entering the three-story house was to climb the brick steps on the front of the building up to the second floor level where I used a big iron key to unlock the double wooden doors. Once inside the second floor level, a short hallway to the left defined the zone controlled by Aunt Eude. Her living room was situated behind a large wooden door that was kept locked at all times. Her bedroom was contiguous with the living room and seemed to be a mere extension of that space. Privacy was provided by large sliding doors that disappeared into the wall, but Aunt Eude never ever closed them.

A stairway at the end of the second floor hallway led to the first floor level where the kitchen, bathroom, toilet, and a second bedroom were located. The backdoor opened onto a grassy area that was enclosed on two sides by the walls of the surrounding buildings, and on the third side by a chain link fence. That backyard served as a small recreational space that Aunt Eude occasionally used to dry clothes on a line that extended across the entire backyard. To the right after entering the double doors on the second floor was a stairway that led to the upper level. This was the stairway to Mag's apartment. Mag was the tenant who occupied the house with Aunt Eude. I lived on Quincy Street for almost four years and I never entered Mag's apartment or even got to know her real name! It was the unwritten rule of good-neighborliness in Brooklyn to never ever encroach on your neighbor's space.

The Adamses and Springers lived further down the street from Aunt Eude. The Adamses were American to the core–very courteous but keep your distance. The Springers were the opposite. They were getting on in age, he was retired and she was a homemaker. I always thought of Aunt Mam whenever I was in her presence. The Springers had immigrated from Barbados many years ago and made Brooklyn their home. Like most elderly Barbadians I encountered in Brooklyn, they had no intentions of ever returning to Barbados!

That summer, I was introduced to some of Brooklyn's other popular shopping areas. My brother-in-law Eldon was the next person to take me shopping. On that occasion, it was along Fulton Street near to Nostrand Avenue. There was a lot of storefront shopping along that street, and plenty of examples of black American culture on display. I came away from that trip with a new pair of very stylish American shoes. There were trips to cricket at Marine Park in Brooklyn as well as to have fun at the Coney Island Amusement Park. My first real trip outside of Brooklyn came when Aletha took me to Lake Hopatcong in New Jersey. It seemed as though it took us forever to get there. This was a typical Barbadian bus outing but to a very swank place that was replete with rides, games, snow cones, lots of hotdogs and hamburgers, and plenty of entertainment. I had a wonderful time, and I remember thinking that this was beginning to look like the America that I had long dreamt about.

On the return trip from Lake Hopatcong however, I was about to see what life was really like for West Indian blacks as they tried to grasp a tiny piece of the American dream. I believe we were in conservative Morris County when our white bus driver decided to pull off the highway at a rest stop. From my window on the bus I could see a restaurant ahead with its neon sign that read "Busses welcome." I particularly remember that sign because I had never seen that word spelled with a second "s." The parking spaces at the side of the restaurant were neatly demarcated with white lines, and the grass was vibrant green and well manicured. Our driver notified all of the passengers on my bus that this would be the only rest room break, and that everyone needed to be back on the bus within fifteen minutes.

Before the first person was able to exit the bus however, a middle aged white man who walked out of the restaurant while the driver was parking, approached the vehicle, and it was obvious to me that he was upset about something. We found out that his anger was directed at our driver who was about to deposit a busload of West Indians onto his property. When he reached the bus, he told us that we would not be permitted to use his rest rooms.

Upon receiving the bad news, several passengers got back onto the bus, but a defiant few that really needed to use the rest room, proceeded to urinate on the beautifully manicured lawn. I thought that the presumed owner would have been outraged by their action, but he wasn't. His concern was to prevent them from entering the facility and he had achieved the outcome he desired! I could not believe what I had seen. The image of a white businessman with an overtly racist attitude and a defiant group of black West Indians intent on showing that man that they were simply not going to assume the role of second-class citizen, was firmly etched in my mind.

During the latter part of the summer, I worked as a plumber's helper with Aunt Eude's friend Mr. Rufus Stuart. The work site was a four-story brownstone in the Bedford-Stuyvesant section of Brooklyn. There was no elevator in the building, and Mr. Stuart needed to have someone run back and forth from the ground floor to the upper level work site with tools and materials needed for the job.

I was also able to make contact with many Barbadian New Yorkers, young and old. I met them at cricket matches at Marine Park and Van Courtland Park. Aunt Eude introduced me to her friends Nellie, Graham, and Glenn. I enjoyed listening to the hit parade on the radio and watching shows like *Queen for a Day* and *Perry Mason* on television.

Summer in New York was hot and humid. The brownstone where I lived absorbed much of the heat during the day and gave it back generously throughout the night. I could not believe how hot and uncomfortable New York was during the summer of 1960.

Chapter 11

My Undergraduate Years

As September approached, I knew I had to find a way to get to NYU on my own so that I could prepare for the beginning of the semester. Before taking the trip to Washington Square, I contacted Jim Wedderburn who was living in one of the dorms at the NYU Washington Heights campus in the Bronx. I recall taking the Lexington Avenue train to Jerome Avenue and then following the signs to NYU. It was a beautiful campus. The academic programs and classrooms were housed in a collection of neo-renaissance buildings that were set back at a considerable distance from the main entrance. The Hall of Fame for Great Americans was the showpiece of the campus. It included an impressive display of bronze busts of prominent American inventors such as Alexander Graham Bell, Eli Whitney, and George Westinghouse.

A large field separated the buildings from the neighborhood streets. The perimeter of the field was defined by a well-maintained oval track, and there were soccer and American football goalposts permanently installed at either end of that oval. My first impression was that the two sports were actively competing for the use of the field.

The day that I arrived on campus, there were two small contingents of student athletes on the field going through their routines as they prepared for the upcoming year of competition. There was a track and field contingent where Jim Wedderburn and his teammates were being coached by Mr. Healy, a white-haired man with a pleasant disposition and a winning reputation as an athletic coach. The second contingent was a small gathering of soccer players under the watchful eye of their coach Mr. Alan Tobin. My meeting with coach Tobin that day would have a significant impact on my life and career.

Soon after I arrived in New York in August, I realized that attending NYU was going to be an expensive proposition. The American Consul at Barbados had expressed his concern about me having enough funds to cover my expenses as a student. The fact that I did not have enough money to pay my tuition meant that I would not be able to enroll that fall. In 1960, tuition at NYU was quite expensive, and I knew that it would be difficult for me to make those payments. I had used most of my earnings from my job in Barbados to assist Mum and Dad with meeting day-to-day expenses. A significant amount of my salary was devoted to paying the monthly installment on the new car, and whatever was left over I used to cover my travel expenses from Barbados to NY. Aunt Eude was adamant that she couldn't help me financially. I thought it was a ploy of hers to hasten my transition towards independence, but I had no way to be sure of that, so it seemed like I was caught between a rock and a hard place.

In mid-August, I made the decision that I would defer entering NYU for one year and instead attend the Manhattan School for Medical and Dental Technology. That school had a reputation for accepting foreign students, and what was most appealing to me, their tuition was within a range that was more affordable than the tuition for NYU. After discussing that option with Eldon, I made a trip to their admission office in Manhattan where I completed an application to change my sponsoring academic institution from NYU to the Manhattan School for Medical and Dental Technology.

So on the day I met Coach Alan Tobin I told him of my change in plans, and indicated that the decision was exclusively driven by financial constraints. His advice was swift and still resonates with me to this day. He simply told me that I should not delay my entry into NYU by one single day. He said that money should not be a barrier to my entering NYU. He reminded me that I had already met the most important criterion–impressing the admissions committee with my academic achievements. Now it was simply a matter of borrowing the money for my tuition and fees either from a family member or a bank. "But I have already obtained permission from the Immigration and Naturalization Service to attend the Manhattan School for Medical and Dental Technology," I responded. "Well," said Coach Tobin, "I wouldn't even go back to the immigration authorities, just register for classes at NYU as you originally intended, and simply let the Foreign Student Office at NYU help you deal with the immigration issues." It was a simple solution, and I followed it exactly as Coach Tobin had instructed. I enrolled in NYU and began my studies there in the fall of 1960.

NYU's Washington Square campus was located at West 4th Street in the heart of Greenwich Village in downtown Manhattan. Greenwich Village was a vibrant community of artists, writers, musicians, and intellectuals. Washington Square Park with its imposing marble arch seemed appropriate to be considered as the gateway to NYU's largest campus in New York City.

There was no quadrangle at the Washington Square site. Instead, several tall, impressive buildings comprised the campus. Those buildings were interspersed between other commercial and residential structures, and housed classrooms, laboratories, libraries, bookstores, and administrative offices. Being an urban campus, NYU at Washington Square had no athletic track or football field, those were reserved for the Washington Heights campus in the Bronx. NYU's Medical School was just thirty blocks away on the eastside of Manhattan. Several schools and colleges comprised the mix of academic offerings at the West 4th Street location. The Loeb Student Center with its gleaming blue glass panels was symbolic of NYU's wealth and prominence in New York City.

Washington Square was a major transportation hub. The A-Train had a stop at West 4th Street. The IRT train station was to the east of campus, and numerous New York City buses completed the network of public transportation options available to NYU students, faculty, and administrators. I remember the Chock Full O'Nuts branch that was just across the street from Main Building on West 4th Street where most of my classes were held. I ate many of their hotdogs and doughnuts, and drank a lot of their freshly squeezed orange juice during the three years that I spent at Washington Square.

Although I majored in biology and minored in chemistry, I wound up taking more liberal arts than science courses. After considerable difficulty, I managed to resolve the differences between the British and American grading systems and was granted one year's transfer credit for the four A Level passes I received in science. Coursework was not as challenging as I expected. I attributed that to the excellent education I received at Lodge School. The professors at NYU, especially in my Biology classes, were very impressive. Drs. Chariper, Mateyko, and Kopac were very demanding and highly accomplished in their respective disciplines. My first exposure to the structure of the deoxyribonucleic acid (DNA) molecule was in Dr. Kopac's class. I even wrote a term paper in my second year on the structure of DNA.

Academically, I did outstandingly well. Books that I read in Latin classes at Lodge School were assigned in English as part of my Classical Civilization Course. I aced that course. I took French and benefited from the firm foundation I received in that language when I was a student at Lodge School. I also did well in English, sociology, psychology, philosophy, and fine arts. I couldn't believe that the College of Arts and Sciences allowed me the freedom to choose the courses I wanted to take each semester.

The average class size at NYU was approximately thirty-five students per section. However, classes in core courses such as English were typically two hundred students or more. I remember thinking that there was no way that my English professor, Dr. Borek could ever know that I was a student in his class. Most of my classes were held in the Main Building, a multi-story structure in the heart of the Washington Square campus. I learned to negotiate all of the stairways in that building in order to get to my classes on time. Waiting on the elevator to get from floor to floor was an impossible task. Students would be packed into those cars like sardines!

In my first semester at NYU, I was required to take a speech test. I also had to make a decision about whether I would enroll in the mandatory physical education course. I was never told why NYU required students to take a speech test but the rumor was that the test was initiated to correct the speech of southern and foreign students who attended the university. I passed the speech test with flying colors and was never required to take any remedial classes in speech. I also was able to avoid taking the physical education course by signing up to be a member of the varsity soccer team.

As a member of the Violets, NYU's varsity soccer team, I quickly learned that winning is the only thing that matters in American inter-collegiate sports. My teammates and I were issued all of our gear–boots, socks, blazers, sweaters, and ties–by the Athletic Division. They stocked more balls and bandages than I ever saw in the years I played for the Barbados Soccer Team. Our season began in September and ended in December. Although soccer was not a traditional American sport, I could hardly tell, especially when I saw how much attention I received from everyone on the campus community, including the faculty.

The NYU campus newspaper–The Washington Square Journal–had three student reporters permanently assigned to cover all of our events, including practice, games, and banquets. The newspaper routinely featured my performance on the soccer field in many of its issues. There were headlines such as "Booters Defeat Elis (Yale), three to two, in Opener Turton, Harewood Sparkle in Contest At New Haven." Or "Violets Tame the Broncs (Rider College), seven to one; Harewood, Souza Lead Attack." My photograph appeared in the Washington Square Journal on a daily basis during the soccer season, and I was selected as a member of the New York All American Soccer Team for three consecutive seasons. I was a real celebrity, a genuine big man on campus.

I played soccer throughout the fall, with home games at Washington Heights and away games at locations such as Ithaca and Syracuse, NY; Washington, DC; and Madison, New Jersey. My team was truly international with teammates drawn from Brazil, Israel, Trinidad, Czechoslovakia, England, and other soccer-playing countries from across the world. It was therefore not surprising that my team finished first in our division every year that I played soccer at NYU.

On one of my away trips, the team traveled to Washington DC to play against Howard University. It was a long trip on the team bus, and after a stop on the New Jersey Turnpike to eat, we resumed our trip to the nation's capital, arriving at our hotel well after midnight. The following morning I was up early, and as instructed, I joined my teammates in the hotel lobby before breakfast. After everyone was accounted for, Coach Tobin led the group in single file into the first floor restaurant. I noticed that the line came to an abrupt halt and my teammates were congregating at the entrance to the restaurant. After a considerable delay, it was obvious to me that Coach Tobin was having a verbal exchange with someone in the restaurant, and judging from his body language the conversation was not going in his favor. Then he turned around and led the entire team out of the restaurant and back into the lobby. I later learned that the restaurant manager had refused to serve the team because there were four black players in the group. That was my second encounter with racism in America, and I could not understand how people with such attitudes of racial superiority could continue to rear their ugly heads in public settings.

NYU's varsity teams produced a number of outstanding athletes in the 1960s. The individuals I came into closest contact with were Happy Hairston and Gary Gubner. Happy was a tall, neatly groomed African American with a very friendly disposition. He grew up in Brooklyn, New York and was an outstanding basketball player on NYU's varsity team. He went on to be a member of the famous Los Angeles Lakers championship team of 1971 and 1972. That team held the record for winning thirty-three games in a row, a feat not duplicated in any other American professional sport. Then there was Gary Gubner, one of NYU's most famous athletes who was ranked number one among the world's indoor shot-putters in 1962. He broke the world indoor shot-put record multiple times that year. He was ranked number two in world outdoor competitions in 1962. I never got to meet Gary, but spent several evenings watching him workout at NYU's University Heights Campus in the Bronx where the soccer team also conducted its practice sessions.

The NYU athlete that earned international attention was Jim Wedderburn. Jim was an outstanding track and field star. He went on to win a Bronze medal at the 1960 Olympic Games held in Rome. Because many of the Caribbean islands were still British colonies, Jim and his teammates Malcolm Spence, Keith Gardner, and George Kerr represented the British West Indies.

Being a student in New York in the 1960s was the best thing that could have ever happen to me. The city was such a vibrant place. Manhattan offered an assortment of museums, theaters, jazz clubs, movie houses, and other interesting venues. When I arrived at NYU for my first semester, the presidential race between Nixon and Kennedy was just heating up. One day as I walked across campus on my way to the Lexington Avenue train to go to the Washington Heights campus, I noticed a large crowd of students had gathered outside of the Loeb Student Center. They were carrying signs that read "Kennedy for President!" I soon found out that candidate John Kennedy was scheduled to appear at a rally on our campus later that day. I waited for almost an hour to get a glimpse of Senator Kennedy, and much to my disappointment, I did not get to see him. If there is one thing I could change today, it would be my decision to leave campus before the candidate arrived. Presidential contender John Kennedy arrived at NYU late in the afternoon, and I was not there to meet him or hear him speak.

The 1960s was also a time that the Civil Rights struggle was gaining momentum. Powerful black leaders like Malcolm X, Martin Luther King Jr. Roy Wilkins, James Farmer, and Stokely Carmichael were regulars on television and talk radio. I listened to Barry Gray on WMCA every night to learn about the latest developments on the political scene. Barry Gray was a clever radio personality who in my opinion had an avowed agenda to use his show to test the mettle of leaders like Wilkins, Farmer, and Malcolm X. His was a classical talk show with an interview format. It was scheduled at eleven o'clock at night. I routinely listened to his interviews and could always discern when he was trying to entrap his guests. I also liked to listen to Gene Shepherd an amazing humorist and raconteur whose program was on WOR radio. He was an exceptional artist who covered topics ranging from normal to the absurd. His descriptions of the Midwest are by far the best I have ever heard. Then there were people like John Neblett and his Passing Parade, and Paul Harvey with his signature reminder to his audience, " and that's the rest of the story!"

I got to meet James Farmer, Malcolm X, Minister Farrakhan, and other prominent civil rights leaders. I frequented the Apollo theater in Harlem to see and hear performers like James Brown, Wilson Pickett, Jackie Wilson, Sarah Vaughan, Billy Eckstein, the Platters, Temptations, Cadillacs, and others, and was entertained by the likes of Richard Pryor, Redd Fox and Moms Mabley. The Village Vanguard and the Village Gate were venues for the best jazz that New York had to offer. Can you imagine having the opportunity to attend a performance by the likes of a Miles Davis, Cannonball Atherly, Thelonious Monk and other phenomenal jazz musicians in a setting where it was so easy to hear and see them?

Then there were the museums–the Metropolitan, Guggenheim, Museum of Modern Art, and the American Museum of Natural History. It was so convenient to take advantage of the many resources the City of New York offered to every student attending any of its numerous colleges and universities. It was a virtual laboratory for almost every course I took, from Fine Art to Foreign Languages.

Meeting tuition expense at NYU was no easy task. For my first and second semesters, I borrowed the money from Eldon and Aunt Eude's friend Mr. Rufus Stuart, respectively. One day as I was exiting the elevator in the Main Building, I bumped into one of the few black students attending NYU. He was a Barbadian whose family was close with my family. His name was Erskine Simmonds and he was in his sophomore year. I remember we had a real businesslike conversation. After exchanging a few pleasantries, I recall him telling me "Harewood, boy, this place will reward academic performance, so if you ace all of your courses, you can apply for an academic scholarship!" I followed Erskine's advice to the letter. I studied as hard as I could, and at the end of my first academic year I was able to compete successfully for an academic scholarship. NYU paid my tuition for the remainder of the time that it took me to finish my bachelor's degree.

I met several West Indian and African students while I was attending NYU. My best friend Alan Hewitt was from Trinidad and so was Ed Turton, Lloyd Ross and Austin Letrin. Philip Daws was Jamaican, and Dennis Paul was Grenadian. The Barbadian contingent included Freddie Earl (St. Michael), Frank Farnum (St. John), Elton Mottley (St. Michael), John Boyce (St. Lucy), Jim Wedderburn (St. Philip), Keith Forde (St. Philip), and Frank Lorde (St. Philip).

During summer vacations, I was allowed to work, and I took full advantage of the multitude of opportunities available in New York, the city that never sleeps. During my first summer vacation, I used NYU's well-organized placement office to find a job on Wall Street. I worked as a clerk in the very prominent Dominick and Dominick firm located at that time in one of the skyscrapers at Sixteen Wall Street. I learned how the Stock Market worked from my coworkers, and was introduced to some of the most powerful computers available then to process the multiple transactions made during a day of active trading in the world's busiest Stock Market.

During the summer of 1962, I got a job running an elevator in one of New York's swank East Side apartment buildings. Again, NYU's placement office provided me with the contact information, and when I interviewed with the manager of the building, he was very impressed when I told him that I attended NYU. His daughter was an NYU student, so in a way, he felt that he was doing a good turn for the institution that was educating his daughter. I was hired on the spot. I worked either the five to midnight shift or the midnight to eight am shift. There was only one manually operated elevator in that multi-story residential building. I was surprised to learn that the operation of that car was not as easy as it seemed. After a couple of sessions with my experienced colleague, I was ready for the task of servicing the building all by myself.

The residents were an eclectic group of individuals who had adopted New York as their home-away-from-home. It did not take me long to become familiar with most of their idiosyncrasies. Several of them were prominent artists and entertainers, and the one I best remember is Merv Griffin. During the 1960s he was hosting his own television show, The Merv Griffin Show. He left the building like clockwork every morning, and would return almost at the same time every evening. Whenever the buzzer to the elevator rang, I knew who would be waiting on that particular floor when I opened the door. As a young coed in the 1960s, I considered it a privilege to get to know a television personality like Merv Griffin. He was a lot skinnier then than the billionaire he became in his later years. The famous movie star Greta Garbo was also a resident in the building where I worked. At that time in her life she was very reclusive, avoiding contact with everyone. I can still conjure up the image I have of her walking down the sidewalk with her back arched, her head facing the ground, and partially concealed by the hood of her raincoat.

My third summer was spent working at the Tompkins Park branch of the Brooklyn Public Library. Located about five blocks from where I lived on Quincy Street, that small branch was a very busy place during the day. My job involved processing requests from residents who wanted to borrow or return books. Restocking the shelves was also a major responsibility for me and my coworkers. I tried to read as many non-fiction books that I could get my hands on that summer. It was at the Tompkins Park Library that I first learned to speak a few words of Spanish. At that time, Hispanics were becoming a visible and vibrant part of community life in Brooklyn, and they comprised a significant percentage of our customers.

I graduated from NYU in the spring of 1963 after spending three years in the undergraduate program in the College of Arts and Science. There was a large gathering of graduates and family attending the outdoor commencement ceremony, which was held at the university's Washington Heights campus in the Bronx. Eudine, Joyce, Aunt Eude, my brother Ivan, and Aunt Eude's friend Mr. Stuart attended. I don't remember who was the keynote speaker or what was the subject of his address. All I remember is that the experience seemed surreal. There was no graduation party, and no ostentatious celebration. The reality of the situation was that I had completed one small step in a very important journey. My ultimate goal was to continue my education until I had earned a terminal degree.

Chapter 12

The Love of My Life

I fondly remember 1963 as the year that I married my dear, devoted wife Eudine. I met Eudine in the summer of 1960 shortly after arriving in NY. The Sons and Daughters of Barbados held their annual dance at the Audubon Ballroom in New York City, and Joyce's friend Aletha and some other Barbadians asked me to accompany them to the dance. When I reached the ballroom, I was surprised to see Barbadians there that I had no idea that they had even left Barbados. One of them was Eudine Austin. I had seen her on more than one occasion when I worked as a technician at the Bacteriological and Pathological Laboratories at the Barbados General Hospital. During that time, I traveled to Bridgetown every day, mostly by car. With my own transportation, I could stay in the city late during the week to attend sports events or go to the movies. On one such occasion, I saw this beautiful, petite young lady walking across Probyn Street on her way to the theater. I always remember that day. So I knew who she was but never had the occasion to meet her.

The Sons and Daughters dance brought us together for the first time, and when we met, it seemed as though we had known each other for a very long time. Eudine was engaging and very easy to talk to, and we talked enough that night to make the dance and evening totally enjoyable. I remember having to juggle my time with her and with the group that invited me to the dance. It was clear to me that Aletha and her friends were expecting me to be their dedicated dancing partner, especially when the band played the popular calypsos of that period. My friend Frank Farnum and his buddies from Brooklyn were also at that dance, and I had to find a way to be with them as well.

The next time I saw Eudine it was at the International Students' Festival at NYU. It was held in the modern, multi-story Loeb Student Center, just on the perimeter of NYU's Washington Square Campus. The festival was always a big hit, with several different international groups showcasing their culture and cuisine before a large, enthusiastic gathering. That year's program included performances by members of the West Indian Students Association, so I felt that it was a good idea to invite a special guest. As the date of the festival approached, I still had not identified the person that I wanted to attend the festival with me. One evening, as Frank Farnum and I were traveling to Brooklyn from NYU's Washington Heights campus, we were talking about the upcoming festival, and Frank suggested that Eudine seemed like the sort of person who might enjoy attending such an event. It was a real no-brainer, and I couldn't wait to get home to call and ask her to be my guest at the festival. I was overjoyed when she accepted my invitation.

The evening was special in every way. The student performances were unbelievable, and so was the food. We were both having such a great time that we did not realize that it was getting really late, and we needed to leave. Once outside of the Loeb Student Center we made our way down towards the subway station at West 4th Street. We had just walked about two hundred yards when Eudine told me that she was having a stomachache, and before I could respond, her stomach simply yielded the exotic mixture of foods she had eaten onto the sidewalk at the perimeter of Washington Square Park! Much later she told me that she never thought that I would ever ask her out again.

Ask her out I did, and I spent many enjoyable evenings with her walking in Central Park, or the Brooklyn Botanical Gardens, or attending a movie on 42nd Street. We became really good friends exchanging stories about growing up in Barbados, and often talking about family members and siblings. I soon got to meet her cousins Esteen and Archie, and their daughter Anita, along with other members of her family. She came to see me play soccer at NYU's Washington Heights campus, and she was my guest at our Varsity Ball. During the period from 1960 to 1963, I made innumerable trips to Harlem on the A-Train to visit Eudine. Sometimes we went to dinner or the movies. Other times we would stroll through Central Park, and spend the evening sitting on one of the benches and enjoying that peaceful setting.

Although we never talked about getting married, it was obvious to me that we had a deep and natural affinity for each other. After I graduated from NYU in 1963, I decided that it was time for us to formalize our relationship. One day I took the train to mid-town Manhattan, walked over to Wexler's Jewelry Store and bought an engagement ring. Later that week, I invited Eudine to Quincy Street. I remember we were talking about graduate school and student visas, and when she least expected it, I presented her with the ring and asked her to marry me. After she regained her composure, her response was clear and concise, "Yes, Ken. I will marry you." We were married at St. Martin's Episcopal Church in Harlem one month after I graduated from NYU.

Our wedding reception was held at the Tuscan Ballroom on the famous 125th Street in Harlem. The ballroom was on the second floor of an old commercial building. My friends helped me decorate the ballroom the day before the wedding. Eudine's Dad flew in from Barbados and made all of the arrangements for the food and drink. He was the typical proud Bajan father who wanted the best for his daughter and new son-in-law. Everyone remembers that he mixed a very potent rum punch using Bajan white rum, which he served at the reception. Instead of plastic glasses, he bought a set of elegant wine glasses. I had a fabulous time greeting friends and dancing to the familiar beat of West Indian music that was provided by a band from New Rochelle that was led by Eudine's cousin Edwin. I drank so much champagne that evening that I am amazed that I was able to participate in the other planned activities before leaving the ballroom for our honeymoon.

I made arrangements to spend our honeymoon at the fabulous Americana Hotel. It was on Seventh Avenue between 52nd and 53rd Streets. Eldon drove us to the Americana where we checked in without any trouble. Our room was a honeymoon suite on one of the upper floors. I remember looking down on the top of some very tall buildings that were part of the midtown Manhattan skyline. We had a wonderful time at the Americana. I thought that we had left the country. There was hardly a sound to disturb us. When we wanted to have a typical Manhattan experience, we simply took the elevator down to the street level and mingled with the Broadway crowd. The two days we spent at the Americana were truly memorable.

Life for us as newlyweds was like a fairy tale. I was now placed in the role of head of household and we hardly had anyplace that we could call a household. After a brief but thoroughly enjoyable honeymoon at the Americana Hotel, we returned to the reality of life on Quincy Street. Aunt Eude was exceedingly kind to us, and she allowed us to occupy the lower level of her apartment. I had lived there during the three years that I was a student at NYU. Now, I was about to share that space with Eudine. At that time, Eudine was working at an accounting firm in Harlem, and I had a job at the Brooklyn Jewish Hospital on Prospect Place.

As a foreign student with a newly minted degree from NYU, my options were limited. I could either enroll in a graduate program, or apply for a job under the practical training provision of the Department of Immigration and Naturalization Services. I never considered the third option, which was simply to pack my bags and return to Barbados. I decided to pursue the second option.

My job search took me to several clinical laboratories in New York. I began with NYU's Medical Center, one of New York City's premier centers for biomedical research. I believed that my training at the Barbados General Hospital would have served me well in that institution! Their interest in my candidacy waned when they learned of my immigration status. I remained optimistic however, and it was perhaps that optimism that was evident as I interviewed for a job in clinical biochemistry at the Brooklyn Jewish Hospital. When I walked into the director's office, I remember he was wearing a full-length white laboratory coat and had a boyish appearance. I liked his friendly disposition, and felt comfortable in his presence. The interview was in no way intimidating. My foreign student status was not an issue. He liked my optimism, and was already playing the role of my boss. "Let me introduce you to the laboratory supervisor, " he said. The laboratory was only a short walk from his office, and within seconds I was in the supervisor's office. He was about five foot six inches tall and visibly overweight. He reminded me a little of the New Orleans musician Fats Domino who rocked our world as teenagers with his rendition of *On Blueberry Hill*. He talked to me about the job, and introduced me to some of the laboratory technicians as we walked by their stations. I liked what I saw, so when the Director offered to hire me, I immediately accepted.

My duties involved conducting routine and special biochemical assays on blood and other biological fluids that were submitted to the laboratory on a daily basis. My colleagues included several talented biochemistry technicians. There was my good friend Charles who had grown up in Alabama. Charles and I have remained friends ever since our first meeting in 1963. I cannot forget the stories he told me about how violent life was when he was growing up in Alabama. His account of how a group of racist white men tied a member of his family to the railroad track and watched the train crush him to death, still gives me the creeps. In spite of the painful memories of his childhood, every holiday he packed his wife and three kids into his car and drove all the way from Brooklyn to Alabama. He would never ever contemplate stopping along the way other than for a bathroom break at a roadside service station.

My other friend at the lab was Carlos. He was a very interesting person. He was from Georgia, which at that time was a satellite state within the Soviet Union. We talked a lot about the differences between Georgians and Americans. Carlos had a genuine affection for life in America and that was reflected in the ease with which he interacted with all of his colleagues at the Brooklyn Jewish Hospital.

In addition to Charles and Carlos, the technical staff in clinical biochemistry included Vito, Kathy, Ann, Ronnie, and Livia. What I remember most about that group was that we worked well together.

There was a contingent of Barbadians working at the Brooklyn Jewish Hospital during my stint there. Archie and Emerson were employed as laboratory technicians, and Neville was the cashier at the first floor coffee shop. I enjoyed visiting with them during the day to catch up on things Barbadian. I also met Alvin and Maurice. They were experienced technicians who were from Jamaica and Guyana, respectively. They taught me how to draw blood so that I could make extra money working as a phlebotomist.

For two years, I took the Nostrand Avenue bus to Prospect Place in the morning and walked the two long blocks to Bedford

Avenue. In the evening, I left work at five o'clock, and rode the bus home, usually arriving well ahead of Eudine. It was pretty much a routine that I became accustomed to and enjoyed very much. Then, the Director created an Assistant Supervisor position and hired a young man to fill it. The new Assistant Supervisor was the exact opposite of the laboratory supervisor. He was stern and aloof, and most of the technicians had a difficult time adjusting to his style of management. I tried my best to get along with him.

In 1965, I was the happiest person on the planet. My application for permanent residence was approved and I received a letter from the Immigration and Naturalization Services informing me of their decision. I would have to travel out of the U.S. to receive my visa. Eudine and I made arrangements to go to Barbados, so in April we were on our way there. I couldn't believe that it was almost five years since I left the island.

When I arrived in Barbados, I couldn't wait to be reunited with my brothers Roger and Philip. I had not seen them since I left home in 1960. I couldn't believe how quickly they had grown up. Philip was a student at Lodge School, and when I drove into the schoolyard to see him I could hardly recognize the person who approached the car to greet me. Then when Roger came to visit me at Eudine's family home in Bank Hall, I was expecting to see a boy. Instead, I saw a man. He was mature, and responsible, and had fully assumed the role of head of what remained of the Harewood household.

When I visited my childhood home, I was very disappointed by what I saw. Because Philip was a minor and Roger was living at his godmother's house in St. Michael, Dad had asked one of the neighbors to keep an eye on the house. That young man was not as trustworthy as Dad thought, and that was evidenced by the fact that many of the things that I treasured as a child were missing from our home. My stamp collection had disappeared. Mum's sewing machine was also gone, along with several pieces of furniture from the living room. I couldn't believe that the entire set of weights I used as a youngster for bodybuilding was no longer there. It was at that moment that I knew that I needed to do everything that I could to get Roger and Philip reunited with the family in New York as soon as possible.

When I returned to work after my trip to Barbados, I had an unpleasant encounter with the new Assistant Supervisor. It was late in the evening. I had just completed my assignments, and was on my way out of the laboratory. The Assistant Supervisor saw me leaving and caught up with me at the door. He told me that he was looking for someone to help one of the technicians finish her work. Apparently, she had not used her time wisely during the day, and as a result, her work was backlogged. The Assistant Supervisor was insisting that I remain behind to help. On any other occasion, I would not have had a problem complying with his request, but on that day, I had promised Eudine that I would meet her at five-thirty, and she was already waiting for me. I explained this to him, and asked if he could get one of the other technicians to help, but he simply would not listen. I felt that he left me with no choice, so I calmly told him that I had to go, and I left for home as planned.

The next morning, the Director was standing in the laboratory when I arrived. He was his usual very cordial self. After some small talk, he invited me into his office, and it was not long before he brought up the issue of the previous evening. I tried to explain what had happened, but it was obvious that he had already made up his mind. He was simply going to support the Assistant Supervisor! As I sat there listening to him speak, I was already envisioning myself in a completely different work setting. One in which I would be viewed as a colleague and not as a pair of hands. I knew then that I needed to move on with my life. When I reflect on the decision I made that day, I realize that it provided me with a new set of options. It was a decision that I would not regret.

My next stop was at the Rockefeller University on 66th Street and York Avenue in Manhattan. I interviewed there and was pleasantly surprised to learn that they had an opening and were prepared to hire me right away. I was assigned to the laboratories of Dr. Lyman C. Craig. Dr. Craig's laboratories were on the fifth and sixth floors in Flexner Hall–a building that housed the research programs of several Nobel Laureates. Dr. Craig was one of those incredibly successful scientists who operated under the radar. I knew very little about him before I went to work in his laboratories. He was the inventor of the Counter Current Distribution System, a powerful devise for separating and purifying molecules, and he was also working on developing an artificial kidney. He was a modest, unpretentious individual who, in spite of his phenomenal achievements, was not overbearing in any way.

My supervisor in Dr. Craig's laboratories was an easy-going scientist, Dr. Jack Goldstein. Jack wore a full beard and was addicted to his pipe. He kept it between clenched teeth whether in the laboratory or in his office. He was trained as a nucleic acid biochemist by Dr. Robert Holley who was a professor at Cornell University in Ithaca, New York. Dr. Holley was awarded the Nobel Prize for Medicine in 1968. He was a brilliant biochemist whose claim to fame was his elegant work on characterizing a group of molecules called the transfer ribonucleic acids (RNAs).

Jack's major focus was on studying the structure and function of low molecular weight RNAs, and his students Tom Scleich and Robert Williams were actively involved in identifying and characterizing two novel RNA species that were isolated in Jack's laboratory. Dan Rifkin, Robley Williams, Kent Stuart and others were the young protein biochemists working in Dr. Craig's group.

It was not long before I felt that I was an expert on isolating RNAs from "frozen cakes" of bacterial cells, and analyzing them based on the way they absorbed light in the ultraviolet range of the spectrum. I learned how to interpret the information derived from the experiments I was performing, and I developed a better understanding of how my research findings could be used to advance our understanding of the molecular basis of life.

Rockefeller University was the ideal place for me to learn about all aspects of the scientific enterprise. The research laboratories were directed by scientists with international reputations, and the research-support organization worked like a well-oiled machine.

The purchasing department was a shining example of how these units should be organized to support basic research. It was effectively managed, and almost everything I needed to get my work done was listed in their catalog and stocked on their shelves. Any order I placed for a reagent was usually filled within twenty-four hours, and this was long before the arrival of overnight delivery companies such as FEDEX. I had easy access to their glassblowing and maintenance shops that usually met all of my needs for customized service. The Caspary Auditorium was a dome-shaped structure where Rockefeller University faculty met to listen to scholarly presentations and exchange ideas on important research topics. I routinely attended lectures in that auditorium that were delivered by some of the world's most accomplished scientists. The Harvey Society held its lectures there, as well as various scientific clubs. Doctoral students frequently used Caspary Auditorium to present their thesis research.

In 1967, Jack interviewed for a job at the New York Blood Center. That was a new, non-profit organization located two blocks west of Rockefeller University on East 67th Street. A group of entrepreneurial physicians had created the center and their vision was to coordinate blood collection and distribution activities throughout the New York Metropolitan area. They bought a large, three-story building across from the Julia Richmond Public School. The building was gutted and later transformed into a blood collection and basic research facility.

Jack was ecstatic when he returned from his morning interview with the new leadership at the Blood Center. He had negotiated successfully to be Director of a new section that would be called the Nucleic Acids Department. He boasted openly that his salary would be twice what he was currently earning at Rockefeller University. After regaining control of his emotions, he casually informed me that he wanted me to join him in his new position. He reasoned that he needed someone with my experience to help set up and manage his laboratory, and promised to pay me a competitive salary.

I shared in Jack's excitement and lost little time in going over to the Blood Center to meet with Ms. Jennifer Fish, the Director of their Personnel Office. Ms. Fish was a very proper middle-aged English woman with a matronly appearance. Her British accent was quite distinct, and I was very much at home in my interaction with her. I was hired instantly at a salary that was significantly higher than I expected.

Working at the New York Blood Center was a unique experience. I would learn all about setting up a laboratory. I worked with the maintenance crew and the purchasing department to have utilities installed and procure equipment and supplies. I developed very special relationships with sales representatives from small equipment companies and large scientific supply houses. I participated in recruiting and training laboratory technicians and postdoctoral fellows.

I was always impressed by the resourcefulness of sales representatives. They could tell me about the research programs at competing laboratories. They knew what pieces of capital equipment our competitors purchased, the kind of data that was being generated, and the competence of the respective investigators. I learned about emerging technologies and was provided with unique opportunities to evaluate equipment prototypes. My friendships with sales representatives like Jules Lux from Savant Instruments and Jack Fried from New England Nuclear contributed immeasurably to my growth and experience as a scientist.

One day, Jack was scheduled to interview a young scientist who was seeking a job as a program director. After the interview, as the candidate left the laboratory, Jack casually urged me to take a look at his curriculum vitae. "He went to the same school as you in Barbados," Jack stated. I looked at the document and quickly found out that he was someone I knew. It was Dr. Colvin Redman, one of the Redman brothers who attended the Lodge School while I was a student there. Colvin was senior to me, but I remembered him as an outstanding athlete. The Search Committee voted unanimously to hire Colvin to direct a new laboratory on Blood Group Characterization. Having Colvin as a colleague and friend was a stroke of good luck. We were both trained as biochemists, and we were also proud alumni of the Lodge School. I placed considerable value in our friendship. I considered Colvin to be someone that I could trust, and I knew that he was a person that I could communicate with freely about research or personal matters.

I met another outstanding scientist/mentor while I was at the Blood Center. His name was Dr. Cyril Moore, and he was the first black biochemist I ever got to know personally. I was introduced to him at a meeting of the New York Enzyme Club. This was a group of very distinguished scientists, drawn from the major universities in the Tri-State area. They met monthly at Rockefeller University, and Jack asked me to join him at one of their meetings.

Cyril was Trinidadian, and like me, he came to the U.S. to pursue a career as a scientist. He was brilliant! He knew everything there was to know about the biochemistry of mitochondria, the organelles in our cells that are the storehouses of energy. He was supremely confident about his discipline and was never bashful to engage anyone in an argument about how enzymes worked. Cyril and I became friends from the day we first met at that meeting of the Enzyme Club. Having Colvin and Cyril, two accomplished biochemists, as best friends and colleagues was invaluable to my career as a scientist.

Chapter 13

Bajan Biochemist

In 1967, Jack introduced me to Dr. Abraham Mazur who was recruited to the Blood Center to develop a protein biochemistry program that focused on the structure and function of the pigment in our red blood cells that is known as hemoglobin. Dr. Mazur was a professor at the City College of New York where he was the Chairman of the Chemistry Department. I believe that it must have been during my first meeting with Dr. Mazur that he told me that the City University of New York had just launched a new Doctoral Program in Biochemistry, and he thought that it was an excellent program for someone like me.

I had a friend then whose name was Larry Loomis. Larry was a technician in Dr. Fred Prince's laboratory at the New York Blood Center. Larry was a student at NYU's Washington Square College at the same time that I attended, and he graduated with a BS in Chemistry. He and I often reminisced about our experiences as science majors. When Larry heard of the program at City College, he was interested in seeking admission. We applied, and were both accepted into the program.

Over the next three years, Larry and I traveled together from the New York Blood Center to City College at 138th Street and Amsterdam Avenue to attend classes. Some of my courses were scheduled at the Graduate Center of the City University of New York, which was on West 42nd Street near to Fifth Avenue. Sometimes, I had to pinch myself to be reminded that I was well on my way to pursuing my dream of obtaining a doctoral degree in biochemistry.

I rotated between the City University of New York and the New York Blood Center to fulfill my coursework and research obligations. I was permitted to adjust my workday at the New

York Blood Center to accommodate my class schedule at City College. Jack was granted Adjunct Professor status at City College so that he could serve as my thesis mentor. I worked in his laboratory during the day, spending every minute working on my project that involved isolating and characterizing a novel species of RNA from the bacterium known as *Escherichia coli*. I routinely perused all of the journals, attended every seminar that was scheduled at Cornell University, Sloan Kettering Medical Center, and Rockefeller University. It was an exciting time to be pursuing a career as a scientist.

The Doctoral Program at the City University of New York was rigorous, and some of the most accomplished scientists were members of the graduate faculty. The combination of an outstanding faculty and the resource-rich setting of New York City made graduate school a very rewarding experience. When I first enrolled, Dr. Jim Hogg was Chairman of the Graduate Program in Biochemistry. He was later succeeded by Dr Aaron Luckton. These were both great administrators. They were approachable, easy to talk to, and very student-centered. Although their home campuses were elsewhere across the New York metropolitan area, they were always available in their office at the Graduate Center to provide me with the best advise possible.

One of the unique features of the program was the way that it was organized. Unlike the University of North Carolina that allows its constituent institutions to administer their graduate programs independently, the City University Graduate Program was inter-institutional in design and fully integrated, drawing on the combined strengths of all of its faculties. Students were accepted into the program by a process that was centralized within the Graduate Center. They were required to take the core courses at the Graduate Center and the specialty courses at the campus where the expertise resided. For example, my course in protein chemistry and my journal club class were taught at the Graduate Center, while advanced organic chemistry and physical chemistry were given at City College and Mount Sinai Medical School. These campuses were widely recognized for their reputations in those areas. Graduate School commencement was the responsibility of the combined program, not the individual campuses.

My classmates and I took full advantage of the many public and private libraries available in Manhattan. I used those facilities routinely as I worked to keep pace with the demands of my classes. I signed-up for German as my second language and had built-in tutors–two Germans who worked as research technicians in Jack's laboratory. Within less than three years I completed all of my coursework; met my language requirements; and satisfied the requirement for successfully conducting an independent research project.

Selecting a project for my research thesis was one of the most important decisions I had to make as a graduate student. I knew from conversations with my mentor Jack that he wanted me to work on something that was novel and innovative. Those were two words that I would hear over and over again during my career in science. I was well aware of the fact that whatever project I chose, it was important for me to have easy access to all of the materials and methods necessary to successfully complete my assignment.

Two additional realities guided my thinking. The first had a lot to do with Jack's earlier work and the reputation that he enjoyed as an expert in studying the structure and function of an interesting group of molecules called the soluble RNAs. He had developed reliable procedures for releasing these molecules from cells, and he had optimized methods for sorting them on the basis of size, weight, and chemical makeup. He had published an elegant report showing that he could separate them into at least four size classes, and he revealed detailed information on two of the size classes that he studied. The second reality had much to do with my conviction that Jack was on the right track. I really believed that the molecules that he was studying might play critical roles in cell growth and division, and I certainly wanted to be one of the scientists associated with any study that could shed light on some of the complex processes associated with life itself.

To ensure that my ideas were sound and well thought-out, I spent several weeks in the libraries of Rockefeller University and Cornell University delving into the large body of work that had been conducted on the RNAs. I tried to read as many manuscripts and review articles on the subject as possible.

I began to feel like I was an expert on RNAs. I found out that these molecules were key components of all cells. I learned that they existed in a variety of sizes and shapes, and that some of them mediated a number of important functions associated with cell growth and division. One of the most powerful bits of information I gleaned from that extensive review of the literature was that RNAs were similar in chemical makeup to DNA molecules. I remember thinking that if their building blocks were so much like DNA's, then it was possible that they could play some vitally important role in cells. After all, it was common knowledge that DNA was the master molecule, and that it was the driving force behind all biological inheritance. What if I could find an RNA molecule in cells that could attract the attention that DNA received?

After completing all of the background work, I finally settled on studying the third size class of soluble RNAs that Jack had identified in one of his earlier publications. I was instinctively attracted to that size class because little was known about its structure and function, and I felt confident that anything I learned could turn out to be important. I was thrilled when Jack and my thesis committee approved my proposal to invest time and energy in studying these molecules.

I wasted little time in launching my project, and was relentless in the pursuit of my stated goals and objectives. I had access to a type of bacterial cell that I was confident that I could use as a reliable source of the material I needed for my proposed study. Bacterial cells were considered to be an excellent model for the kind of investigation that I was about to launch. Most of what had been known about the biology of human cells had been learnt from studies carried out on bacteria. I bought several frozen packs of bacterial cells from one of the biological supply houses so that I had enough material to begin my work. I began by thawing the frozen packs until they were transformed into a soft mushy blob to which I added an inert abrasive material that proved to be very effective in breaking the majority of the cells open. I then utilized a number of well-established biochemical techniques to separate out the soluble RNAs for further scrutiny. It then took me only two additional steps to get to the molecules that were of greatest interest.

I was able to carry out detailed studies on every aspect of the molecules that I purified from elution region three. I calculated how much they weighed; took precise measurements of their size and shape; determined the percentage of each of the individual building blocks from which they were assembled; and generated information about their origin and function. It was gratifying when I learned that these were considered to be breakthrough discoveries that scientists were beginning to view with considerable interest. It was really flattering when Jack asked me to submit my findings to the Federation of American Societies for Experimental Biology (FASEB) for external peer review. I was thrilled when I learned that national experts in the field had found my work acceptable for publication. An abstract of my study appeared in the official program at FASEB's annual meeting that was scheduled for Atlantic City, New Jersey later that year. When I saw my name along with Jack's in my first peer-reviewed publication, I was ecstatic!

The national exposure I was receiving made me even more comfortable with the body of work that I completed, and I welcomed the opportunity to meet with my doctoral thesis committee to present my results and defend them to the best of my ability. Finally, the day of reckoning came. Although I knew that I was very knowledgeable about every aspect of the study, I was still a bit apprehensive about having a team of experts scrutinize every experiment that I had carried out and the conclusions that I had drawn.

The venue was the conference room at the New York Blood Center. My committee comprised Drs. Tom Haines, Michael Fishman, and Abraham Mazur, all members of the chemistry department at the City College of New York. It also included Dr. Ezra Shahn who was a Professor in the Department of Biological Sciences at Hunter College. Jack served as chairperson. He was Head of the Nucleic Acids Department at the New York Blood Center and Adjunct Professor of Chemistry at City College of New York.

After we were all comfortably seated around a large oval conference room table, I was invited to speak. I began by reviewing the entire field of soluble RNAs, highlighting some of the important earlier findings, and explaining why I felt that a more detailed investigation of these molecules was necessary. I presented the rationale for my work and thoroughly reviewed my results. I concluded by making some reasonable predictions about the potential role these molecules might play in regulating the complex behavior of cells. At the end of my presentation, the committee members grilled me for over an hour. Most of their questions were directed at obtaining additional information on specific aspects of my talk. I found the committee to be really fascinated by my work and I was pleased with my performance.

After the last committee member finished questioning me, I was politely asked to leave the room. I was exhausted and not sure of what the next step(s) would be. As I remained in the hallway pondering my fate, the door opened and Jack motioned me to come in. As I entered the room, I was seeking some signal from their faces as to the outcome of their deliberations, but none was evident. Then the moment came. Jack broke the silence. With his pipe tightly clenched between his teeth he simply said, "congratulations Drrrrr Harewood." Those were magical words to me. They signaled the end to one of the most challenging but exciting times of my career.

As I drove home to Brooklyn that evening, thoughts of Eudine, Mum, Dad, Aunt Mam, Aunt Eude, Joyce, other family members, mentors like Mr. Gittens, Mr. Gooding at Lodge, and Mr. Tobin, raced through my mind. I reflected on the fact that it was almost ten years since I left Barbados to set out on this journey. I had withstood the challenges of undergraduate college, and done everything I needed to do to survive and thrive in the City of New York. My hard work had finally, paid off. I had successfully defended my thesis, and would soon be invited to attend the City University of New York's Graduate School Convocation where the Board of Higher Education of the City of New York would confer on me the degree of Doctor of Philosophy. I knew then that the events of that day, July 30, 1970 would fundamentally change my life.

Graduation day finally came on June 3, 1971. My devoted wife Eudine, our daughter Dionne, and Mum accompanied me to 57 West 42nd Street where the commencement ceremony was held. I remember that compared to my graduation from NYU, this was a less elaborate ceremony with a small number of graduates, guests, and university faculty in attendance. The program was conducted without much fanfare, and I am unable to recall any major speeches. In many ways it was a low-key event. When the moment came, and my name was called, I walked up to the platform slowly, trying desperately to conceal as much as possible the rush of emotions that had engulfed my entire being. After shaking Dean Luckton's hand, I turned around to face the gathering holding my degree firmly with both hands. I could see the pride in Eudine's, Dionne's and Mum's, eyes as I left the platform to return to my seat. I was one of the first two students to ever receive the Ph.D. Degree in Biochemistry from the City University of New York, and I have always been proud of that distinction.

In 1964, just one year after my marriage to Eudine, Aunt Eude announced that she was taking early retirement from her job with the City of New York Welfare Department. She went on to say that she was planning to go back to Barbados for an unspecified period of time. I did not fully comprehend how this would affect me, so I was not particularly worried. I tried to find out when the rent was due and exactly how much money I needed to pay the landlord. I also sought information on emergency measures I needed to take in the event the landlord failed to come over to stoke the coal-fired furnace in the basement. Everything else went according to plan, and I enjoyed having complete control of both sections of the duplex while Aunt Eude was away. I was about to find out what it meant to be the true head of household.

Soon after our marriage, Eudine and I developed a habit of meeting in downtown Brooklyn every Thursday evening. We usually ate dinner in the restaurant at Abraham and Strauss, one of the largest department stores, or at Bickford, a modestly priced restaurant located at the major intersection of Flatbush and Atlantic Avenues. My favorite dish at Bickford was their beef stew.

One Thursday, Eudine and I had an early dinner at Bickford's. After dinner, we shopped a little, and then took the Gates Avenue bus home to Quincy Street. When we reached our stop at the intersection of Marcy Avenue and Quincy Street, we got off the bus and headed for home just across Marcy Avenue. As I approached the main entrance to the duplex, I noticed that the outer door was slightly ajar. Then when I reached for my key to unlock the inner door, it became clear to me that the lock on that door was broken. My heart raced uncontrollably as I entered the building and cautiously descended the stairs to our first floor apartment. My worst fears were soon realized because as I reached the landing, I saw a steel tool that resembled a claw hammer on the ground in the hallway. I surmised that the intruder had used that tool to pry open the door to our apartment. Once inside the room, my heart sank. The drawers and closets were left wide open, and our personal belongings were strewn all over the floor. Our new Magnavox television was missing and so was the shortwave Zenith radio. I was mortified. The wedding gifts that Eudine and I treasured so dearly were either missing or violated by an unknown intruder.

I quickly sprung into action and placed a 911 call to alert the Brooklyn police. The next person I called to notify of my predicament was my Barbadian friend Wilton Bushell. The police officer that was dispatched in response to my 911 call was white, in his late twenty's, and very casual in the way he reacted to the crime scene. I briefed him about what I saw as I arrived home earlier that evening. I showed him the broken doors at the main entrance to the building as well as to our downstairs apartment. I took particular pains to let him know that I found the tool in the hallway and that I had not touched it for fear of smudging any fingerprints that the intruder might have left. He listened carefully to what I said, remaining silent throughout my entire statement. When I completed my account of what happened after we entered the house, he spoke for the first time and said, "I noticed from your diploma hanging on the wall that you graduated from NYU. You have a good education, so I am wondering why you have chosen to live in a neighborhood like this one?" He went on to tell me that there were several robberies in that neighborhood every day and it was impossible to chase after all of those criminals. I was so shocked by his nonchalant reaction to our predicament that I wasn't ready for what he would say next. In the same calm and seemingly uncaring manner he said, "this is not the movies! There is no way that we can investigate every robbery that takes place in this neighborhood. We would only conduct an in-depth inquiry and assign a detective to the case if someone had been injured or killed, so why don't you leave this neighborhood?" I will always remember that policeman and the way he admonished Eudine and me for living on Quincy Street.

When Wilton arrived, I told him what had happened and showed him the broken doors. There was not much that he could do to repair the damage, but his mere presence comforted us in ways that he could not have imagined. Eudine and I spent the rest of that night on the second floor where the door had not been damaged. I had an axe under my pillow, and I was determined to inflict considerable pain on anyone who might seek to violate our privacy for a second time that evening.

The experience of being robbed was extraordinarily traumatic, and it dawned on me that I could no longer live in that neighborhood. I began to search for a new apartment almost immediately. Eldon invited me to take a look at an empty apartment he had in a brownstone that he and Joyce owned on Amboy Street, in East New York. He promised to take me over to see it one evening during the week. With the exception of some worn tiles and a missing refrigerator, the apartment at Amboy Street seemed well-suited for Eudine and me.

I immediately took on the task of arranging to have the floor tiled; but I was not destined to live in the Amboy Street apartment. As fate would have it, one evening Eldon asked me to accompany him to Amboy Street. He wanted to check on the progress of ongoing repairs, and thought it would be a good thing to have me there. On his way, he stopped on Nostrand Avenue to speak with his real estate broker. He invited me into the office, and I sat in a chair that was within earshot of their conversation. I was stunned when I learned that Eldon was moving aggressively to sell the house that I was preparing to occupy. I couldn't wait to share the news with Eudine when I got home later that evening. We both agreed that it made little sense for us to continue with the repairs on an apartment in a house that was up for sale. What if I did not like the new owner? Suppose the new owner did not want to honor our lease arrangement? There were too many uncertainties. I decided that I would cancel all arrangements with Eldon as soon as I could reach him.

Our conversation went better than I thought it would go. He was definitely not upset by my decision to opt out of the rental arrangement. What surprised me most about his reaction was the alternative he wanted me to consider. Apparently, he had some very big plans to sell the houses he owned on Amboy and

Herzl Streets. His intention was to buy a multi-story apartment building on Rutland Road. He had been negotiating the deal for sometime and was optimistic that he would soon complete the purchase of that investment property. He asked me to consider purchasing the Herzl Street property. I thought his suggestion was so absurd that I quickly dismissed it, telling him that I did not have enough savings to even consider such an arrangement. Eldon, the consummate entrepreneur, simply responded; "You don't need savings to buy a house, just apply to the Dime Savings Bank of Brooklyn for a loan, and if you are short with the down payment, I will lend you the money that you need." That simple exchange with my brother-in-law was all that I needed to become a homeowner in 1964.

My good friend Elwin Griffith, a Barbadian attorney at the Chase Manhattan Bank, represented us at the closing. I was amazed by the simplicity of the transaction. I wrote several checks, all with other people's money and at the end of the session I was handed the keys to a two-story brownstone on Herzl Street in the Brownsville section of Brooklyn. My days as a landlord were only just beginning. Eudine and I quickly made arrangements to move into the vacant one-bedroom apartment on the first floor of our Herzl Street home. The beautiful two-bedroom apartment on that floor where Eldon and Joyce lived before their move to Rutland Road was occupied by Little Eva, a popular singer whose hit song *Loco-Motion* sold over one million copies and reached number one in the U.S. in 1962. One of the two apartments on the second floor was vacant, and I immediately sought to find a tenant for it. Our neighbor was Mr. Roland Fuller, a pudgy, no-nonsense fellow with a passionate involvement in community service. The Campbells, a Jamaican family owned the house on the other side of us.

Our first order of business was to renovate our apartment. Dad helped us build a sliding door closet, and we hired Mr. Stewart, Aunt Eude's friend, to replace the bathtub and re-tile the bathroom. I also tiled the kitchen and bedroom floors, and installed new carpet in the living room. I was pleased with the way the new tiles and carpeting transformed that tiny apartment.

Soon after we moved to Herzl Street, I learned that the neighborhood was in transition. The term that was used to describe what was happening is "white flight." With the departure of middle class whites, blacks and Hispanics were rapidly becoming the new homeowners in that formerly Jewish community. The new residents formed a neighborhood association, and Mr. Roland Fuller became the leader of our Herzl Street block. He was a rotund guy, short in stature, and businesslike in his demeanor. His familiarity with local politics made him ideally suited for the position of block leader. His first act was to purchase flashlights and walkie-talkies for every homeowner on our block. Each of us was assigned a time slot to patrol the neighborhood at night, and we were instructed to notify home base of any unusual persons or activities we encountered. Our nightly neighborhood patrols provided all homeowners with a real sense of security.

I soon had all three apartments rented. The Prices and Mrs. Mason were upstairs, occupying our nicest apartments, and Little Eva and her husband occupied the downstairs apartment. We lived in the one bedroom apartment on the first floor next door to Little Eva.

John Lindsay was Mayor of New York at that time, and his administration had embarked on an aggressive campaign to enforce the city's new building codes. This was my first encounter with the bureaucracy of New York City, and it took a toll on first time owners like Eudine and me. First, there were new rules for illuminating rental properties. The city even recommended wattage and location of lights. Then, there was a requirement for enclosing furnaces, and installing steel doors at the entrances to basements.

It was a hectic time for landlords, and the building inspectors capitalized on the vulnerability of the owners of rent-controlled properties. To avoid arbitrary citations for violation of the city's housing code, it is alleged that landlords routinely gave the New York building inspectors tips that they graciously accepted. Rumor had it that failure to tip meant that the full wrath of the inspector would be directed at the delinquent landlord. West Indian homeowners in Brooklyn had to be very creative during the John Lindsay administration years. I remember getting a steel door that was discarded from a major renovation project. I tied that door to the top of my Dodge Dart and drove it all the way from Manhattan to Herzl Street in Brooklyn. As usual, Dad came to my rescue. He installed the steel door, and built the concrete enclosure around the furnace. My brother Philip was working at an architectural firm in New York and he drew the design for the enclosure!

Two years after we moved into our apartment at Herzl Street, Eudine became pregnant with our first child. She continued working until late in her pregnancy before taking maternity leave. Mum and Dad were living at Rutland Road, and I was able to draw on their support during this critical time of need. Late one evening when Eudine was dutifully monitoring her contractions, she noticed a dramatic increase in their frequency. It was real cause for concern. I called her obstetrician Dr. Bloomfield to let him know what was happening and he advised me to take her to the hospital as soon as possible. St. John's Hospital was about a fifteen to twenty minute drive from where we lived, so I packed a small bag, got Mum, and we were on our way to St. John's. It was a harrowing experience and I remember that Eudine and I were so nervous that we were both visibly shaking when we reached the check-in desk. The nurse on duty that evening did not help matters when she panicked, believing that Eudine was about to deliver the baby right there in the waiting room.

Eudine was quickly admitted, and much to my surprise, I was not allowed to accompany her to the maternity ward. I left and took Mum to Rutland Road, then I went home to Herzl Street. As soon as I reached the apartment, I called Dr. Bloomfield to let him know that Eudine had been admitted to the hospital. After calming me down, he asked me to remain at home, and assured me that he would call periodically to update me on Eudine's condition. It was almost twelve hours before the call came informing me of Dionne's birth, she arrived late the following day. Eudine always reminds me that I was scheduled to take a graduate school exam on the day that she was in labor. It was an examination that I could not reschedule, so I was at City College on 138th Street in upper Manhattan during the entire time that Eudine was in labor. Dionne was born on the day I took and passed my second-level exam. She was a real blessing, cute and very well-behaved for a newborn.

About a year or so before Dionne's birth, Joyce and Eldon moved into a very attractive townhouse in a new community in Brooklyn called Spring Creek. From the first time I saw those homes I fell in love with that new community. While most of the houses in Brooklyn were multi-family brownstones built in another era, the homes in Spring Creek were modern, single family structures, with baseboard heating and attractive bathrooms and kitchens. There were even small patches of grass at the entrances that gave the neighborhood an up-scale appearance. The one thing I really liked about Spring Creek was its distance from the subway system and the commercial section of East New York.

Chapter 14

Spring Creek

One day, I got a telephone call from Joyce urging me to try to get over to Schenck Avenue as soon as possible. The reason, one of the homes on her block was up for sale. The family that lived in that house had been involved in a bitter divorce and had moved out. The house was empty, and Joyce assured me that she could get the keys to show me the interior. The moment I entered that house on Schenck Avenue, I knew I wanted to live there. Eudine liked it too, so we both felt that it made good sense for us to try to purchase that house. I did not hesitate to make an offer that the owner accepted without any hassle. All I had to do next was find a good lawyer. One day as I was on Nostrand Avenue shopping, I noticed a sign for a lawyer's office and walked in. Rose Hart was an elderly Jewish attorney who was obviously very knowledgeable about New York Real Estate law. I told her that we were interested in purchasing a house on Schenck Avenue and asked if she would represent us. She accepted without hesitation, and told me what I had to do to ensure a timely closing.

I can't believe how easy it was to complete the transaction. I remember sitting at the closing listening to the attorneys talk, and responding to my lawyer's request to write check, after check, after check. In less than an hour, I was handed the keys to our new home. On the day after the closing, Eudine checked out of St. John's Episcopal Hospital, and we moved into the Schenck Avenue home with our adorable daughter Dionne.

Eudine and I now owned two houses, a rental property on Herzl Street and a family home on Schenck Avenue. It was a very busy time for me. I was a doctoral student, a landlord, a husband, and a dad. I had apartments to paint, garbage cans to remove from the sidewalks, and rent to be collected. The

Scroggins' moved into our one bedroom apartment at Herzl Street. With four tenants in the house, it was increasingly difficult to keep up with the calls for service. Every time my phone rang, I was reluctant to answer. Ninety percent of the calls after nine o'clock in the evening would be about some frivolous issue. It did not take long before I realized that in order to maintain my sanity, I would have to get rid of the Herzl Street property. My neighbor Roland Fuller eventually came to the rescue. He offered to buy the property for the same price that we paid for it five years earlier. It was a deal that I could not refuse. When I walked out of the lawyer's office after closing on the sale, I felt like a gigantic weight had been removed from my shoulder.

Life on Schenck Avenue was all that I had envisioned it would be. I found the house to be very user friendly. It was a two-story building with a finished basement. A small eat-in kitchen with built-in oven and dishwasher. Eudine and I bought an attractive dinette set with four chairs and a beautiful bluish chandelier for the kitchen. There was a half bathroom on the right of the main entrance. I remember how difficult it was to turn around in that room because it was so tiny.

The central hallway opened into a very large living and dining room complete with hardwood floors throughout and a large picture window at the back. We covered the hardwood floors with a red carpet that we purchased from a store on Flatbush Avenue. We thought that the red would go well with the black and white wallpaper that decorated the hallway at the entrance and the stairway leading to the second floor. There were three bedrooms on the upper level and one full bathroom. A master bedroom with a single closet and broad picture window, and the full bathroom with an enclosed tub and shower faced the front of the house. Two smaller bedrooms were located at the back of the second floor. A small, wrought iron ladder on the second floor hallway provided access to the roof in case of fire.

To the right of the hallway on the first floor was the stairway that led to the finished basement. Half of the basement wall was covered with an attractive, light brown wallpaper and the other half with a white plaster that was molded to look like a brick wall. There was a full bar built into the back right corner of the basement. It had very attractive wooden accents, and recessed ceiling lighting. A small boiler room and washroom completed the basement level. We covered the basement floor with a plush attractive carpet and painted the doors in tomato red and green. Our back yard was finished with poured concrete, and it had a sprinkler that came in handy during the summer.

Schenck Avenue was an entirely new experience for us. That was our first single-family home and we enjoyed the privacy it offered. It was a warm, cozy place to come home to. We decorated it with elegantly framed prints that I purchased through my membership in the International Graphics Arts Society in Manhattan. We bought our dining room furniture from Korvettes, a major department store in downtown Brooklyn. We also had the home decoration division of Korvettes install an attractive wrought iron divider in our living room area, and an awning fabricated from hardened plastic and aluminum to protect the front patio from rain and snow.

I fondly remember our neighbors on Schenck Avenue. When we first moved in, the neighborhood was almost completely white. On our right were Harry and his wife. Harry was a barber with a very pleasant disposition. I cannot remember much about his wife. The Goldman's lived on our left. They were a family of four, Mr. and Mrs. Goldman and their two sons. They were very apprehensive when we first moved next door, and later confided that their fear was significantly reduced when they learned that I was a doctoral student at the City College of New York. Other neighbors included the Rodriguez family who were Hispanic, the Campos who were from the Philippines, and the Scotts who were Jamaican. Across the street there was one black family, a Haitian family who later attracted much attention when the husband declared himself a serious candidate to replace Papa Doc Duvalier as president of Haiti.

There was much to talk about and celebrate on Schenck Avenue. We let Dionne play on the front lawn. In the summer, our neighbors could be seen sunning on folding chairs, or barbecuing on their porches. Then one summer, for-sale signs began to appear up and down Schenck Avenue, signaling the beginning of a mass exodus of whites from the neighborhood. They called it "blockbusting." One or two real estate agents went through the neighborhood scaring whites into believing that blacks were about to takeover their community. They urged them to move before losing the equity in their homes. It worked, and before the end of that summer, most of the neighbors sold their homes to black families.

Our new neighbors were middle class blacks, largely from the West Indies, and with money to invest in improving their homes. Chain-link fences and gates sprung up all over the neighborhood along with wrought iron bars at the windows, and at the sliding glass doors at the rear of the house. Hurleigh and Vickie moved into Harry's house, and Leroy and Eslyn bought the Goldman home next door. Sylvia and Ruben and Owen were just down the street from us. Maurice and Headley, Margerie and Eudine's sister Barbara were on the other side of the street. Eudine's sister Maria moved into the other block, and Peggy moved next door to the house that Joyce previously owned. I was living in a real West Indian neighborhood. I read the Barbadian newspapers on the weekend, ate fishcakes and pudding and souse, and listened to the latest recordings of the Mighty Sparrow from Trinidad and Gabby from Barbados.

In the 1970s, summers on Schenck Avenue were very different than when we first moved into the neighborhood. We were entertaining friends and family on a weekly basis, and there was always someone dropping by to visit. One day, I went into the backyard to turn on the sprinkler and to my amazement I came face to face with one of my old school friends from the Lodge School, Patrick Grosvenor. Patrick and his wife had bought a home on the next block and their backyard was across from ours. Whenever I think about that meeting, I find it hard to believe that in a city as large as New York, my neighbor would be a Barbadian and a former Lodge School student. There was so much for us to talk about. We reminisced about the years we spent at Lodge, our careers, and our families. I remember telling Patrick that we were planning a trip to Niagara Falls, Canada; and before I could complete the sentence he had already decided that he would be interested in joining us with his family.

We left Schenck Avenue early one summer morning and traveled north across the Tappan Zee bridge and into New York state. Our trip took us through rural New York, into Buffalo and across the Peace bridge that connects Buffalo to Ontario. We then continued on to Niagara where we found a nice hotel on Lundy's Lane, a major tourist strip with lots of small hotels and restaurants. We loved the Canadian side of the falls. There was the excitement of visiting the falls and watching thousands of gallons of water cascade over the U-shaped rim of that most impressive natural attraction in North America. After spending a few days at the falls, we set out again, this time for the city of Toronto where there was a large West Indian community. Our trip to Toronto was planned to coincide with the summer Caribana celebration. Caribana showcased Caribbean culture through music, cuisine, and the performing arts. We loved the experience, especially having the opportunity to get together with so many of our childhood friends who were living in Canada.

From Toronto it was off to Ottawa and a visit with the Barbados High Commissioner Owen Rowe and his wife Joan. Owen was a good friend of Patrick's and we all knew Joan from schooldays in Barbados. After a most delightful visit with the Rowe's it was off to Quebec City and a stay at an old hotel called Louis Jolliette. We spent only one night at Louis Joliette, moving the next day to an attractive small hotel located in the shadow of the Chateau Frontenac–a major landmark in Quebec City. We used Quebec City as a base for exploring the Gaspee peninsula where we had a chance to visit the Basilica at St. Anne De Beaupre, a major Catholic shrine approximately thirty miles east of Quebec City. Our trip back home took us through Montreal for a visit with Patrick's sister, and then back down Interstate-87 to New York City.

Our second trip to Canada with the Grosvenor's took us from Brooklyn through Connecticut and the other New England States, and on to St John's, New Brunswick where we stayed at a local Holiday Inn. As soon as we checked into our hotel, the entire city was engulfed by a thick fog that made it almost impossible to see objects thirty feet ahead. It was an experience that I could never forget. From St. John's we traveled on to Halifax, Nova Scotia where we enjoyed many of the major sites such as Peggy's Cove and the Citadel. I had my first jumbo lobster dinner in Halifax. It was served on a tray and was easily the largest lobster I had ever seen.

From Halifax we traveled to the city of Dartmouth where we saw a West Indian community that resembled many of the small communities in the South Carolina Low Country or in Barbados. There were clusters of small homes that looked like Barbadian chattel houses. I was surprised to see so many bicycles leaning on the sides of these homes. It was eerily similar to scenes that were so common when I was growing up in Barbados. We were surprised to see West Indian culture reflected in that Dartmouth community. I learned that Dartmouth was one of those locations where West Indian men deserted their merchant ships many years ago to remain in Canada. Apparently those deserters chose to remain in that tiny community where they lived in much the same way as they had lived back in the Caribbean.

Our trip to Nova Scotia was among our most memorable vacations in Canada. On the way back to the U.S. from Halifax we spent one night at a hotel in Oromocto, New Brunswick. The accommodations there were simply atrocious. The room was sparsely furnished, and the beds were old and uncomfortable. We survived Oromocto and learned from that experience to work more diligently on reading reviews on hotels before committing to staying at them. I have strictly adhered to that practice on all of my subsequent trips to eastern Canada.

Life on Schenck Avenue afforded me an excellent opportunity to organize the Lodge School Alumni Association. Patrick and I often talked about our days at the Lodge School, and it was during one of those conversations that the idea of starting a Lodge School Alumni Association was first discussed. Philip was a real resource. He helped contact the alumni from his generation, while Patrick and I went after our contemporaries. We were able to get commitments from Lolly Walker, George Bispham, G. B. Taylor, Keith Forde, Miles Brown, Bertram Catwell, Tom Marsh, Jerome Jones, Colin Mayers and others. Patrick Medford would join us later to the delight of everyone.

Our meetings were held at my Schenck Avenue home. Imagine having a house full of different generations of Lodge School alumni reminiscing about school days in Barbados. We talked at length about all of the characters we had as former classmates and the idiosyncrasies of the masters who taught us. Eudine organized the food, and I took care of the Mount Gay rum. It was at that gathering that everyone felt that forming an alumni association was an excellent idea. I purchased a copy of *Roberts Rules and Procedures* and we set a date for our first formal meeting. That meeting was held at my home, and was very productive. We made plans to draft a constitution, and set a date for electing officers. The group elected me as the first president of the newly formed Lodge School Alumni Association of New York. George Taylor was elected to serve as the first vice president. George and I collaborated on planning events and identifying ways to raise funds for the association. We organized basement parties and used the money to buy books for the library at Lodge School, and clothing to help flood victims in Barbados.

Our first major event was an independence dance sponsored by three Barbadian organizations–Somerset Cricket Club; the Queens College Alumnae; and the Lodge School Alumni. The planning was thorough. Dorothy Yearwood was president of the Queens College group, and Basil Barrow was the spokesperson for Somerset. The venue was the Manhattan Center on the west side of Manhattan, close to Madison Square Garden. Our keynote speaker was the Honorable Val McComie, Barbados Ambassador to Washington and former master at the Lodge School.

We packed Manhattan Center with Bajans of all descriptions. When all obligations were met, we collected enough donations to enable us to make sizeable contributions to needy Barbadian causes. One of the causes we supported without reservation, was the library at our alma mater. I made many trips to Barnes and Noble bookstore in Manhattan to purchase a variety of books that we shipped to Lodge School to be added to the library's collection. After the obvious success of the event at the Manhattan Center, the visibility of our association within the U.S. increased dramatically making it easier for us to raise funds to support other worthy causes in Barbados.

I declined to seek office when my term as president expired. Bertrand Catwell was elected to succeed me, and I passed the baton to a younger generation of Lodge School alumni. The venue for our meetings shifted from my home, and enthusiasm for the organization began to wane. Fundraising events were not well-attended and there was much criticism of the new leadership. It wouldn't be long before the organization lost its momentum and monthly meetings were suspended.

After graduating from the City College of New York, I elected to pursue my post-doctoral work with Jack at the New York Blood Center. By that time, the Blood Center had grown in stature and funding, and its founders had taken the bold step of consolidating ongoing research programs to form a new institute that was named "The Lindsey F. Kimball Research Institute" after a major donor. Jack had just hired a new post-doc from Columbia University Dr. Judy Christman, and her arrival enabled us to broaden the research focus of the laboratory to include studies on the differentiation process of red blood cells. Judy brought considerable expertise on how cells are able to regulate their own growth and division. It is a fascinating area of research that, if successful, could help explain the molecular events associated with memory storage, or tissue repair after injury. Judy was trained in the laboratory of Dr. Ernest Borek, a noted expert in the field of nucleic acid methylation. Together, Judy and I developed a highly productive partnership that yielded important new insights into the red blood cell maturation process. In their immature state, the cells are called reticulocytes, and as they differentiate they jettison their nuclei. In spite of the absence of a nucleus, the mature red blood cell still has the capacity to successfully carryout all of the vital functions associated with the transport of oxygen and the removal of carbon dioxide from the vital tissues and organs of the body. By the time Judy arrived, there were seven people in Jack's laboratory, the technical staff included Rotraud and Rosa who were both from Germany, Ahmed from Egypt, and two young American males, Jack and Allan. Judy and I were both designated as post-doctoral fellows.

Under the advice of one of my thesis mentors, Dr. Shahn, I sought and was offered a position as an adjunct professor at Hunter College. Dr. Richard Mawe, chairperson of the department of Biological Sciences thought I would bring a unique perspective to his faculty, and he welcomed me with considerable enthusiasm. My first assignment was to teach the lecture and laboratory sections of an undergraduate Histology course. Although I was definitely up to the challenge, I did not want to take any chances, so two weeks before the semester started, I spent evenings at the Cornell University library reading every histology book I could find on their shelves. On the first day of class, I was pleasantly surprised to discover that most of the students were mature individuals, much older than the average college student, and several of them were employed in full-time positions during the day. One of my students even worked in the city's forensic laboratory. With a roster of such experienced students, I was forced to invest even more time preparing for my lectures. I studied every organ and tissue in the human body in such detail that I was able to respond to any question posed by my students. It was my first formal teaching experience, and I must confess that I was so well prepared that I frequently encouraged the students to probe me for greater detail on any of the material I covered in the lecture or laboratory sessions.

My mentor Jack was not pleased when he found out that I was teaching the Histology course at Hunter College. I expected an entirely different reaction from him. I thought that he would have been elated to learn that the Biomedical Science department at one of the respectable institutions in the City University System had chosen me, a student whom he had mentored, to serve as a member of their adjunct faculty. Our differences on this issue quickly escalated, and neither of us could put together an argument that was persuasive enough to win the other over. Because we had reached an impasse, Jack asked me to either give up the adjunct appointment at Hunter or my Research Fellowship at the Lindsey Kimball Research Institute.

I was not convinced that this should have been an either/or situation because both experiences were enabling me to grow as a scientist. The teaching position was very challenging. I worked hard on preparing for my weekly lectures, and I learned so much from interacting with my students during the laboratory sessions. My work at the institute was also gaining considerable traction, and I was keenly interested in continuing to break new ground in my collaboration with Judy. I knew that I did not have a lot of time to make a decision on such an important matter.

As the fall semester approached, I sought the advice of one of the other program directors in our building, a highly successful research investigator whose laboratory was down the hall from Jack's. He was an unconventional scientists whose star was on the rise in the Blood Center and nationally. His work focused on trying to understand how the Hepatitis virus was transmitted, and the mechanism the virus used to cause that debilitating disease. He had already identified Hepatitis viral particles in the blood obtained from individuals with the disease, and he had gathered impressive data on virus morphology and biochemistry. Additionally, he had developed a sub-human primate model for Hepatitis that was yielding new insights into the molecular events associated with infection and disease progression.

My conversation with him was very constructive. He was impressed by my adjunct appointment, and thought that my work on the Hunter faculty was career enhancing. I told him of my ultimatum from Jack, and inquired about the possibility of transferring to his group. He was visibly excited when I told him of my desire to explore an opportunity to join his group. He certainly displayed considerable enthusiasm for my proposal during our conversation in his office at the Blood Center. I left the meeting feeling encouraged by his positive reaction to my request. I was optimistic about my chances to transfer to his laboratory where I could continue to work in the area of viral biochemistry while retaining my teaching appointment at Hunter College. He promised that he would get back to me the following day. The next day however, I was unable to find him in his laboratory or in the building. Instead, I found a note in my mailbox that simply stated, "Ken, prospects seem dim!" I realized that it was time for me to look beyond the New York Blood Center if I was going to continue to build my career as a scientist.

I am still amazed at how quickly I learned that there were some very attractive organizations seeking someone with my training and qualification. The first opportunity was at a company called Ciba-Geigy. It was a pharmaceutical company with major research facilities in Ardsley, New York. Ardsley was maybe forty minutes north of New York City and easily reachable by car. Judy, my post-doctoral colleague, had interviewed there earlier in the year, so she was able to brief me about the job in considerable detail. They were looking for a biochemist with experience in separations technology. Judy assured me that I had the skills and expertise necessary for that job. I contacted the Human Resources department at Ciba-Geigy and was thrilled to learn that they were interested in having me come in for a formal interview.

My interviews with the Director of Human Resources and the hiring manager went very well. It was obvious to me that the focus of my research and the training I received from Jack made me exceedingly marketable. At the end of the day, after numerous conversations with scientists and corporate executives, it was easy for me to surmise that there was considerable interest in my candidacy. I was told by the Director of Human Resources that she would be in touch within a week or so. Based on the reception I received from the Ciba-Geigy interview, I was convinced that the time was indeed ripe for me to broaden my job hunting campaign.

My next stop was at Rockefeller University. I was invited by the Biology Club to be a speaker in their highly focused seminar series. I talked about the work I did for my doctoral thesis. I was now much more experienced than when I was a graduate student, and that maturity was reflected in the way I was able to discuss the implications of my work and the ease with which I cited specific journal articles to corroborate my findings.

This was early 1971, and at that time proteins were believed to be the key molecules responsible for controlling all aspects of gene expression regulation. I believed that a growing body of information was available to suggest that the regulation of cell behavior would involve additional types of molecules, and the RNAs that I was studying were prime candidates for such a role. Dr. Palade's laboratory was widely known for its work on describing how material was transported from one compartment of a cell to another, and he was working diligently on trying to understand how molecules were transported across the cell's membrane. It was not surprising to me therefore that after my seminar, I was approached by one of the members of Dr. Palade's group who wanted to talk about some of the issues I had raised.

That young scientist was a tall, handsome young man who spoke with a distinct German accent. His name was Dr. Gunther Blobel, and he was fascinated by the size of the RNA molecule I described in my presentation. He had undertaken a similar study and was puzzled by the fact that the size of the molecule he identified was larger than he had predicted. He was so excited by the similarities between my findings and his that he invited me to his laboratory to show me what he thought was a very interesting phenomenon. At that time, neither Gunther nor I knew that his observation would lead to the discovery of "signal sequences" on messenger RNA molecules that facilitated movement of proteins across cellular membranes. Gunther went on to win the Nobel Prize in 1999 for his discovery of intrinsic signals on proteins that regulate their transport and localization in cells. I remember Gunther inquiring about my interest in applying for a post-doctoral position in his laboratory. He wanted me to join the team that was attempting to reconcile the differences in size between mature messenger RNA molecules and the messenger RNA molecules that he was studying. He was obviously impressed by my expertise in nucleic acid biochemistry, and thought I would be an excellent fit for his group. I declined his offer and have never regretted that decision.

Chapter 15

Pfizer Central Research

My next stop was at a company called Pfizer. I learned of the job at Pfizer through a small head-hunter company that had its main office on 42nd Street and Seventh Avenue in Manhattan. The owner was an affable man who seemed almost too young for the position that he held. But somehow I trusted him when he said that he thought that I would be an excellent fit for Pfizer. While I was sitting in the office, he placed a call to someone at Pfizer to schedule an interview, and later that week I was on my way to a small town in northern New Jersey called Maywood, to explore job opportunities with that company.

The Pfizer Operation in Maywood, New Jersey was housed in a cluster of low-lying, nondescript buildings sequestered behind an eight-foot tall chain link fence. Dr. Keith Jensen, director of the facility met me at the main gate. He was a man of small stature with a friendly disposition. Although he was very serious and business-like, I felt comfortable in his presence. He did not conform to the cold, impersonal image I had of corporate executives.

I was ushered into a room where several scientists in white coats were sitting around a large table. This was the room in which my seminar would be held. I had given that talk several times in New York before expert audiences, so I was very confident with the material I was about to present. My talk was divided into three sections. I had learned that format from listening closely to the great scientists who spoke at the Caspary Auditorium at Rockefeller University when I worked in Dr. Craig's laboratories. I began in my usual fashion by providing them with an overview of the field. I then presented them with detailed information on the work I had done, and I concluded with a broad discussion on the implications of my findings.

There was hardly any interruption of my presentation, and I was able to finish in the hour that had been allotted. I felt good about my talk and my interactions with those scientists. Dr. Jensen assured me that my visit had gone well and the scientists seemed to be very impressed with my candidacy. In fact, Dr. Jensen told me that he was impressed to the point that he wanted to invite me to give another seminar. The venue for that talk would be Pfizer's Global Research Headquarters in Groton, Connecticut.

Arrangements were quickly made and I was soon a guest of Dr. Jensen at the Groton site. That was an expansive, immaculately landscaped campus with a collection of modern buildings and numerous employees, many at the Ph.D. level. I gave a similar talk at Groton to the one I presented at Maywood. My audience was a small group of Pfizer scientists, and the venue was a well-equipped conference room in the main research building. I was again surprised by how well my talk was received and how gracious they were to me in the question and answer period. When my talk was over, I met with several key members of the Central Research Division's senior scientific team. It was interesting to see how focused everyone was on drug discovery. It seemed that they all saw the scientific world in only one dimension–taking an idea from the laboratory into the clinic and then into the market place. Wherever I went that day, scientists were telling me about their efforts to establish a connection between the research they were conducting and the business of the company.

At the end of the day, Dr. Jensen was so pleased with my candidacy that he made me an offer before I left Groton. The offer was a job at either site, Groton or Maywood. I tried desperately not to reveal how excited I was by his generous offer. I knew what my answer would be, but delayed a little before giving him a response. The Groton Team that I was most likely to join was interested in discovering drugs that could be used to elevate the level of a substance called interferon that the body produces. They reasoned that higher levels of interferon would be protective against virus infections. The Maywood job was more about conducting basic research on cancer, and would afford me an opportunity to become part of an exciting quest to understand how a group of viruses called retroviruses caused cancer in animals. The scientists at Maywood believed that information obtained from the animal studies could provide valuable insights into how cancer may develop in humans. I told Dr. Jensen that I wanted to join the research program at Maywood, New Jersey.

With a job offer firmly secured from Pfizer, Eudine and I decided that it would be an excellent opportunity to get away with the children for a while. We felt that Barbados was the ideal place for such a vacation. That summer, we rented homes by the seaside at Worthings and Silver Sands, and thoroughly enjoyed the sea and the balmy island breezes. Mum came along and helped out with the children.

Upon returning from Barbados, I met with Jack on my first day back at work to inform him of my decision to resign from my position at the New York Blood Center. Our conversation was frank but very cordial. I thanked him profusely for all that he had done for me, and told him that it was time for me to move on to the next phase of my career.

I went to work at Pfizer's John L. Smith Memorial for Cancer Research in Maywood, New Jersey in August. I felt a natural affiliation for that particular job, and the trip to Barbados helped me to engage the decision-making process in a way that I couldn't have done if I had remained in New York. I no longer thought about the prospect of working at Ciba-Geigy, and I never once revisited my decision to decline to consider an appointment at Rockefeller University. My journey as an independent scientist was about to begin, and I couldn't wait to get started.

The John L. Smith Memorial for Cancer Research was named after a former Pfizer President and Chairman of the Board who died from cancer in 1950. In 1956, Pfizer dedicated the John L. Smith Memorial for Cancer Research at Maywood, New Jersey in his honor. The facility occupied the site of the former Pfizer Therapeutic Institute. By the time that I arrived, the institute at Maywood had become one of the major players in the battle to understand the cause of human cancer.

There were approximately one hundred employees at Maywood when I joined, ten of whom were Ph.D. scientists. The facility got its start in vaccine research and then transitioned to studying cancer viruses. Dr. Jensen's simple statement to me was that he just knew that he wanted to hire me, but he did not know exactly how he would use my skills and experience.

Maywood was divided into three units: Dr. J. Olson, ran the Administrative unit; Dr. Sami Mayyasi headed all of Viral Oncology; and Dr. Keith Jensen served as the Director of Virology and Oncology. Under their leadership, the team of scientists, with the assistance of a talented group of research technicians and virus production specialists, played a vital role in the national effort to study how viruses caused cancer. Maywood supplied the Special Virus Cancer Program at the National Cancer Institute with customized biological reagents that were then distributed to cancer research scientists nationally and internationally.

Maywood's virus laboratories were organized into five sections: breast cancer; animal leukemia and lymphoma; human lymphoma and sarcoma; molecular biology; and electron microscopy. Additionally, a production staff coordinated the processing, and shipment of viruses and cultured tumor cells to researchers all around the world.

My first day on the job was spent in a laboratory with Dr. John Wulff. I believe that he was awarded his Ph.D. in immunology from Ohio State University, and he had established an impressive research program that was generating some important data on cancer causing viruses. John was a really nice guy, and I was grateful to Dr. Jensen for choosing him as my partner. I was assigned a technician, Carla Higdon, and given responsibility for establishing a group within the molecular biology section that would be called Molecular Virology. I set to work immediately assembling the tools and strategies that would enable me to meet that formidable task.

As a nucleic acid biochemist, I was well-equipped for the challenges I faced as I sought to help unravel the secrets of cancer. My closest ally in that quest was my friend Dave. One month after arriving at Maywood, a young, chunky Ph.D. scientist called Dave Larson reported for duty. Dave was built like a wrestler with solid arms and legs, and he approached his work with a sense of purpose similar to that displayed by a professional athlete. Dave and I became friends instantly. Our personalities simply clicked, and we soon joined forces in tackling any problem, research or research-related.

My efforts were centered on the biochemical characterization of viral and cellular nucleic acids. I began by studying the RNA from a virus called the Mason-Pfizer Monkey Virus, an agent that was implicated in the genesis of breast cancer in monkeys. That virus was isolated as a result of a collaboration between the Mason Institute in Massachusetts and Pfizer's John L. Smith Memorial for Cancer Research from which it got its name. It was considered to be the prototype Type-D retrovirus because of the way its membrane was assembled inside the cell, as well as the budding pattern it displayed as it exited the cell. Those features differentiated it from the classical retroviruses that were known as Type-C viruses.

My colleagues at Maywood were considered to be the world's experts in studying the Mason-Pfizer Monkey Virus, and I thought it wise to try to extend their studies to the viral RNAs. I also undertook a careful analysis of the RNA isolated from a human cell line called NC-37 after it was infected with the Mason-Pfizer Monkey Virus. Like the Mason-Pfizer Monkey Virus, NC-37 Cells were established and initially characterized at Maywood. They were lymphoblastoid cells established from peripheral blood obtained from a Caucasian male.

When I joined the Maywood team, NC-37 cells were the workhorse for virus production because they represented one of the best characterized normal human cell line available at that time, and they were ideally suited for growing and producing the agents that we were studying. I believed that the work that I was carrying out on the RNAs of the Mason-Pfizer Monkey Virus would help increase understanding of how a virus was able to infect a human cell and cause it to lose control of its regulatory machinery. I devoted considerable time to developing highly sensitive and reliable analytical procedures to determine how viruses were able to alter the rate at which cells grew in size and numbers.

Virus purification was another area that I thought to be important for me to study. Because cellular particulate material was widely reported to contaminate virus preparations, I was determined to develop a more effective virus purification strategy than the one that was routinely used. Those efforts were remarkably successful, and within my first year at Maywood, I was able to use my experience to refine the procedures that we used to purify the viruses we produced for the National Institutes of Health.

In my second year at Maywood, I discovered a unique property of the Mason-Pfizer viral RNA that had major implications for the field of viral biochemistry. I detailed those findings in a manuscript that, after peer-review, was published in a major national journal. I also developed, and routinely used a new quality control procedure to test all batches of virus produced at Maywood. The method facilitated rapid screening of virus preparations for a number of unique biochemical parameters. No such screen was previously available. That method turned out to be of singular importance in the testing of virus samples before shipment to outside investigators.

That same year, I also participated in several intramural collaborative research efforts, extending my studies to a rat virus, and to a monkey virus known as the Simian Sarcoma Virus Type-1. I prepared and submitted two manuscripts detailing my work on the characterization of those retroviruses.

My successes at Maywood as documented in my publications, began to attract national attention. My hard work was paying off, and Dave and I were submitting abstracts of our latest findings for presentation at the annual meeting of the American Society for Microbiology. It was not surprising that in my second year at Maywood, Dave and I were in Miami Beach attending the annual meeting of the American Society for Microbiology. I was selected to give a presentation on my work describing a procedure for the rapid isolation of viral RNAs. A large crowd was in attendance to listen to my presentation. When I completed my talk and left the podium, I was immediately surrounded by a group of scientists, several of whom wanted to get my contact information. One of those conferees invited me to interview with a very prominent scientist who was a Branch Chief at the National Institutes of Health in Bethesda, Maryland. I spent a day visiting with that scientist, but declined his offer for me to join his research group. Somehow I felt that my work at Maywood afforded me a unique opportunity to be at the frontline of retroviral research. After all, Maywood was the primary site for characterizing all new virus isolates. That access was invaluable, and it enabled me to be a part of a growing international effort to discover the first human cancer virus.

Within three years, I was promoted to the position of Head of the Laboratory of Molecular Biology. That was the first clear signal that my contributions to the field were being recognized by Pfizer senior management. As the leader of the most visible section at Maywood, I was able to make decisions about project priority, and I had full control of the budget that was allocated to meet programmatic needs. I initiated a job enrichment program for the technical staff, and that program was exceedingly successful, resulting in a dramatic increase in both the quantity and quality of the work produced by my team. The "rapid electrophoretic procedure" that I developed for biochemical analysis of cancer viruses was gaining wider acceptance within the molecular virology community.

It was around that time that my laboratory began to take on a more visible role in the national effort to discover a human breast cancer virus. We utilized the Mouse Mammary Tumor Virus and the Mason-Pfizer Monkey Virus isolates that were implicated in the development of breast cancer in mice and monkeys, respectively, as models for studying the cause of breast cancer in humans. I established biochemical assays to probe human breast tumor tissue for evidence of virus-related information, and along with my Maywood colleagues, I developed a highly sensitive immunological assay to corroborate our biochemical findings. That work brought me into contact with a number of prominent researchers at the National Cancer Institute.

The War on Cancer that was launched by President Nixon in the early seventies, propelled Maywood into a position of prominence nationally and internationally. The discovery of an enzyme called reverse transcriptase in 1971 by Drs. Temin and Baltimore marked the beginning of a revolutionary change that transformed the thinking within the entire biological world. Up until that time, the Central Dogma of Biology was based on the belief that DNA was the master molecule. Encoded in the sequence of that double stranded molecule that is found in the nucleus of our cells is the entire library of information that determines our unique phenotype. It contains in its linear sequence the genes that make us look like our parents and grandparents. The Central Dogma stated that DNA begets a molecule called messenger RNA and it is from that informational transcript of DNA that our proteins are derived through a process called translation.

It was considered heretical to believe that the flow of genetic information could occur by any other mechanism. What was revolutionary about the enzyme discovered by Temin and Baltimore was the fact that it provided for the first time a clue that explained how a virus having an RNA genome could cause cancer. Because the genome of RNA tumor viruses encodes a gene for the production of the reverse transcriptase enzyme, they have the unique capability of making complementary copies of DNA after they invade human cells. They could then utilize a remarkably precise cutting and splicing machinery to insert those complementary DNA sequences permanently into the host cell chromosomes, converting normal cells to neoplastic or cancerous ones.

The discovery of reverse transcriptase marked the first time that scientists could conceive of an RNA molecule as a repository for genetic information. The ability to convert that RNA molecule into a DNA molecule by a process that reversed the flow of genetic information was a major breakthrough in molecular biology. For that seminal discovery Temin and Baltimore were awarded the Nobel Prize.

As a biochemist, I was trying to understand the manner in which such vital processes as cell growth and division are regulated. I felt that if I could gain some insight into how those processes are controlled, then I might be able to determine the precise manner in which physical, chemical, or biological agents might alter them during cancer development. I was convinced that without knowing exactly what molecular event triggered cellular transformation in the various types of cancer, it was necessary to investigate all possibilities. Our group at Maywood played a key role in studying biological agents as potential triggers of human cancer.

As the War on Cancer was heating up, my colleagues and I were using an assortment of molecular probes to prove that retroviruses were the etiological agents of cancers such as leukemias, sarcomas, and carcinomas. We used probes from the Mouse Mammary Tumor Virus to analyze human cells for a putative breast cancer virus. We employed a similar strategy to determine whether human leukemia would be caused by a virus that was related to the Rauscher Leukemia Virus, the agent that caused leukemia in mice. Almost every month, there was an announcement that attracted national attention. There were reports on virus "host range" that sought to explain why a virus isolated from a mouse could not easily infect a rat cell, and similarly why a rat virus could not infect a monkey cell. Then there were claims for tissue specificity that taught us that retroviruses like the Mouse Mammary Tumor Virus only caused breast cancer in mice and not leukemia. Conversely, the Rauscher Leukemia Virus would only induce leukemia in mice, not breast cancer.

The march up the evolutionary ladder attracted significant attention. Scientists reasoned that the closer they could get on the evolutionary ladder to humans, the more likely it would be to obtain clues about the characteristics of a putative human cancer virus. Almost every week, reports of new virus isolates heightened the drumbeat for a possible victory in the War on Cancer. I remember the first report on the isolation of a virus called the Simian Sarcoma Virus Type-1 that caused cancer in monkeys. Another publication showed that it was possible to coax a virus out of Baboon cells called the Endogenous Baboon Virus. Then we learned that an agent called the Gibbon Ape Lymphoma Virus was able to cause lymphomas in Gibbons. All of those new virus isolates were quarantined at the government facility on Plum Island in the Long Island Sound, and then released to the Pfizer laboratories at Maywood for further characterization.

We had the unique capacity to mass produce those agents in quantities that permitted routine analysis of their morphological, immunological, and biochemical properties. We had powerful electron microscopes that enabled our scientists to study their size and shape. Our immunological assays helped us to look at their relatedness to known viruses, and we developed sensitive biochemical assays to look at nucleic acid and protein similarity.

The group that I headed was charged with developing many of those assays, and with assistance from Dave, we created a complete profile of the protein and nucleic acid composition for all new virus isolates. I could also rapidly assess their relatedness to previously characterized viruses. We earned the reputation for being the best-equipped and the most reliable national facility for large-scale virus production and characterization. Maywood's pre-eminence as a center for high quality research on retroviral molecular biology persisted throughout the entire War on Cancer period. As Dave would say in his inimitable fashion, "everything we touched turned to gold."

One day, Dr. Jensen received a very important call from a senior administrator at the National Institutes of Health. It was a call informing him that President Nixon was going to be traveling to Russia and he needed to present the Russians with some samples of well-characterized virus. The request was transmitted from Washington to Maywood with the firm requirement that we provide the president with the highest quality virus preparations possible, and that we deliver those samples in a timely fashion. My section had the unenviable task of confirming the purity of all virus preparations to be delivered to the president.

No one at Maywood wanted to have the President of the United States deliver viral preparations from Maywood to the Russians that failed to meet the highest standards of purity and activity. We were very sensitive to the political fallout that could result from such a shortcoming. A slipup of any sort could irreparably damage our reputation within the scientific community, and might even result in the loss of all of our National Institutes of Health funding. It could also be extremely embarrassing to President Nixon, and could possibly exacerbate any strained relationship that might have existed between the two superpowers.

Our colleagues in the Maywood production facility, in their inimitable fashion, met their production targets without fanfare or fuss, and then it became my responsibility to assure the quality of all production lots. My team of scientists worked around the clock, testing and retesting all virus lots to certify their biological quality, before they were shipped to Washington DC. The effort was a huge success, and several weeks after President Nixon's visit to Russia ended, we received word that the Russian scientists were completely satisfied with the virus preparations that they received from the American president. Although these developments were not brought to the general public's attention, they did not go un-noticed by the American scientific community. Maywood's reputation went through the roof. Calls of congratulations were coming in to our switchboard from all over the country.

Dr. Robert Gallo was so impressed by our work that he wanted to enter into a strategic partnership arrangement with us to determine whether human leukemia was caused by a virus. He felt that if a virus was indeed responsible for causing the disease in humans, then it should be possible to detect footprints of that virus in extracts derived from human leukemic patients' cells. To test his hypothesis, he wanted to have us use our highly sensitive and reliable immunological and biochemical assays to probe batches of coded human samples for evidence of virus related information.

The Gallo offer represented a real breakthrough for us, especially because he had identified Maywood as the organization that was best suited to provide the desired technical support. Based on data that I had already gathered from my own research, I was quite convinced that human leukemia could have a viral origin, and was honored to have an opportunity to collaborate on such a project.

My colleagues and I lost little time in developing a response to Dr. Gallo's solicitation. Our proposal highlighted the advances that we had made in developing a battery of state-of-the-art assays that enabled us to sensitively and reproducibly detect virus related information in biological tissue. It detailed the type and scope of the services that we could provide to the Laboratory of Tumor Cell Biology through a strategic partnership arrangement. It included language that we felt would convince Dr. Gallo of our interest in the project, and our commitment to working collaboratively with him and the members of his scientific team until the project was satisfactorily completed.

Our proposal was favorably reviewed, and as soon as the contract was formally approved, my group began receiving batches of coded samples from Dr. Gallo's laboratory. On average, they shipped between ninety to one hundred samples to us every week. Although the identity of the samples was not revealed until the analysis was completed and the results submitted, the agreement stated that each batch of samples would include extracts from human leukemic patients' cells; normal human cells; and viruses. The virus samples were intended to serve as positive and negative controls.

Our first approach was to screen the extracts for virus related proteins. To accomplish this, we used what is called a competition radioimmunoassay. We had developed and described that procedure in a peer-reviewed publication. We would simply add a portion of each sample to a mixture containing one of the structural proteins isolated from a known leukemia virus along with its corresponding antibody. Because the virus protein was radioactively labeled, we could easily track it's binding by measuring the radioactivity associated with the complex formed when the protein bound its cognate antibody. If any of the coded samples contained proteins that were related to the virus protein then they would compete for the same antibody binding sites, reducing the radioactive signal emitted by the complex. Samples containing proteins that were not related to the virus protein would display no affinity for binding to the antibody and would not displace any of the radioactive signal from the complex.

The second assay we employed was a molecular hybridization assay. It detected sample relatedness based on nucleic acid sequence homology. When DNA isolated from a coded sample was incubated with complementary DNA derived from a virus that caused leukemia, complementary sequences would anneal to form DNA duplexes, and the stability of the duplexes would vary directly with sequence homology. In other words, if the cellular DNA shared one hundred-percent homology with virus DNA, those duplexes would be extremely stable. If, on the other hand, the cellular DNA samples diverged in sequence from the virus DNA, then the stability of the duplexes would decrease in a manner that reflected that divergence.

Each week, we noted that we could conveniently identify samples that were positive in both assays, and when we reported our findings to Dr. Gallo, we learned that the samples that we scored as positive were consistently those that were isolated from human leukemic patients' cells.

Our ability to detect the presence of virus related information in extracts obtained from leukemic patients cells was mind-boggling. The data certainly suggested that leukemia in humans might be triggered by a putative virus that was immunologically and biochemically similar to the agent that caused leukemia in rodents and sub-human primates. We continued to probe human tissues for putative human cancer viruses for the remainder of the time we collaborated with Dr. Gallo's laboratory. I traveled to the National Institutes of Health Campus in Bethesda, Maryland on a monthly basis to attend Dr. Gallo's research team meetings. Many members of that team were scientists who worked directly for Dr. Gallo. Others, like me, worked for organizations that were engaged in research partnerships with him. Then, there were scientists from companies with operations in the Washington, DC area, as well as faculty from universities in Boston, Europe, and even Russia, who attended those meetings. We devoted the entire day to reviewing the latest data; reporting on competitive activities and findings from other laboratories; and carefully planning the next series of experiments.

Once per year, we all gathered at a large farmhouse in Maryland to participate in what began as a retreat and later became a major annual symposium devoted in its entirety to the study of viruses and cancer. I was very impressed with the work that I was fortunate to be involved in during the years of our partnership with Dr. Gallo. There was never any doubt in my mind that his organization, with its many different players, would one day be the first to identify a virus that caused leukemia in humans.

Gallo's belief that human leukemia would have a viral origin was based on a large body of evidence that had accumulated from studies conducted on mice, rats, monkeys, and gibbon apes. In each of those instances, evidence of the agent's ability to transform cells in culture or induce tumors when injected into the respective host was clear, convincing, and highly reproducible. Dr. Gallo also told me that he thought that the low incidence of leukemia among Caribbean blacks could be a hint that those individuals might harbor a virus inhibitor in their plasma. It was an intriguing thought that was worthy of further exploration. He wondered if I could help him gain access to serum from a cohort of Caribbean blacks. The initial reason for wanting to examine blood samples from Caribbean blacks would later change, after the discovery of what was called Acquired Immunodifficiency Syndrome or AIDS.

Gallo would eventually be credited with the discovery of the first retrovirus that was associated with the development of human leukemia. He called that virus the Human T Lymphotrophic Virus-1 or HTLV-I. That was the first RNA tumor virus that was implicated in the etiology of Human T Cell Leukemia. That discovery was widely celebrated by retroviral molecular biologists, and to many, it seemed like an appropriate way to justify all of the effort and resources expended by the War on Cancer initiative. The celebration was short-lived however, and the spotlight quickly turned to studies on a possible virus involvement in the development of AIDS.

Because of the new technologies spawned by the War on Cancer program, and the highly sophisticated resources available to scientists, it was very convenient to probe peripheral blood samples from AIDS patients for evidence of retroviral involvement. As a consequence, interest in studying retroviruses increased dramatically, and laboratories nationally and internationally quickly joined the search for a putative AIDS virus. Everyone wanted to be the discoverer of that highly sought after human retrovirus.

The laboratories of French scientist Dr. Luc Montagnier that had collaborated freely with Dr. Gallo during the 1970s was now locked in fierce competition with his group. Dr. Gallo continued to prove the resourcefulness of his laboratory by reporting on the discovery of a second agent, which he called Human T Lymphotrophic Virus-2. That virus, though similar to HTLV-1, was sufficiently different that he felt the probability of it being involved in causing AIDS was quite high.

While Dr. Gallo's new virus was attracting significant attention within the scientific community, Luc Montagnier published a paper in which he reported on the isolation of a virus from human cells that he called Lymphoadenopathy Virus. My recollection is that the Montagnier manuscript did not generate much interest among tumor virologists. It represented another of those seemingly endless reports on the isolation of a putative human cancer virus that could not be corroborated. But opinions would change radically after Dr. Gallo requested a sample of the Lymphoadenopathy Virus from Montagnier to undertake a comparative analysis between that virus and the candidate viruses isolated by his laboratory. The results of that study showed Montagnier's Lymphoadenopathy Virus to be remarkably similar to Dr. Gallo's Human T Lymphotrophic Virus-2. Further examination of the two viruses showed that they more closely resembled the so-called foamy viruses than the classical retroviruses. Did this mean that the viruses were similar or even identical? Was it likely that they could indeed be candidate AIDS viruses? The answers were not immediately evident.

The international battle that ensued pitted the Montagnier laboratory against Dr. Gallo's laboratory and the French against the Americans. Each group was claiming to have been first to isolate the virus that caused AIDS. The dispute was finally settled when an International Committee recommended an independent analysis of the genomes of both the Human T Lymphotrophic Virus-2 and the Lymphoadenopathy Virus. After the sequences were compared they were found to be almost identical. The second recommendation issued by the committee was to rename the new virus the Human Immunodeficiency Virus or HIV. That brought an end to one of the greatest political upheaval in science since the controversy over the discovery of the three-dimensional structure of DNA.

In 1984, President Reagan's Secretary of Health and Human Services Margaret Heckler addressed the American press promising an AIDS vaccine in a few years. Her message was clear, as a result of American ingenuity, the War on Cancer had yielded its second major victory–the discovery of the agent that was associated with the development of AIDS. The promise made to the nation at that public appearance was that America would produce a vaccine to treat AIDS as soon as possible. That goal would prove to be much more elusive than anyone imagined when Secretary Heckler made her projection.

In 1976, I was promoted to Project Leader, a position that significantly expanded my scientific and managerial responsibilities within Pfizer's Department of Cancer Research. As a Project Leader, I assumed responsibility for overseeing the activities of a group of ten research scientists. The group included biochemists, immunologists, and molecular biologists. I also served as Head of the Molecular Biology Project Team where, in collaboration with my Pfizer colleagues and scientists at the National Cancer Institute, I pursued a variety of research projects on cancer causation, prevention, and treatment. I devoted approximately eighty percent of my time to research, fifteen percent to administration; and the remainder to assorted other responsibilities. My research duties included planning, performing, and evaluating data generated from numerous research projects. I prepared reports, wrote manuscripts, and presented my work to various scientific groups.

In order to meet the challenges of my new assignment and effectively coordinate the technical planning and work effort of my group, I spent much of my time perusing the literature in the program focus areas, as well as drawing on the knowledge and experience of my colleagues, internally and externally. During that time, I was also designated as Principal Investigator on a major contract between our company and the National Institutes of Health, Office of Resources and Logistics. We were phenomenally successful, and much of that success was due to our creativity, initiative, hard work, flexibility, and active and effective communication of program accomplishments.

In March of that year, I was invited by the American Society for Biological Chemists' Lecturer/Recruiter Program to address a group of biology majors at Kentucky State University, and in May, the National Consortium for Black Professional Development invited me to address their annual convention in Chicago. I was asked to speak on the issue of "Developing Mechanisms for Channeling Blacks into Specific Areas of the Life and Biological Sciences." I chose that occasion to talk about what I called a "negative psychology" that pervaded our schools, and I also talked about the problems black students faced when seeking financial assistance to obtain a college degree. These were subjects that I was very familiar with, and I wanted to try out my ideas on the more than three hundred educators, business executives, government agency representatives, scientists, corporate recruiters, religious leaders, and students that attended those proceedings in Chicago.

By "negative psychology" I meant the sum total of negative feelings and attitudes communicated by many teachers and administrators to black students during their progression through their middle, high school, and undergraduate years. I had personal experience with such negativity during my undergraduate years when an insensitive academic Dean at NYU cautioned me against applying to NYU's Medical School because he thought that it would be unlikely that more than two black students would be admitted into the school's freshman class. Then there were the negative messages promulgated at the national level emanating from some very prominent college professors whose ideas about race, eugenics, and IQ that were widely disseminated in the 1970s, sought to prove that blacks were inferior to whites.

With regard to the financial barrier, it was clear that given the economic realities of the educational system, black students often faced the prospect of lacking the funds necessary to meet the financial demands of a college education. I used my own experience when I first arrived in New York to illustrate how lack of financial resources can influence decision making about college. Fortunately for me, my soccer coach, Mr. Alan Tobin was there to help me stay on track with my plans to enroll in NYU. My presentation was so well-received that the Executive Director of the National Consortium Mr. Hanford Stafford invited me to serve on the Board of that prestigious organization.

In 1976, I was named as one of two Pfizer Black Achievers in Industry honorees by the Harlem YMCA. Eudine and I, along with my childhood friend Wendell Kellman who was then serving as Consul-General for Barbados at New York, and some of the senior administrators from Pfizer's New York's Corporate Headquarters, were in attendance at the ceremony that was held at the New York Hilton Hotel. There were many prominent Black Achievers who shared the stage with me that evening. I vividly remember Jane Tillman Irving and Gil Noble both of whom went on to become major television personalities in the New York City Media Market.

Chapter 16

Teaneck

One of the most attractive developments resulting from my joining the Pfizer Cancer Research Organization at Maywood was my eventual relocation to Teaneck, New Jersey. I worked for almost five years in Maywood, commuting daily by car either up the East Side or West Side drive in Manhattan and then across the George Washington Bridge through the Palisades, Hackensack, Paramus, until I reached the town of Maywood. I took every opportunity during those five years to familiarize myself with the various New Jersey communities, scouting for neighborhoods that I believed would best meet the needs of my family.

Our son Kevin was born in the same year I went to work in Maywood, and Eudine and I did not want to move to New Jersey during that most critical stage of his development. So we sent Dionne to the Brooklyn College Early Childhood Center. Eudine took her there every morning and picked her up in the afternoon. Although we liked the school, it was a challenge for Eudine to get her there, and moreover, it was an even more challenging proposition as Eudine prepared to return to work on a full-time basis. So we transferred Dionne from the Brooklyn College Early Childhood Center's program to a private school in the Flatbush section of Brooklyn. A lady called Mrs. Butler ran that pre-school program.

The school was operated out of a church on Bedford Avenue near to Rutland Road where Mum and Dad lived. Mrs. Butler was a lovely black lady with a matronly approach to managing her students. Peggy was working at Downstate Medical Center then, and either she, or one of my nieces would pick up Dionne in the afternoon, and take her to Mum and Dad until Eudine came home from work. One evening when we arrived at Mum and Dad, Dionne was not there. It was the first time that had ever happened, so we naturally panicked. Mrs. Butler had a rule that all children had to be picked up before five-thirty in the evening, and for some reason Peggy had forgotten to get Dionne. I can't describe the feeling of total panic that I experienced as I left Mum's house to go in search of Dionne. My fear was quickly erased when I entered the church and learned that Mrs. Butler had taken Dionne to her home.

When Dionne was old enough to enter elementary school, we sent her to St. Stephens, a Lutheran School in the Flatbush section of Brooklyn. It was a school with an excellent reputation, and we believed that Dionne enjoyed being a student there. By that time Kevin was ready for Kindergarten. We sent him to the ABC Preschool on Rockaway Avenue in Canarsie, Brooklyn. We never felt comfortable about our decision to send Kevin to that school, so as soon as he was old enough we transferred both he and Dionne to a school called Prince of Peace. Prince of Peace was also a Lutheran School, but the difference between it and St. Stephens was that the school was run by West Indians. The Assistant Principal happened to be a Barbadian. Finding that school was a stroke of good luck for us because it provided Dionne and Kevin with an excellent academic foundation.

After five years of house hunting in almost every northern New Jersey Township, I was able to find a house that met all of my expectations for a family home. I was shown that house by the owner of a small real estate company whose office was on Main Street in Teaneck. There was so much value and character to that house, that at first, I didn't want to believe what I was seeing. Call it luck or providence, but that evening after a thorough walk-through, I was shocked to find out that the house was priced within a range that we could afford. I couldn't wait to give Eudine the details when I reached home. However, I thought it best to provide her with a much understated description of the house. I told her that I thought that it was a good idea for us to arrange to see the house the next day.

The drive from Main Street in Teaneck to Palmer Avenue was less than three minutes. As soon as we pulled up in front of the house, Eudine's demeanor changed. Her body language communicated her mood. “Why did you bring me to see this house?” she asked, “you know we can’t afford it!” I tried to calm her down by saying, “Let’s take a look anyway before you decide.” The owners were obviously very proud of their home, and wanted to sell it to a family that shared their feeling. In order to make the deal as attractive as possible, they were offering to leave the custom drapery at the living room window and the wooden shades in the Florida room.

We loved the design of the house; it was a split level, four corner brick with a sunken family room and a gas fireplace. There was a glass enclosed Florida room that was heated and air conditioned. It had three bedrooms and two bathrooms on the second level, and there was a partially finished room in the attic. The heating and air conditioning system was a high-quality, gas-fired Bryant unit. There was a high-tech air-filtration system that removed particulate material from the circulating air, and there was a humidistat that maintained the moisture at a comfortable level year-round. I thought that our house on Schenck Avenue was our dream home, but now this house on Palmer Avenue proved me wrong. We did not hesitate to instruct our Broker to make an offer, and were pleased when we learned that the owners had accepted.

Queen Anne Road, Teaneck Road, and Chadwick Lane would soon become our stomping ground. Dionne entered the Thomas Jefferson Middle School and Kevin enrolled in the Bryant School. Teaneck’s schools had earned a national reputation for their progressive stance in promoting diversity, and we were really pleased to be living in a community that valued all of its citizens.

Eudine kept her job in Manhattan and commuted daily by bus through the Lincoln Tunnel. It was an easy commute that took approximately thirty minutes from door-to-door, thanks to an express lane in the Lincoln Tunnel that was dedicated exclusively to buses.

My trip to Pfizer in Maywood was about fifteen minutes. I drove Dionne to school first, and then returned to wait with the other parents for Kevin’s school bus to arrive. In the afternoon, we arranged to have Kevin bused to the neighborhood Lutheran church where he remained until I could picked him up after work. When we learned about the Copley School from a friend, we transferred Kevin there, and he was happy to attend that program along with his friend Chaka. As usual, I would pick him up in the evening.

When Kevin graduated from the Bryant School, he joined Dionne at Eugene Field. After school, Dionne and Kevin waited for me in the Teaneck Public Library, just across the parking lot from their school. The arrangement could not have been better. It exposed both of them to a wealth of resources available in that library. The librarians got to know them well and included them in many of the activities sponsored by the library. Dionne learned to quilt by attending their afternoon class, and Kevin participated in their chess program, becoming a very skilled player. He won most of the tournaments he entered, and was so good that he was able to teach me everything I know about the game. I enjoyed the friendly rivalry that developed between the two of us, and I really looked forward to challenging him at least twice per week.

Springtime in Teaneck was simply delightful. The magnolias and the forsythia, and lilacs decorated the landscape filling the air with the most distinctive fragrances. I loved driving down the narrow, two-way streets with Dionne and Kevin singing a song that we would make up as we went along. If we were traveling on Chadwick Lane then the first verse would begin with a reference to, *"Chadwick Lane, oh how I love you Chadwick Lane.*" The lawns and shrubbery in our neighborhood were neatly manicured, and the public parks would be ablaze with dogwoods and the occasional cherry and pear tree. I often loaded the bikes onto the back of the car and drove to the park where we spent quality time riding and jogging.

We never really got to know our immediate neighbors in Teaneck. A lawyer and his family occupied the house to the right of us. He had a young Jamaican lady who was a live-in maid. She cared for their young daughter. Occasionally, when I was mowing the lawn or raking the leaves we would exchange pleasantries. The family on our left was friendlier. The husband was a medical doctor and they had a daughter who was around Dionne's age. She and Dionne spent many evenings playing on the lawn between our houses, and through their friendship we were able to develop a relationship with her parents. In the back of us was a mixed-race family. The husband was black, and his wife was white. They had two sons both around Dionne's age. I remember them being so unfriendly that on the rare occasion when we talked with them our conversation was, at best, superficial.

There were other neighbors with whom we had excellent relations. The Dorsey's lived a few blocks away. Eudine met Mrs. Dorsey on the bus to Manhattan and they became good friends. Her husband Tom was a real gentleman, and he and I got along well. He worked at Giants' Stadium in the New Jersey Meadowlands and he would get us tickets to the soccer games. I remember taking Kevin to see the Cosmos play at the stadium. They had recruited world-class players like Breckenbaur and Pele, and had taken American soccer to another level. Tens of thousands of fans would be in attendance, and after the game, Tom would arrange to have us meet the players in the lounge.

Downtown Teaneck was a collection of small shops, a movie house, an old-fashioned bakery called Butterflakes, and a fish store. We enjoyed going down to Main Street to purchase our weekly supply of the delicious pastry that was available at Butterflakes, and when I was away on business, Eudine would take the kids to the International House of Pancakes where they enjoyed most of the entrees listed on their glossy menu. Our trips to Pathmark, the largest supermarket serving the Teaneck community, were most enjoyable. On Saturdays we went to a pizza parlor in Hackensack called Ginos where they served some of the most delicious pizzas. Sometimes we ate fast-food at Arthur Treachers or Long John Silver, or we would visit our favorite Chinese restaurant in Paramus. The biggest treat however, was a trip to the Paramus Mall. There we would shop at Stern's department store until we dropped; and we enjoyed eating lunch in their second floor restaurant.

Living in Teaneck also brought us closer to the families of my Maywood colleagues. Richard and Elise, Dave and Sandy, John and Elizabeth, and others. We attended company picnics and dinners, and developed close friendships with several other Maywood families.

The annual company picnic was held at Rye, New York. Rye was an amusement park that was just outside of the New York City limits on the way to Connecticut. We would invite the children's cousins Richard and Gia to join us. Mum always went along with us to those picnics. We would spend the day enjoying the rides; trying our luck with the games of chance; and enjoying the sumptuous buffet that the company provided.

In 1971, President Nixon in his State of the Union address informed the nation of his intention to ask Congress for an appropriation of an extra $100 million to launch an intensive campaign to find a cure for cancer. The discovery of the enzyme reverse transcriptase was announced to the world one year before President Nixon's promise, and the scientific community was already poised to take advantage of the molecular tools that retroviruses made available. In preparing for the task ahead, the National Institutes of Health converted the Army's Biological Warfare Facility at Fort Detrick, Maryland to a Cancer Research Center. President Nixon delivered on his promise and signed the National Cancer Act in December 1971.

As the decade of the seventies wound down, the War on Cancer was loosing its punch. President Jimmy Carter occupied the White House, and an increasingly restless Congress was expressing considerable concern about wasteful government spending. Many elected officials were prepared to make massive reductions in monies appropriated to conduct the War on Cancer. Clearly, no one had yet found the magic bullet. Ironically, the late seventies was also a time when revolutionary changes were taking place in the world of science. While a new technology called "Recombinant DNA" was being ushered in, laboratories all across the U.S. were moving away from conducting research that was focused on the biology of retroviruses. Some of the best retroviral biologists changed the emphasis of their research programs. The Cancer Research Center at Fort Detrick began to lose its luster, and several prominent investigators moved back to the home campus at Bethesda, Maryland to pursue different interests.

As I reflect on that period in my career, I am intrigued by the fact that revolutionary change in science is usually triggered by findings that appear to be innocuous when first reported, but have the capacity to fundamentally alter the way the business of science is conducted over the long run. The discovery of a family of enzymes called restriction endonucleases illustrates this point. The first report on the isolation of a restriction endonuclease appeared in the literature in 1970, but the significance of that report was only fully realized in 1978 when the Nobel Prize in Medicine was awarded to Daniel Nathans, Werner Arber, and Hamilton Smith for their seminal work on the characterization of restriction endonucleases.

Restriction enzymes have the capacity to cut DNA at specific nucleotide sequences called restriction sites. As bacteria evolved, they developed the capacity to produce these enzymes as a defense mechanism against viruses. In 1979 when I moved from Maywood, New Jersey to Pfizer's Global Research Headquarters in Groton, Connecticut, some of these enzymes were already available commercially. That availability ushered in a new technology called recombinant DNA.

The second development that occurred in the 1970s was the refinement of gene cloning strategies. The drivers of this progress were circular DNA molecules called plasmids. Dr. Joshua Lederberg first proposed the name plasmid. He was one of those brilliant microbiologists that I learned about when I was an undergraduate at NYU. Dr. Lederberg had used the designation plasmid to describe an extra chromosomal genetic element that he first isolated in 1967. Later, another prominent scientist Dr. Stanley Cohen working in the Department of Genetics at Stanford University demonstrated that he could use plasmids to "transform" bacterial cells by a process that involved inserting a "foreign" gene into the plasmid and using the "chimaeric" or hybrid plasmid to introduce the foreign gene into bacterial cells.

After reading the language of Stanley Cohen's application to the U.S. Patent and Trademark Office in 1978, it was obvious that a new era of Molecular Genetics was about to begin. The Abstract of that application was brilliantly constructed and described the methods used to cut the circular plasmid, insert the foreign gene, and reattach the ends of the replicating structure to form a larger circle. The next step involved inserting the modified plasmid into a bacterial cell and then coaxing the cell to produce multiple copies of the "foreign" gene. The authors went on to state that the method would prove to be a convenient and efficient way "to introduce genetic capability into microorganisms for the production of nucleic acids and proteins, such as medically or commercially useful enzymes, which may have direct usefulness, or may find expression in the production of drugs, such as hormones, antibiotics or the like, fixation of nitrogen, fermentation, utilization of specific feed stocks, or the like."

As is clearly evident, the claims were comprehensive and all encompassing. No one had any idea in 1978 whether a patent would be granted. The possibility that if approved, the patent owner could prevent pharmaceutical companies from accessing this emerging technology without paying large sums of money in licensing fees was frightening to consider.

Although the patent was not issued until 1984, the filing of that application accelerated the development of a new type of company–the biotechnology company. Every major pharmaceutical company realized that in order to maintain their competitive advantage, they needed to acquire a small start-up company or create a group within their organization that could import the new technology and disseminate it across the various therapeutic areas. To do nothing was simply not an option. Pfizer's reaction was to assemble a group of scientists and senior managers to form a taskforce that was charged with conducting an in-depth study of these new developments; and to recommend a set of actions to the leadership of its Central Research Division. I was invited to be a member of the taskforce, and I began my assignment by attending a number of focus group meetings that were held at the company's Global Research Headquarters in Groton, Connecticut. My Director Dr. Keith Jensen was the first to make me aware of those developments. He called me into his office one morning, and in his inimitable fashion he told me that the War On Cancer was losing favor with the Congress. He said that there was talk about moving away from the sole-source contract arrangement that the John L. Smith Memorial for Cancer Research in Maywood had enjoyed since its founding. He further stated that he didn't know what would happen, but was willing to assume that if the sole-source contract mechanism that supported the bulk of Maywood's production operations ended, it would be hard to convince the company to keep the facility open. He then went on to tell me about the scheduled taskforce meetings, and the fact that I was invited to participate in those discussions.

I arrived in Groton on the day of the first meeting of the taskforce filled with mixed emotions. On the one hand, I was flattered to be selected from among my Pfizer colleagues to serve on such an important group. On the other hand, I couldn't help thinking that change was in the air for my friends and me at Maywood, and that it was likely that our roles within the company would soon be different. The science we were practicing was rapidly being replaced by a new set of technologies, and if we did not quickly begin to adapt to that reality, we would most certainly lose our competitive advantage, becoming the dinosaurs of a modern scientific era.

The meeting at Groton lived up to its billing. I was amazed at how much the field had changed since I was awarded my doctoral degree. Our invited guests reported on work that had not yet been published. They told us how investigators were already using the new technology to manipulate bacterial genes in ways that altered major metabolic pathways. Yeast genes were being cut and spliced, and there was talk of doing the same with plant, animal, and human genes. New tools were available to read all of the letters in the DNA alphabet, a development that permitted scientists to gain unprecedented insights into the structure and function of genes. As I sat there for the two days that the taskforce met, I realized that the age of biotechnology was dawning, and the way we practiced science was about to change forever.

Shortly after my two-day trip to Groton ended, Dr. Jensen again approached me with a simple proposal. He was inviting me to consider moving from Maywood to Groton to be a part of a new Recombinant DNA Group that Pfizer was planning to launch. There was no effort to coerce me into accepting the offer, but Keith's reminder that the War on Cancer program was in its last throes, was enough to capture my attention.

I really didn't want to move my family to Groton. We loved Teaneck very much, and any move to Connecticut would mean that Eudine would have to give up her job in New York. Then, we were both reluctant to move Dionne and Kevin from their schools and the many friends that they had made since we lived in Teaneck. It seemed like I was between a rock and a hard place. This was all happening during my fourth year as the principal investigator of a major grant awarded to the Maywood team. That was the year when I had a manuscript accepted for publication in the International Journal of Cancer, and my abstract to present my most recent findings to a gathering of international experts at Pitsunda, Russia had already been accepted. I was also serving as the Chairman of the Cancer Research Department's Professional Development Committee, and I was my company's representative on the Board of the National Consortium for Black Professional Development. There was so much that I wanted to protect and preserve. So I quickly began to carefully think through all of my options.

There was a state senator who lived in our neighborhood in Teaneck and he wielded considerable influence in Trenton, the capitol of New Jersey. I approached him at a cocktail party one evening and inquired about employment opportunities for scientists within the New Jersey Department of Health. He urged me to contact the Office of Health and Safety in Trenton to schedule an appointment with the director. My request was granted without any problem, but my meeting with the director was brief and very discouraging. The work of the department was uninteresting, and the location was so unattractive that I believe I would have turned down an offer if one was forthcoming. I politely thanked the director for his time and quickly made my exit to the parking lot. I was becoming more and more convinced that Groton could be a reasonable option.

Then one day at work, I was having a conversation with one of my colleagues. George was an experienced individual. He had worked at Pfizer several years before leaving to take a job in Frederick, Maryland. Later, he returned to Pfizer and was now serving as one of the five section managers at Maywood. George counseled me to stay with Pfizer. He told me of the error he made when he left Pfizer before he was fully vested in the company's retirement plan. When he returned, because he had been gone for more than two years, he found out that those earlier years of service were not counted, and he simply lost the benefits that had accrued based on his previous employment with the company. "Never leave before being vested," he told me! I needed two more years to be vested, and George's advice seemed to make a lot of sense.

After that, my interest in finding a job in New Jersey waned; I lost enthusiasm for job hunting altogether. I began to draw on Keith's experience as a senior administrator within the company. I contacted my friend Dave who had relocated to

Groton in 1978, and sought his perspective on what life was like at that site. I made several trips to Groton before finally convincing my family that a move there would be in our best interest. Eudine was very supportive and she helped me to gain the support of Dionne and Kevin. We planned to have her give up her New York job and remain at home until the kids were comfortably adjusted to their new environment. We put the house up for sale, and to soften the impact of our plan to leave Teaneck, I decided to take the entire family on a trip. First we traveled to Los Angeles where I attended a meeting of the American Society of Microbiology. After the meeting ended, we went on to Honolulu. Our house appeared on the Teaneck Real Estate Listing just before our departure for Los Angeles.

We arrived in Los Angeles after a long flight from New Jersey to learn that President Carter was visiting that city and the hotel had assigned our room to a member of the presidential party or to the press corps. They offered us accommodation at a small hotel in Pasadena or at the Los Angeles Athletic Club, which was only a few blocks away. We opted to stay at the Athletic Club. That turned out to be an excellent choice. We simply loved the surroundings there. The room was spacious and attractively furnished. The entire facility was immaculate, and they even had a well-maintained athletic track on the upper level that was accessible to all guests. By staying there we were afforded a unique opportunity to see how elegantly the members of that exclusive club lived.

My brother Roger who had moved to Los Angeles in 1971 was there to show us around the city. We took the children to Disney Land, and he treated us to some of the most sumptuous brunches available in Malibu and Rodondo Beach. Our stay in Los Angeles ended too soon, and we were quickly packing our bags and preparing for the second leg of our trip. This time it would be Honolulu, Hawaii where I was scheduled to attend a joint meeting of the American and Japanese Societies of Microbiology.

I had signed up with the tour group that handled all aspects of our visit to Hawaii. Our flight arrived in Honolulu very late in the evening. It seemed like we were transported to some enchanted land. I remember a gigantic reception with

Polynesian girls swaying, delightful music playing, and the beautiful leis that were placed around our necks as we disembarked from the plane. I learned that the flowers that were carefully linked together to form each lei were called Plumeria. On close examination, I noticed that those beautiful leis were made from flowers that we called Frangipani in Barbados. Frangipani trees grew abundantly in Barbados, especially in graveyards. The distinct fragrance of their five-petaled flower was associated with sadness, and it is perhaps for that reason that I never played with those flowers when I was growing up. What a contrast in cultures–in Hawaii I was being welcomed with a lei made from Plumeria, a flower that the Polynesian people celebrated, while in Barbados I kept my distance from the Frangipani tree and its flower because of its poisonous sap and its ubiquitous presence in graveyards.

Upon arriving at the hotel, before I could even check in, I was told by the clerk at the check-in counter that they had a message for me. Both Eudine and I felt that it was from our real estate agent back in Teaneck, but I did not anticipate that it would be an offer on our house. Ordinarily, news about a generous offer on your house is greeted with enthusiasm. In this case however, I was saddened to learn that someone had found our home so attractive that they wasted little time in trying to acquire it. I knew that if I accepted the offer it would mean that when I returned to Teaneck I would be packing to move to Connecticut. Saddened, but at the same time very optimistic, Eudine and I decided to accept the generous offer on our Teaneck home.

During the first part of our stay in Honolulu, I participated in the joint meeting of the American and Japanese Societies for Microbiology. It was a continuation of the meeting that started back in Los Angeles. While I attended the sessions during the day, Eudine and the children were busy enjoying the luxurious Hilton property.

In 1979, Hilton Hawaiian Village was the epitome of what a vacation resort should be. Our room overlooked the beautiful Waikiki Beach with its elegant palm trees and lush white sand. The gardens were ablaze with tropical plants of every description, and the paved paths led to so many delightful shops and restaurants. The kids enjoyed playing on the sand, building castles and soaking up the sunshine. One day, as Kevin and Dionne played on the beach, a couple walked by with a young boy about Kevin's age. As the youngster approached Kevin he seemed to be more than simply curious, and then he said "Hi Kevin!" We couldn't believe what we heard. A youngster all the way in Hawaii who knew Kevin. Like any curious parent I asked "who is that Kevin?" and he nonchalantly said, "Oh he goes to my school in Teaneck!"

The island of Oahu offered up some other interesting surprises. Our trips to the Polynesian Cultural Center, and the Pineapple Factory were memorable. When we visited the Arizona Memorial it was difficult to keep a dry eye especially when I saw my son bawling as he heard about the tragedy that befell those brave servicemen. Then there were dinners in restaurants whose names are impossible to pronounce. And then it was off to the Big Island of Hawaii.

We landed at Kona and were transported to the Kona Lagoon Hotel, a beautiful resort that was built right at the water's edge. I found Kona to be very touristy. The beach was rocky and black from several years of larval flows. I remember being able to walk quite a distance into the shallow coastal water perched precariously on those jagged black rocks. The breakfast buffets at the Kona Lagoon Hotel lived up to my expectations. It included all sorts of tropical fruit, succulent and sweet, and served on trays decorated with orchids that were attractive enough to be eaten! I shopped in the town for souvenirs and visited the waterfront just in time to witness the conclusion of a marlin fishing competition. Dionne and Kevin got a chance to have their picture taken alongside a four hundred-pound marlin that was the first prize winner.

From Kona it was off to Hilo by bus. We explored larval tubes, Volcano National Park and a nursery that produced most of the anthurium lilies sold on the mainland. Hilo was not as touristy as Kona, and it seemed to be misting or raining all of the time. We left Hilo for our trip back to Honolulu, and the long, overnight crossing to the mainland. We arrived at San Diego early in the morning of the following day, where we had to wait for several hours before catching our connecting flight back to New Jersey.

I find it difficult to remember what happened after we returned to Teaneck. I recall that the closing on our house was held in New York City, and it was then that I learned that the buyer was a popular newscaster that I listened to regularly on WABC Radio. My heart sank when our lawyer told us that the buyer's wife was planning to remove the beautiful gas fireplace from the den.

On returning to Teaneck from New York City, we packed our bags and waited for the moving truck to arrive. I was so flustered on the day of our move that I slammed the lid of the trunk to our Chevy Malibu shut with the ignition keys inside the trunk. I then had to wait until the American Automobile Association could send a locksmith to Teaneck to help me retrieve the ignition keys from the trunk. It was a sad time when I left Teaneck.

Chapter 17

Niantic

The trip by car from Teaneck to Niantic was quiet and uneventful. My niece Gia came with us, and I believe that her presence made it easier on Dionne and Kevin as they confronted the reality of moving from a home and neighborhood that they really loved. Several months before our move, Eudine and I had undertaken a protracted search for a home in Southeastern Connecticut. Through arrangements made with the Pfizer Human Resources Department, we had engaged the services of a real estate agent named Mr. Kiley. He was a very accommodating individual who responded promptly and professionally to every request we made. On our first meeting with Mr. Kiley, he took us on a guided tour of the region. He showed us the U.S. Submarine Base at Groton, the Coast Guard Academy in New London, the aquarium in the popular vacation town of Mystic, and several other places of interest in the area. On subsequent house-hunting trips, we restricted our search to the town of East Lyme because it had the reputation of having the best public schools.

East Lyme was approximately halfway between New York and Boston. The town comprised two villages, Flanders to the north and Niantic along the shoreline. Eudine and I fell in love with Niantic. We were attracted to its small size; its picturesque bay; and its beautiful, sandy beach. It did not take long before we made an offer to buy an attractive center-hall colonial home in Laurel Hill, a small Niantic community. That home sat on approximately half an acre of land on Greencliff Drive. The owners accepted our offer without any hassle, so our destination on the day of our move was Greencliff Drive in Niantic.

Greencliff Drive was a circular street. The Hollidays occupied the house on the corner, then there was our house, then the Lyons' then the Lidsky's, and then the Greens'. On the other side of the circle our neighbors included the Heilweils, the Kisers, the Glowakis, the Kestlers, the Woodwards, and the Ballentines. It was almost nightfall when the movers off loaded the last box from their truck. When they drove off, it was just my family and me and a sea of boxes waiting to be unpacked.

When we moved to Niantic, the village's population was approximately fourteen thousand residents. That number would double every summer because of the village's attractive coastal location. Niantic had its own private beach that was dotted with small cottages and historic mansions that remained vacant during the winter, but would be crowded with tourists as summer arrived.

Laurel Hill was one of the nicer developments in Niantic. The Green family owned most of the land that was developed there. Our neighbors included officers from the Navy and Coast Guard Academy. Several Pfizer senior directors also lived in Laurel Hill. It was an eclectic group of individuals, and most of them came out to greet us shortly after we arrived. They brought gifts for our home, cakes, cookies, and friendly conversations. One of our neighbors who lived on the other side of the Greencliff Drive circle reached out to us immediately, later becoming very close friends of ours. In my first meeting with them, they told me how the neighbors had caucused when they learned that a black family had bought the house on Greencliff Drive and would be moving into the development. Their fears were quickly assuaged when they learned that I was a scientist who was transferring from Pfizer's facilities in Maywood, New Jersey to fill a senior level position in the Central Research Division at Groton.

Our home in Niantic was large enough to accommodate family members for weeks at a time. We had four large bedrooms, and a full basement. Eudine and I consciously decided to buy a large enough home so that we could entice relatives to visit and even stay awhile. I would soon realize that things that I took for granted in New York and New Jersey were real challenges in Niantic. I had a very hard time finding a barber, and Eudine could not find a hairdressing salon. There was only one black barbershop in New London and that's the only place I could get a reasonably good haircut. Eudine got her hair done by a lady who had a small salon near to the town of Norwich, Connecticut.

I used an Energy Harvester continuous burning woodstove to supplement the baseboard oil fired furnace that heated our home. I would light that stove sometime in October every year, stoke it an average of twice-a-day with the hardwood logs from the neatly stacked wood pile that we kept on the side of our two-car garage, and I burnt it non-stop throughout the entire winter.

Holidays in Niantic were really special, particularly Thanksgiving and Christmas. Our house would always serve as the venue for the entire family. There would sometimes be as many as twenty to twenty-five family members visiting our Connecticut home during those holiday weekends. Typically, the family members would arrive on the night before the holiday, and Eudine would greet them with a hot bowl of her signature fish soup. It contained a variety of fresh seafood specialties that I purchased from Cappy's, a very popular seafood market in nearby Flanders. She would also served fresh ears of boiled butter-and-sugar corn along with fresh apple cider that we obtained from Scott's Farm.

On the day of the holiday she served the traditional pigeon peas and rice dinner, supplemented with pudding and souse, and coconut bread, and several other Barbadian specialties. I always looked forward to the Christmas holidays. We would start as usual with the fish soup on Christmas Eve, and then we all held hands and sing Christmas carols for about an hour, ending the session with our favorite carol–Silent Night. I videotaped all of those gatherings at our home in Niantic, and I am sure that future generations of Harewoods will one day get a sense of what those Connecticut reunions were really like.

As I mentioned earlier, we chose to live in East Lyme after conducting an in depth analysis of the school systems in Southeastern Connecticut. East Lyme schools had the best reputation in the area, by far. So it was off to school in the fall of 1979 with Dionne and Kevin. Dionne was entering East Lyme Junior High, which was a middle school, and Kevin was assigned to the Lilly B. Haynes Elementary School. Both schools shared the same campus that was located off the busy thoroughfare leading to downtown Niantic. The site was much larger than the grounds at any of the schools Dionne and Kevin previously attended. It was secluded, with lush green playgrounds surrounding a cluster of one-story brick buildings. The kids made friends easily, and had little difficulty getting adjusted to their new environment. Kevin's best friend was the Lidsky's son Harry, and Dionne's best friend was the Krom's daughter Laura who lived only one street over from our home. My niece Gia would soon come to live with us in Niantic. She attended the Lilly B. Haynes Middle School with Kevin, so Eudine and I had our hands full shuttling three kids from one venue to the other.

School at East Lyme was challenging for me and for the children. There would be incidents in which students on the school bus made really nasty remarks to Gia or Kevin, and I remember being very upset when I heard of those hurtful incidents. Then there was the time when Kevin's English teacher recommended that he be moved from the "A" group in her class to the "B" group because she thought that he was easily distracted, and that the move would give him more time to socialize! How offensive! I was down to the school the very next day to complain to the principal who shared my outrage at the teacher's action. That misguided teacher did not have her way, and Kevin was permitted to stay with the "A" group.

The most troubling thing that happened during that difficult time of adjustment was an essay that Kevin wrote for one of his classes. It was about a family that left its comfortable digs in a big city and set out on vacation. According to Kevin's narrative, the dad made a wrong turn off the major Interstate and, after several unsuccessful attempts to find an entrance ramp, was unable to reach his destination. The penalty for his mistake was complete isolation from civilization, and years of being forced to adapt to living in a very primitive setting! When I heard of this story, I was very confused. I felt that I might have done my family an injustice by moving them to Southeastern Connecticut. Although I worried about that before we moved from Teaneck, I always felt that we were such a close knit family that we could adjust easily to whatever challenge we encountered. It was now time for me to sit with my son and let him know about the resilience of his ancestors.

Kevin and I did have that heart-to-heart conversation. I told him about our rationale for moving to Niantic. I talked about the pros and cons of our move to Connecticut, and promised him that we would always remain grounded in the culture that had sustained several generations of Austins, Kidneys and Harewoods. I pledged that I would maintain contact with the world that he had grown accustomed to while living in Brooklyn and Teaneck. In keeping my promise to him, every weekend I took Eudine and the kids to New York, or found a way to get some member of the family to visit with us in Connecticut. It was a challenge, but it was for a worthy cause, and I was prepared to use every ounce of energy I had to ensure that my children did not succumb to the pressures of living in a setting that lacked the diversity to which they were accustomed.

Eudine and I immersed ourselves in all of the children's activities. Tennis, track, soccer, band, crew, Indian guides, cub scouts, everything! Dionne and Kevin joined the marching band, Dionne as a flag and Kevin as a trombonist. The East Lyme band was legendary in its accomplishments on the field whether in formal competitions or during halftime at football games. I became an active member of the fan club, traveling to competitions all over the state and region. In keeping with the tradition, I supported Eudine's decision to buy a large bell that we would ring at high points during the band's performance. I even enjoyed sitting in the frigid stands during the annual Thanksgiving Day game between the East Lyme and Waterford High School football teams.

Approximately six months after we moved to Niantic, Eudine set out in search of a part-time job to fill the time between Bible study with the neighbors and the children returning from school. She found a job with the family that managed the New London Mall. She kept their books and got to learn about the operation of that for-profit business. The mall owners who lived in Massachusetts, subsequently established an office at the New London site and asked Eudine to become their full-time manager.

In 1980, the Edward Malley store anchored the mall. There was also a large department store called Two Guys. Several small stores and boutiques filled out the space in that 39-store mall. Edward Malley and Two Guys eventually closed and were replaced by Marshalls and Bradleys, respectively. It would not be long before the mall attracted a Red Lobster restaurant. The entire Southeastern Connecticut area soon underwent a mini renaissance, attracting a major mall–Crystal Mall, several large hotels, and subsequently two very popular casinos, Foxwoods and the Mohegan Sun.

When I first moved to Connecticut, my family and I worshiped at the Pleasant Street Baptist Church in Westerly, Rhode Island. This came about through an accidental meeting with the pastor of that church (Pastor Lamb) while I was on one of my house hunting trips. I had taken Eudine and the children to dinner at a restaurant called Sailor Eds in Mystic, Connecticut, when an African American man walked up to my table and introduced himself. I believe that we were the only other African Americans having dinner in the restaurant that evening, so I was delighted to have him come over to greet us. After introducing myself and the members of my family, I told him that I was looking at houses and would soon be moving to the area. He saw us as potential new members of his congregation and offered me his business card. He told me that he would be delighted to have my family worship at his church when we moved to Connecticut. Eudine and I remembered Pastor Lamb's generous invitation, and shortly after we moved to Niantic, we decided to pay a visit to the Pleasant Street Baptist Church.

Westerly was a twenty minute ride north of Niantic on Interstate-95. It is just across the Connecticut state line on the southwestern end of Rhode Island. Like many small towns in the region, Westerly was a delightful coastal community. Pleasant Street Baptist Church was built near to the charming Victorian village known as Watch Hill, which seemed to be a favorite place for Italian families who migrated to that area many years ago. They lived in elegant homes tucked behind high privacy fences and their names were prominently displayed on attractive signs that decorated the entrance to each property. Watch Hill and the entire town of Westerly were favorite seaside vacation spots.

I developed a friendship with the Simmons family who were members of our congregation. Downey worked at Pfizer in the large manufacturing plant that was located on the bank of the Thames river. His wife was a very friendly lady who always made us feel so welcomed when we worshiped at her church or when we were guests at her home. On my first visit to their home, Downey spent a lot of time showing me his grandfather clock. It was made from solid black walnut and had a very beautiful, brass movement. The amazing thing about his clock was the fact that he built it from a kit that he bought from a company in South Carolina. Before the evening ended, he provided me with the address of the company he purchased the clock from. I was so impressed by Downey's wood working skills, that I did not lose any time in placing an order to the South Carolina company for a similar clock. That was the beginning of my wood working career. The black walnut grandfather clock that adorns the corner of our dining room, and the Butler Tray Table in our family room are examples of the success I had with assembling my own furniture during the time I lived in Connecticut.

Pleasant Street Baptist Church was a very small church with an aging congregation. I enjoyed worshiping there so much that I was not worried about the distance from our home in Niantic, and the time it took us to make the round trip. When Mum and Dad visited, I took them to worship at Pleasant Street. After several months of driving back and forth from Niantic to Westerly for morning worship service and then for Sunday school, I began to realize that we were spending most of our weekend on the road. It was around that time that I felt that I would have to look at other options for worship nearer to our home.

Trying to find a place of worship that was racially mixed and committed to diversity was a difficult proposition in Southeastern Connecticut in the late 1970s. I attended Sunday services at the Episcopal churches in New London and Niantic where I found the congregations to be inhospitable and overtly unwelcoming. It seemed to me that those churches were part of a different denomination to St. George's Episcopal Church where Eudine and I worshipped when we lived in Brooklyn. Then, one Sunday, as I was flipping through the pages of the New London Day, the local newspaper, a story about the mayor of New London caught my attention. It indicated that Mr. Leo

Jackson, an African American who was then the elected mayor of the City of New London, would be a guest at the Second Congregational Church the following Sunday. He was going to speak on the topic, "Growing up Black in New London." I told Eudine that I thought that it would be a good idea for us to go and hear what the mayor had to say, and she agreed. So on the following Sunday, I attended the morning service at Second Congregational Church, and also participated in the fellowship hour where I heard a very enlightening story about what life was like for blacks in New London during the 1960s.

I found the congregation to be warm and friendly, and particularly liked the message delivered by the Reverend Donald Frazier. He and his wife were serving as interim ministers at the time, and it was easy to tell that they occupied a warm spot in the hearts of the church members. Overall, I liked the experience and left with a positive impression of the church. Because I was not familiar with the Church of Christ, which is the denomination to which Second Congregational belonged, I felt that it was important for me to learn as much as I could about the church and its history.

Established in 1835, Second Congregational Church was the direct beneficiary of the wealth of a group of prominent New London businessmen. Those city leaders recognized that as New London's population increased as a direct result of the rapid expansion of its whaling and banking industries, its First Congregational Church that was founded in 1642 was no longer able to meet the needs of the community. They therefore built a second church on lands located at the southwestern corner of Huntington and Jay Streets that was donated by a prosperous whaling agent. The church historian told me that eight "proprietors" contributed to the building fund. The records indicate that, "in its origin, the Second Congregational Church was an overflow from the fullness of the First Church", and that "it did not grow out of dissention in doctrine or party strife or schismatic recklessness." In view of the fact that temperance and the abolition of slavery were major issues in New London at that time, the leadership of Second Church felt a need to assuage any fears that its membership might have about a possible schism within the Church of Christ. The building that was finally constructed reflected the grandeur of that time in

New London's history. Second Congregational Church with its elegant façade and impressive steeple was an important addition to the city. As the years went by, it survived financial problems during the Gold Rush and the Civil War. It was rebuilt after two devastating fires in 1868 and 1926; and the restored building remained a "beacon on the hill" at the conclusion of the first and second world wars.

I joined Second Congregational Church in 1981, shortly after Wallace Anderson Jr. entered the life of the church as pastor. I became a member of the Board of Deacons, and served the congregation faithfully until 1987. Ethyl Diaz was the only other African American serving on the Board, and we worked diligently to expand the missionary work of Second Congregational Church to the entire City of New London. Dionne and Kevin were welcomed into the Sunday school and they participated in a variety of the youth activities, including ski trips to Middlebury, Vermont. They both joined the Confirmation Class and received their first communion as members of Second Congregational Church.

I was keenly interested in getting to know the few black people who lived in Southeastern Connecticut. When Pfizer asked me to be the company's representative on the Board of the New London Community Resources Commission, I quickly accepted. The commission was one of several agencies funded by the Thames Valley Council for Community Action, a private, non-profit corporation in Jewett City, Connecticut. Thames Valley Council for Community Action advocated for many of the needy and disadvantaged residents of New London County, and the New London Community Resources Commission met an important need for the residents of the City of New London.

New London is one of the small cities in Southeastern Connecticut. It is a seaport city and a port of entry on the northeast coast of the U.S. The city is over three hundred fifty years old, and judging from its name and the name of the river (Thames) that separates it from the Town of Groton, and the name of the region (New England) it is obvious that its earliest settlers wanted to remember the city and country that they once called home. New London is bounded on the west and south by the Town of Waterford, and on the north by the Thames River and the Town of Groton. The Thames river flows into the city harbor before emptying into the Long Island Sound. Because the New London Harbor was once one of the best deep water ports on the Long Island Sound, it is not surprising that New London became a base of American naval operations during the Revolutionary War.

When I arrived in Southeastern Connecticut, New London was home for the U.S. Coast Guard Academy, Mitchell College, Connecticut College, and the Underwater Sound Laboratories. In the years since I left the area, it became home to the second site of Pfizer's Global Research Headquarters in Southeastern Connecticut.

Residents of Southeastern Connecticut are constantly reminded of the role New London played during the Revolutionary War. Aided by the notorious turncoat Benedict Arnold, the British fleet raided the city in 1781 and engaged the local militia in the bloody Battle of Groton Heights. After sneaking into the harbor under cover of darkness, the British set fire to the city. Fort Griswold located across the Thames River in Groton was New London's main defensive stronghold. Its well-fortified walls were considered to be more than adequate to protect the local militia from enemy attack. Unfortunately, Norwich native Benedict Arnold who had previously been a member of the local militia that was charged with protecting the city, would betray his fellow citizens. Because he was aware of the signals used to notify the locals of an impending attack, it is believed that he sounded the all-clear signal, rendering the Fort essentially defenseless when the British soldiers came ashore. One summer when Aunt Eude and Eudine's cousin Anita visited us in Niantic, I took them to see the re-enactment of the Battle of Groton Heights at Fort Griswold. I can still remember how realistic it was to see the professional actors dressed in full battle regalia locked in mortal combat, reminding everyone in attendance of that tragic battle and the notorious traitor known as Benedict Arnold.

For several decades beginning in the early nineteenth century, New London became one of Connecticut's important centers for commerce. During that period, the city was reported to be the second busiest whaling port in the world after New Bedford, Massachusetts. Evidence of its pre-eminence as a whaling port is still reflected in the city's architecture. Many of its historic homes were constructed with a small room called a "widows lookout." This is where a whaler's wife would maintain a constant vigil to see when her husband's whaling ship was returning to the port of New London after a long trip at sea. In fact, some of the blacks that still resided in New London when we lived in Connecticut were believed to be descendants of the men who worked on the whaling ships that used that city as their homeport.

My work on the New London Community Resources Commission and the Thames Valley Council for Community Action Boards was very rewarding. I got to feel the pulse of those small communities. I met the leadership of major social service organizations, and served as a liaison between Pfizer and needy Southeastern Connecticut residents. Names such as Vernice Cook, Eunice Waller, Ken Crosby, William Garcia, Jean Etienne, and Mrs. Norma Albright were synonymous with social service and community outreach. They worked tirelessly to help the needy in the City of New London. I will always remember my colleagues Ken, Leslie and Ronnie with whom I served on the Board of Thames Valley Council for Community Action.

On several occasions, I was invited to speak to community groups about my experience in cancer research, and I thoroughly enjoyed the meetings I had with church groups, in particular. I also was a regular speaker during Black History Month at The New London Middle School where Bettye Fletcher served as principal. She was a dedicated teacher and administrator. As one of the few African American principals in New London, she radiated a sense of confidence and purpose that I had rarely seen in Connecticut. She and her husband had three sons who were close in age to our daughter Dionne. I got to know the entire Fletcher family very well.

One summer, there was a major story in the local newspaper about the scholastic and athletic achievements of one of Bettye's sons. Alphonse Fletcher or "Buddy" as we called him, had graduated at the top of his class from Waterford High School, and he was also one of the school's outstanding athletes. I thought that "Buddy" would be an excellent candidate for an internship in my laboratory at Pfizer, so I called Bettye and asked if she would agree to such an arrangement, and she was thrilled. Soon after that conversation, "Buddy" joined my group where he worked on an interesting biochemical problem for that entire summer. "Buddy" went on to pursue a bachelors degree at Harvard, and after graduating, wound up as one of the top traders at Kidder Peabody on Wall Street. The company he founded, Fletcher Associates, was considered to be one of the most successful Asset Management companies in New York City in 2009.

Chapter 18

Cloning Genes and Discovering Drugs

In August 1979, my move to Connecticut had profound implications for my career as a scientist. In addition to settling into a new home, I was responsible for establishing a biotechnology laboratory at Pfizer's Groton site. Pfizer Central Research at Groton was the Global Research Headquarters for one of the world's largest pharmaceutical companies. It shared a sprawling, attractive campus with a large manufacturing plant that was located on the bank of the picturesque Thames River. The research campus was a cluster of modern buildings situated in a residential neighborhood complete with golf course and tennis courts. It was a gated campus with guards stationed around the clock at its two major entrances. A freight train line bisected the campus and transported bulk products to and from the large, bustling manufacturing plant. The grounds of the campus were immaculate. Neatly manicured lawns; attractive, colorful shrubbery; and well-paved walkways were everywhere, giving the campus a country club appearance. As I drove into the parking lot on my first day of work, I could not help remembering what Eudine's director told her when she learned that we were moving to Groton, "you're going to Groton to rotten!" When Eudine told me how her director felt about our impending move, I was determined to prove that director wrong.

My work at Rockefeller University, the New York Blood Center, and the John L. Smith Memorial for Cancer Research had prepared me well for what I would be facing in my new position as project leader in the newly established Microbial Genetics Group. The formation of that group was a direct outcome of the recommendations made by the taskforce on which I served.

I was one of two scientists chosen by senior management to form the new group. Our charge was to do everything possible to import recombinant DNA technology into the Central Research Division and to disseminate it throughout the various therapeutic areas. I was permitted to bring only one of my technicians from Maywood with me to Groton. I offered the opportunity to Carla Higdon. She was the first technician assigned to my laboratory when I joined the company at Maywood, New Jersey, and she had worked well with me for the past eight years. My colleague Alan Proctor, a microbiologist who joined the company in the Process Development Group was permitted to bring his two technicians, Greg and Tom, into the group. Together we were a team of five persons.

I initially shared a laboratory space of approximately five hundred square feet with Alan. It was on the first floor in Building-118 where our new program was housed. Alan had a nice office on the front of the building with a large picture window. My office was located within a suite operated by the Laboratory Animal Group. I will always remember Stan Purcell and Walter his able assistant who worked in the offices next to mine. They placed all of the orders for the large animal vivarium and supervised the operation of an extensive network of animal support facilities. I remember taking Dionne and Kevin into work with me to let them see my laboratory and tour the research division. It was around my birthday and they spent lots of time at my desk working on birthday cards for me. I may still have those cards somewhere in my collection of memorabilia.

After my first year at Groton, when two additional laboratory spaces became available, I was assigned my own laboratory, and Dennis, one of the new Ph.D. hires was given the second. The compromise for moving into one of the new laboratories was giving up my nice office for a tiny, windowless room on the interior of the building just off one of the corridors. Having my own laboratory space was much more important to me than having an office with a window, so I cheerfully accepted the new arrangement.

At that time, the Microbial Genetics Group seemed to have an unlimited budget, and we had a green light to hire additional scientists. We were constantly interviewing and hiring new personnel. In addition to Dennis we hired John, Lance, Art, and

Peter. There were exchange visits involving scientists from Pfizer's research facility at Sandwich, England. I remember that Iaian and Eric were valuable additions to our team of scientists. Later, Gaston and Glen transferred from other Groton units to join our group. Needless to say, I was the only African American Ph.D. working at that time in the Drug Discovery Group at the Central Research Division. It was not a diverse environment by any means, and I had to draw on that deep reservoir of self confidence and self-assurance that I had built up during the course of my career.

Looking back, I recall that the only charge that senior management gave our group was to import the new technology into the Central Research Division and to disperse the acquired capabilities across drug discovery groups. We were not given a mandate to do anything else! Alan seemed to be very comfortable with that assignment but I wasn't. After all, I moved from Maywood to Groton after eight years of having successfully managed a highly visible and very successful program. My work at Maywood was focused on studying cancer, and every success I had, helped to expand my understanding of the molecular events associated with cancer causation. I therefore wanted to continue to use my creative energies to address the myriad therapeutic areas that my colleagues at Groton were working on. As a result, I did not want to spend my time working on technology only, instead I envisioned our group playing a more central role in moving the drug discovery agenda forward at a more rapid pace than was possible with the old way of doing things.

During my first year at Groton, I met with experienced scientists like Archie Swindell, and Michael Paige, Malcolm Morville, William Hoffman, Dave Larson (my buddy from Maywood) and Ivan Otterness, and others trying to identify the ideal project. I sought support for epidermal growth factor, vasoactive intestinal protein, platelet derived growth factor, fibroblast growth factor, and several other proteins that were known to be involved in a number of important metabolic pathways. I spent a lot of time in the library perusing recently published articles and collecting detailed information on all potential leads.

My efforts however, failed to elicit any interest from my colleagues. I was told in no uncertain terms that Pfizer was a company that focused on synthetic small molecules in all of its drug discovery initiatives. The ideal drug was always considered to be a small molecule chemical administered once a day, that was orally active and did not cause any major side effects. Proteins were not considered to be ideal drugs because of difficulty with delivery, stability, and cost of production. I was told that I needed to choose a project that was well-aligned with Pfizer's current business interests. It was difficult for me to find a project that satisfied those criteria.

Then one day, purely by accident, I learned that a group called the Enzyme Task Force was planning a meeting at the Groton site. It was a Pfizer group comprising scientists, staffers, and corporate managers from Groton, New York, and Milwaukee Wisconsin. They met on a monthly basis at a different Pfizer location to talk about matters that were relevant to the operation of the company's Chemical Products Division. I was curious to learn about the types of products included in their production portfolios, and soon found out that production and sale of milk clotting enzymes was a major thrust of Pfizer's Milwaukee Operation.

My contact at Groton told me that I should get in touch with Paul Stenke, one of the managers in Milwaukee, if I wanted to obtain additional information about the milk clotting enzymes business. I called Paul and questioned him about the Milwaukee Operation. I specifically asked him about the types of milk-clotting enzymes they produced. I told him that I was planning to contact the Secretary of the Enzyme Task Force, and I queried him about the date of the group's upcoming Groton meeting. What was amazing to me was the speed with which I could gain access to important information within the Pfizer organization. Paul readily provided me with detailed information about the enzymes produced at the Milwaukee site. He talked about the processes involved, and he even offered to give me some samples of his source material. A piece of key information he provided was the name(s) of the vendors he used to obtain the starting material. Paul also provided me with contact information that I sought.

The Secretary of the Task Force was an amiable, attractive lady called Holly Evans. She shared the date of the group's next meeting with me, including the time the meeting was scheduled to begin, as well as the building and room location. She even offered to allocate some time on the agenda for me to make a brief presentation on the new technologies I was involved in developing. That was the break I was seeking. I had finally identified a protein in which Pfizer had significant commercial interest, and was already actively involved in marketing competitively. That seemed like an ideal candidate for a project in our Microbial Genetics Group. A summary report provided by Holly Evans proved to be extremely useful. It listed all of the enzymes currently in use by cheese manufacturers to trigger effective coagulation of milk in the first step of cheese production. I was amazed to learn that some of those enzymes were extracted from fungi! I also learned that Pfizer and other companies even held patents on some of those enzymes. There were several big players involved in producing milk clotting enzymes, and Pfizer was keenly interested in maintaining or improving its market share during what was predicted to be a very difficult time for companies involved in the sale of such products. The standard of the industry was an enzyme called chymosin or rennin. It was extracted from the stomach of un-weaned calves, and its ability to bind and cleave kappa casein, a protein component of whole milk, was well established. Cleavage of kappa casein set up a cascade that resulted in clot formation. The limited digestion of the kappa casein fragments was critical for the production of high quality cheese. Other enzymes were not ideally suited for cheese production because after the initial cleavage of the casein molecule, they continued to digest the smaller fragments. When present in cheese, those small casein fragments produced a bitter taste.

When rennin was used for cheese production, its action on kappa casein was limited, and the final product never had the bitter after taste. I was convinced that rennin was an ideal target for a recombinant DNA project. It was already a product that was being marketed by the company's Chemical Products Division, so the commercial requirement was no longer an issue. Then, it was a protein that was extensively studied, so information on its composition was already available. Finally, because its mechanism of induction was well known, it was quite likely that its messenger RNA would be sufficiently abundant in the calf's stomach to increase the probability of successful isolation.

On November 24, 1980, I wrote and submitted to senior management a formal proposal to clone the gene for bovine rennin into bacterial cells. I told my senior management team that the application of recombinant DNA techniques to cloning genes was already offering new opportunities to study how these genes were regulated. The new technology was also facilitating production of important pharmaceutical, chemical, and agricultural products. I further told them that one protein that represented an ideal target for cloning was the enzyme rennin that is produced by the stomach of the new born calve to help with the digestion of its mother's milk.

I reminded them that rennin was widely known as an enzyme that was almost exclusively used as the major milk-clotting enzyme in commercial cheese production. I pointed out that during the past two decades, substantial shortages of calf stomachs had resulted in the use of rennin substitutes to meet the needs of an expanding cheese industry. I tried to convince them that the most attractive reason for targeting rennin was its known structure. I indicated that I knew almost everything there was to know about the molecule. I had information on its size, where it was produced, how it was activated, and much more. I felt that those features made it most attractive to initiate a project that was directed at cloning the gene. There were other arguments that I used to make my case. I told them that rennin was the predominant enzyme secreted by the young calf to enable it to digest its mother's milk. I specified that during the first four to five months after birth, calves produced rennin almost to the exclusion of other enzymes.

I reasoned that it would be very convenient to isolate the RNA molecules from homogenates of calf stomachs that were responsible for producing rennin. The fact that the complete sequence of the rennin protein was known made it easy to design molecules that could be used as probes to find the rennin gene. The next point I made was that I could use a partially purified preparation of rennin to induce antibodies in rabbits, and I could use the rabbit serum to positively identify bacterial cells that were producing the rennin protein.

I concluded my argument by stating that successful execution of the proposed project could pave the way for developing a recombinant DNA process for rennin production. I predicted that the other anticipated advantages included: a homogeneous product as opposed to the seventy percent purity that was available from conventional methods; lower production costs; and the possibility of producing a kosher product that would not be subject to cyclical shortages.

When I presented those ideas to the members of the Enzyme Task Force at their Groton meeting, you could have heard the proverbial pin drop. There was absolute silence in the room. I was very much aware of the mood of that group. Everyone, without exception, had read the recently published Report on the Milk Coagulant Market. That report discussed markets and market segmentation in the early 1980's. It provided general information on suppliers operating within the market, and it attempted to make realistic projections of future market trends. Of everything projected in that document, what I remember best was the statement that the coagulant market was changing as a result of rennin shortages, new needs of the industry, and changes in consumer preferences for specific cheese varieties. It was therefore projected that the trend to move away from calf rennin to microbial sources of milk coagulants would continue, with those alternate sources sharing over seventy percent of the market by 1982! What if I could pull this off and prove them wrong.

One of the directors in the room who understood the potential of what I was proposing, immediately stated that he would support my project, if only for defensive reasons. All of the funding for that effort would come from Pfizer's New York headquarters. My Groton management was dragged kicking and screaming into supporting the proposed initiative. They would later state that although it was not a sexy project, they were prepared to embrace it because it afforded the division an excellent opportunity to showcase the new and emerging technologies. It was viewed as the perfect demonstration project. Central Research Division was prepared to show the world that it had the capacity to harness the new technology and use it to enhance any area of the company's drug discovery business.

Those sentiments were expressed by my Senior Vice President in a brief memo he wrote to the President of the Division. He simply stated, "...we have identified a project for expression of a mammalian protein of commercial interest–the enzyme rennin. Ken Harewood has developed the proposal prepared in Project Abstract Form... The project has been discussed in principal with U. S. chemicals (Regan) who strongly supports it!"

I launched the project to clone the gene for Bovine Rennin in 1981. My technician and I started out early in the morning with our scalpels, dry ice, and several packages of disposable gloves, and we headed to the slaughterhouse in North Branford, Connecticut. That was where my contact from Milwaukee told me that I could obtain a plentiful supply of fresh calf stomachs.

North Branford was a small town approximately forty-five minutes south of Groton on Interstate-95. The slaughterhouse was in an inconspicuous one-story building that I would never have suspected to be used for that purpose. When I arrived, there was an unmarked truck backed up to the loading dock, but I could not detect any sign of livestock until I entered the building. Once inside, I could see the calves being off loaded and prepared for processing. It was such a well-organized procedure that it was impossible to focus on any single step. Before Carla and I could unpack our supplies, one of the men came to me in the outer room with his outstretched hand in which he held a tiny, pink object. It was a calf stomach.

My first reaction was one of complete surprise. That calf stomach was smaller than I had imagined. It was warm and slippery, and I had considerable difficulty keeping it in my gloved hand. My plan was to remove the lining from the stomach, and rapidly freeze the tissue in dry ice. It turned out to be much more difficult than I had envisioned. I spent the next two hours detaching the linings from numerous stomachs until I felt that we had a sufficient supply of tissue. That day, I found out that a pound of freshly slaughtered veal was less expensive than one of those tiny stomachs. It was almost lunchtime when we left the slaughterhouse and headed back to Groton.

Over the next year and a half, I successfully carried out all of the cloning steps as specified in my proposal. With the able assistance of my technicians Carla and Anjani, I characterized the genetic material that was produced, and completed all of the major objectives of the bovine calf rennin cloning project. I developed a simple method for identifying the different forms of the enzyme, and was able to confirm the sequence of the active and inactive forms of the gene. My experience from Maywood enabled me to design a sensitive immunological assay to detect trace amounts of the cloned protein, and I collaborated with my colleagues in the production group to develop a recombinant DNA process for making large-scale amounts of rennin. It was gratifying to see how effectively the project team method worked. For example, my colleague Art was assigned the task of constructing expression vectors; Glen was asked to develop a synthetic strategy for assembling the entire rennin gene; Keiren worked on a method that employed fluorescence to distinguish between the allelic forms of the protein; and Ting Po optimized the process for its production at plant scale.

On December 1, 1987, Pfizer reported that its first food additive petition involving a fermentation process using a genetically engineered microorganism had been accepted for filing by the U.S. Food and Drug Administration. The petition covered the milk-clotting enzyme rennin. It informed the agency that rennin was the active component of calf rennet, which has long been recognized as the premier milk coagulant used in the manufacture of high quality cheese. It indicated that calf rennet was traditionally obtained by extraction from calf stomachs, which at the time were fluctuating in availability and price. It further noted that the new fermentation process, developed in the company's Central Research Laboratories in Groton, Connecticut was expected to provide the rennin enzyme economically in a consistent, stable and highly pure form. According to the petition, rennin prepared by the new fermentation process was shown to be identical in all respects to the product obtained from calf stomachs. The petition further stated that rennin's efficacy in cheese making was demonstrated repeatedly at plant scale. It indicated that the development of Pfizer's fermentation-produced rennin involved a number of significant technical achievements, including development of a commercially practical process, and synthesis of the nature-identical prorennin gene, a major feat considering its complexity.

The company went on to state that recombinant DNA techniques were used to insert the prorennin gene into a host microorganism, used in the fermentation process. It assured the agency that the microorganism was not present in the final rennin product. Assurance was also given that the company would manufacture rennin under appropriate NIH Guidelines for recombinant DNA research in a new state-of-the-art facility under construction at the company's manufacturing plant in Terre Haute, Indiana. The petition concluded with the company revealing that it would utilize its Diary Products Group that was headquartered in Milwaukee, Wisconsin to manage worldwide marketing of rennin.

In an article published in one of the Research Division's periodicals, I learned how big a deal this really was. The part of the story that really caught my attention was when it was reported that, "meanwhile, painters applied a final coat to the gleaming interior of the new plant... This facility was designed to efficiently produce product in an automated, fully enclosed system, where all process streams are closely monitored to assure product integrity and to minimize, if not completely eliminate, inadvertent losses. As plumbers worked amid the glittering network of stainless steel piping, engineers tested each piece of equipment and instrumentation in almost constant consultation with engineers and designers from Groton and New York's Corporate Engineering Division." That was a description of the new plant that Pfizer built and dedicated to the production of rennin.

There were other articles written about the success of my project, and many of them reflected the optimism that industry analysts shared about the potential of the new gene cloning technology. The article I remember best was one published by U.S. News and World Report. It included a photograph of me holding an X-ray film that displayed a partial sequence of the rennin gene. That was the same photograph that the company placed on display in one of the street level windows at corporate headquarters in midtown Manhattan. I had no idea that my picture was being used as part of a major public relations campaign. Then, one day, Joyce called me from NY to tell me that she was standing at the bus stop outside of Pfizer's Corporate Headquarters waiting for the cross-town bus. As she wiled away the time, she turned to look into the company's product display window, and to her surprise she saw a giant-sized picture of me looking down at her on the sidewalk. She said that she jumped up and down uncontrollably, pointing to the picture, and shouting, "that's my brother, that's my brother!" After regaining her composure, she realized that everyone at the bus stop must have thought that she had lost her mind.

Back in Groton, my technicians and I were beginning to come to grips with the significance of our achievement. We knew that I had taken a bold step when I proposed to clone the rennin gene. Additionally, we were acutely aware of the fact that I had placed the reputation of the Molecular Genetics Group on the line when I promised to develop a process that would yield a commercially-useful product. That was all behind us now. The pressure was off. I had succeeded beyond my wildest dreams. I felt that my colleagues at Groton and elsewhere within the division would be so proud of our breakthrough accomplishment that there would express their appreciation in some tangible way. There were no celebrations, however, just a group picture of the Project Team and an article in the division's monthly publication. I do not remember receiving any congratulatory notes from the leadership within the Central Research Division. I was not even invited to the dedication of the new plant in Indiana, but got to read about it long after it had occurred.

As the spotlight shifted from research and development to the marketing of rennin, I realized that the linkage between my laboratory and the company's first successful recombinant DNA product was waning. I shared that concern with one of my Groton colleagues and he advised me to write a comprehensive review of the rennin project and issue it as a special report. I thought it was a brilliant idea.

The Central Research Division's policy required each investigator to write a report detailing progress on work conducted in his or her laboratory during each quarter of the year. My quarterly report had already been submitted and included highlights of all of my research projects, including the rennin work. My colleague's idea was to submit another report that focused exclusively on rennin.

I spent the next several days assembling that report. Because I was the only one at Groton who had a complete record of the rennin project, I had easy access to all of the key pieces of relevant information. I had invested almost two and a half years in conducting the research. I was the investigator that met with the senior administrators in the Chemical Products and Central Research Divisions. I wrote all of the letters to scientists who had authored publications on rennin, especially in Japan and Denmark. I visited technology transfer offices in Wisconsin with my licensing and development colleague John Wolff. John and I had shared an office while we were in Maywood working as members of the Cancer Research Division. I had taken a short sabbatical from my job in Groton to spend some time at the Massachusetts Institute of Technology in the laboratory of one of our consultants learning how to sequence the rennin gene. After assembling all of the sections, I mailed the final report to key members of the research directorate. As I look back at that period of my Groton experience, I realize that the special report I prepared then, was the most comprehensive document written by anyone on the rennin project. It brought closure to one of the most challenging and rewarding experiences of my entire career at Pfizer.

It is very interesting how quickly reality sets in after a seminal achievement such as the cloning of the rennin gene. With that task completed, project team members would have to move on to new areas of research investigation. It was not difficult for me to meet this challenge. I definitely did not want to lose any of the momentum I had built up since arriving at Groton, so I turned my attention to proteins as potential therapeutants. I felt that I was ready for such a challenge, and I was confident that this would be an appropriate way to deploy the gene cloning technology. I knew that it was very difficult to get buy-in from my colleagues at Groton because the research culture there was dominated by synthetic organic chemists. My most powerful weapon however, was my trusted friend Ron who had wisely advised me to write the interim summary report claiming full ownership of our group's only successful project.

I remember my first meeting with Ron. Keith Jensen had hired him to serve as project leader of the new Groton Tumor Immunology Group. Ron was trained in New York and knew many of the same people that I knew. We shared similar concerns as members of so called minority groups living in communities that were lacking in diversity. Ron's laboratory was down the hall from the Microbial Genetics Group, and I was a regular visitor.

One day soon after Ron arrived in Groton, he and I were going to lunch in the main cafeteria. It was a day when Thanksgiving lunch was being served and there was the usual crush of employees filing into the cafeteria. What happened next was something I could never forget. The security guard whose duty it was to ensure that only Pfizer employees gained entrance to the cafeteria, looked in my direction and demanded to see my ID. At first, I couldn't believe that he was singling me out of that very large crowd of employees. Then it dawned on me that he was really asking me to prove that I was indeed a Groton employee. I was outraged. First, I was walking with Ron a new employee, and I noticed that the security guard was not even interested in checking Ron's ID. Second, I had been at Groton almost seven years when this happened, and could not understand what was motivating this action by the security guard. So I instinctively responded by asking a question. "How do you know who is an employee?" I inquired. "Why are you not asking to see the IDs of anyone else on this line?" In order to let that security guard know how serious I was, I told him that I would report the matter to the Director of Human Resources as soon as I returned to my office. I was vindicated. The Director of Human Resources was quick to repudiate the guard's action, assuring me that he had already transferred him to work on the manufacturing side of the sprawling Groton campus.

Ron fully appreciated the power of the technology that I was practicing, and on a daily basis, he and I perused the scientific literature seeking new opportunities to positively project those unique capabilities. On another occasion, he came to me with what was a very attractive proposal. In his inimitable fashion, he told me that he had just received news of a report that would reveal the entire sequence of a protein called Tissue Plasminogen Activator. Tissue Plasminogen Activator was a highly selective clot-buster protein, and he knew the Belgian scientist who had done the work. Ron felt that this represented the break we were looking for, and suggested that we should immediately develop a proposal to gain senior management support for launching a project.

My response was instantaneous. Here was an opportunity for us to be first in an area that could bring distinction to our division and company. Ron and I collaborated on developing a brilliant proposal. I had learned what was expected from such a proposal based on my experience with rennin, so we did a thorough analysis of the clot-buster market. We knew all of the proteins and their mechanisms of action. Furthermore, we learned that a small biotechnology company in California had an interest in cloning the gene for Tissue Plasminogen Activator.

Senior management was prompt in its response to our proposal. We were asked to meet with two of the Executive Assistants to the President of Central Research. Neither of them was convinced that Tissue Plasminogen Activator could ever become a commercially viable project. They pooh-poohed its action and potential selectivity, and argued strenuously against the claims we made in our proposal. Ron and I were shot down, but we went down fighting. After a heated conference call between the leadership from Groton and our counterparts in Sandwich, England, we knew that senior management would not support our proposal. Ron refused to go down without having the last word. He marshaled all of his creative energies and wrote a blistering rebuttal to all participants expressing his disappointment at their lack of vision! A California biotechnology company went on to successfully clone the gene for Tissue Plasminogen Activator, and that small biotechnology company made a fortune on the product. In the jargon of our business, "we were scooped!"

The rejection of our proposal to clone Tissue Plasminogen Activator meant that synthetic small molecules would continue to dominate our company's drug discovery pipeline, and it was time for me to set my sights on new biological targets, not on new biopharmaceuticals. Based on my interest in cancer research, and my training in biochemistry, I began to re-focus my interest on cancer drug discovery. I knew that senior management was not interested in discovering another cytotoxic compound to treat cancer. Their goal was to discover and develop agents that were highly selective for destroying tumor cells without harming normal cells. That would only be possible if the biological target for such drugs was present in cancer cells and absent from normal cells.

The *ras* family of oncogenes seemed to me to be the perfect target that I could use to launch a project in the cancer drug discovery area. An altered form of the *ras* gene was thought to be involved in the cause of some forms of cancer. I reasoned that if a drug could be developed to target the altered form of *ras* found only in cancer cells and not in normal cells, then I would be well on the way to discovering the elusive magic bullet. I wrote a proposal detailing reasons why *ras* should be considered as a target for cancer drug discovery. It was a very persuasive document, powerful enough to gain senior management support. Even Alan, who by that time had been promoted to Manager of the Molecular Genetics Group was supportive of this effort.

Alan's commitment was amply demonstrated by his willingness to assign Lance, one of our smartest new hires, to work with me on the project. Ron and I negotiated successfully to have the cancer group expanded by one laboratory, mine. In fact, I had already sought support from George who at that time had risen to the position of director within the Division. I asked George if I could move into the wing that the cancer group would occupy. He cautioned me to be patient in my desire to switch groups, but assured me that I could get one of the laboratories in Building-118W that had been designated as the cancer wing.

When I broke the news of the impending move to my technical staff they were delighted. I had spent six years working in the Molecular Genetics Group and was now anxious to use the technology for drug discovery. So I welcomed the move, especially because it meant that I would once again get to work in an area in which I had so much success while in Maywood. So I moved to Building-118W and resumed my work on cancer.

Lance's role was to design a yeast screen, and mine was to construct a mammalian cell model. We were both immensely successful, and within our first year we had developed models that could be placed in use to identify potential anti-cancer agents. Ron and I worked closely during those years to advance the goals of the Groton Cancer Group. We were breaking new ground, and taking on new challenges, but that would not last for very long. Major changes within senior management resulted in significantly different views on how the cancer group should be managed, and before long Ron was packing his bags and heading off to a very attractive position as Assistant Director of a major cancer center in Pittsburg, Pennsylvania.

Following Ron's departure, the Cancer Group never regained its footing as a program destined for great things. Leadership was turned over to Paul, who was a strong proponent of drug screening. He hired his best friend Jim and together they began to radically change the direction of the program. It was not a good time for the Cancer Group. This lack of focus was evidenced by the type of personnel hired and the new partnership arrangements formed. Another shakeup in top leadership placed the Cancer Program under the control of Molecular Genetics. Alan was promoted to director and Ian became manager with responsibility for cancer. This was a completely new assignment for Ian and the learning curve was going to be steep.

One night, as I was thumbing through one of the major scientific journals, I came across an advertisement for a job at City College of New York, my alma mater. The job was for a director of their Center for the Study of the Cellular and Molecular Basis of Development. The deadline for response had already passed. I was so attracted to the job that I called Eudine over to share the information with her. I lamented the fact that I did not have a chance to respond to that advertisement. Eudine immediately told me that I should apply anyway. That turned out to be the best advice she could have given me. I applied for the position as she suggested, and could not believe it when I received a letter from the Dean of Natural Sciences inviting me to the campus for an interview. The Chair of the Biology Department hosted my visit. I made two trips, gave one formal seminar, and met with the deans, the provost, and the president. They all liked me for the position. I received a formal offer from the Dean inviting me to join the Biology Department as a tenured professor and Director of the University's Research Centers in Minority Institutions program.

Chapter 19

Back To Academia

After spending fifteen years in Southeastern Connecticut, it was difficult to even think about returning to New York City. The offer letter from the Dean at City College was real, and it meant that I would have to respond with my decision. By that time both of our children were away at college, and neither of them had ever expressed any desire to return to Southeastern Connecticut. That made it easier for me to contact a real estate agent and begin the process of looking at houses in the tri-state area of New York, New Jersey, and Connecticut.

I could not believe how difficult it was to find a house that we liked. We looked in small and large towns; we even went back to our old neighborhood in Teaneck, New Jersey. We looked at high-rise apartments in Manhattan and New Jersey. One day it dawned on me that I was moving a bit too fast. For the first time I began to think of the offer from City College as providing me with an opportunity to take a year off from Central Research to gain some valuable experience in a highly respected academic institution. After working there for a year, I felt that it would be easier for me to determine whether a move to academia would offer me the opportunity for career advancement that I was seeking. Furthermore, I knew that if I pursued such a strategy, I could take advantage of the company's sabbatical program that permitted senior scientists to take up to a year's leave without interruption of pay or benefits. I was prepared to ask for a year's sabbatical, and I was confident that senior management would approve my request.

Eudine and I prayed in earnest for guidance in this matter. I even confided in some members of Pfizer's senior management to get their perspective on the action I was planning to take. My conversation with the City College Dean did the trick. I remember selling him on the idea of a partnership between the two institutions. I could take on the role of Gene Center Director while retaining my position at Central Research. I agreed to spend four out of five days per week at City College. It was an idea that was attractive to both parties. I drafted a letter detailing the terms and conditions of my yearlong sabbatical, and it was signed by my director. The Dean was thrilled by the prospect of the proposed partnership with Pfizer and approved the arrangement without hesitation.

I moved into a very swank one-bedroom suite on the seventeenth floor of the Corinthian Towers on the eastside of Manhattan. This was advertised as the largest modern apartment complex in the City of Manhattan. It had the appearance of three contiguous piles of casino chips stacked in the configuration of a cloverleaf. That was the same building where my Pfizer colleagues and I stayed when we visited the New York headquarters of the company. I furnished the apartment through a lease arrangement with a furniture rental company that operated out of Westchester, New York. I was able to move in at the beginning of the 1991 academic year. I commuted to Manhattan on Sundays and returned to Niantic on Thursdays. On Fridays I worked at Central Research, caught up with my mail, and tried to stay in touch with what was going on at Pfizer.

The work at City College was both challenging and rewarding. I was immediately thrust into the position of managing a multi-million dollar research center. There was a multi-disciplinary faculty to support, and lots of interactions with the National Institutes of Health. I wrote grant proposals and progress reports, attended program directors' meetings, and managed a complex set of core facilities. I learned how the City University of New York Foundation worked, and I collaborated with the directors of the numerous programs that represented the various schools and colleges at my home campus. I developed close working relationships with the deans and department chairs.

I taught classes at the graduate level and shared my experiences with students and faculty. I enjoyed having the opportunity to provide them with a corporate perspective on science, and I tried to show them how important it was to embrace the project team mode of operation in conducting biomedical research. I helped several minority students launch their careers in science, and I was able to expand the base of support for the center's programs from both government and corporate sources. I must admit that it felt quite strange working with my former mentors, putting the finishing touches on grant applications or making decisions about the type of equipment the center needed in order to keep pace with emerging technologies.

In addition to the rich experiences I gained as the center's director, I benefited tremendously from having the opportunity to live in Manhattan. Eudine and I looked forward to spending the occasional weekend in the city. She would arrive at Pennsylvania Station by Amtrak and we would take a taxicab over to the Corinthian. The entire weekend would involve window shopping on the avenues, lunch at any of the eastside cafes, and routine visits to Broadway to enjoy some of the most spectacular productions. Life in the big city was everything it was advertised to be.

I remember going to the popular World Trade Center restaurant *Windows on the World* with Don who was a Pfizer Vice President and a friend of mine from East Lyme, Connecticut. I did not know then that I would never have another opportunity to visit that iconic eating place. On another occasion I was able to join Joyce at the New York Hilton Hotel to briefly participate in Bill Clinton's campaign for the presidency in 1992. That was the year that the Democratic National Convention was held at Madison Square Garden in New York City, and Joyce was actively working in support of women's causes.

As Director of City College's Center for the Cellular and Molecular Basis of Development, I traveled to Bethesda, Maryland frequently and I attended numerous meetings to promote the center's programs. The most interesting meeting I participated in that year was a program directors' retreat that was held in Honolulu and hosted by the University of Hawaii Campus at Manoa. It was a well-organized meeting at which I got my first chance to meet the administrator of the Research Centers in Minority Institutions (RCMI) Program. He was an affable, white-haired middle-aged African American widely known for his direct, no-nonsense style of communicating. I distinctly remember the Dean introducing us and stating his reason for requesting the opportunity to meet with the RCMI Administrator to discuss some programmatic issues. Rather than responding directly to the Dean, he simply looked at me and stated, "you are the director of this program," and then he asked, "what are your priorities?" From that moment I knew that he expected me to be the major spokesperson for the City College Center.

I also met the directors from the other RCMI programs that were located at some of the large Historically Black Colleges and Universities (HBCUs). It was an excellent meeting for networking at which we sought solutions for the myriad challenges facing HBCUs and other minority serving institutions. It was at that meeting in Honolulu that the Dean and I pledged to host the next Directors' Meeting at City College. There was considerable support for our proposal. Everyone thought of New York City as the ideal venue for such a meeting. In addition to the working sessions that we were required to schedule, there would be ample opportunity for the directors to enjoy the City of Manhattan. The Sociology Department collaborated with the Dean and me in organizing and hosting the meeting at City College. It provided us with an opportunity to showcase our research programs, and elevate the image of the institution as a national model for conducting high-quality research in the biomedical sciences.

As Director of the City College Center, I organized field trips to the Merck campus in Rahway, New Jersey, and to Pfizer's Central Research Division in Groton, Connecticut. My lectures to the faculty and students always sought to emphasize the fact that science is a business, and that the pharmaceutical drug discovery process best reflects how the different disciplines of science collaborate to address a common problem. That year, I arranged a special seminar series at City College that brought many of my Groton colleagues to the campus to talk about their research and the impact their work would have on human and animal health.

At the end of the year I knew that it was time for me to return to Pfizer. I learned a lot about being a tenured professor and senior administrator at a major academic institution. I was able to develop valuable grant writing skills, and I networked extensively with administrators at the National Institutes of Health and other academic institutions. Most important, I was able to establish a partnership between Pfizer and City College that would profoundly impact student training long after my service as center director ended. I was proud of what I had accomplished on my year's sabbatical. It was a sad day when I turned in my keys to the concierge at the Corinthian, and when I said goodbye to my colleagues at City College to return to Niantic and Pfizer.

During the last four years that I spent in the Central Research Division of Pfizer, I managed to persuade the leadership there to allocate a fund in the amount of $200,000 that I used to launch a minority student training initiative. I always had a passion for minority student training, and was able to make a real difference quite early in my career.

It was at an American Society of Biochemistry Meeting at Atlantic City, New Jersey that I made my first major commitment to minority training. I had seen a meeting of the Associations' Minority Affairs Committee listed in the program, and out of sheer curiosity I thought that I would attend. On the day of that meeting, I entered the small salon expecting to see a room full of minority scientists. Instead I saw more white scientists in that room than black scientists. Everyone however, seemed totally convinced that there was a problem with attracting minorities to science, and wanted to contribute time and effort to rectify the problem. The chairperson of the session was a middle aged African American scientist with a very distinguished persona. His baritone voice and the manner in which he spoke identified him as a man of letters, a real scholar. At that time, I did not know that I was in the presence of Dr. Harold Amos, Chair of the Department of Microbiology and Molecular Genetics at Harvard University. He held the distinction of being the first African American to head a department at Harvard Medical School. He later served as Chair of the Division of Medical Sciences there. He remained a member of the faculty at Harvard Medical School for almost fifty years. Dr. Amos became one of my role models from the date of our first meeting, and he remained a major mentor and advisor until his death in 2003.

At that meeting in 1971, Dr. Amos was trying to identify scientists who were interested in joining what he called "the Lecturer-Recruiter Program." It was an initiative that sought to link research-active scientists with students and faculty at predominantly minority institutions. All he needed was contact information from scientists interested in participating in the program, and he sent those names along with the investigators' areas of specialization to administrators at targeted minority institutions. Several white scientists expressed a strong desire to participate in the program and quickly signed up. I was one of the black scientists who saw that as a real opportunity to make a difference.

At that time, I did not know how deeply I would become involved in the work of that committee, and the satisfaction I would derive from contributing to such a worthy cause. The first minority institution I visited was Kentucky State University in Frankfort, Kentucky. Dr. Gertrude Ridgel, Chairperson of the Biology Department had selected my name from the list she received from Dr. Amos. She wrote me a very nice letter inviting me to her campus. I accepted her invitation, and prepared for my trip to Frankfort. I took a flight from Newark, New Jersey to Louisville Kentucky, and then I traveled from Louisville to Frankfort by taxi.

The trip from Newark was routine, and I arrived at the Louisville airport on schedule. It was a small airport with no jet bridges. The small aircraft pulled up approximately one hundred yards from the terminal and we were asked to disembark and select our luggage from the cluster of bags that was off-loaded onto the tarmac beside the aircraft.

Once outside the terminal, I noticed that a line had already formed, and a stocky cop wearing a broad-rimmed felt hat with a leather hatband and chinstrap was controlling the flow of traffic. He had a pock-marked, reddish face, and deep southern drawl, and was clearly demonstrating that he was in control of that entire space. I joined the line behind a very tall, young, black man. The line inched forward slowly until it was soon our turn. "Where are you two boys going?" the rotund cop asked disparagingly? Under other circumstances, I would have been insulted to be referred to as a "boy," but in Lexington, Kentucky in 1975, I was very careful not to reveal any negative emotions.

We responded in unison, "Frankfort!" A sharp whistle from the cop signaled our taxi driver, and within minutes the tall young man and I were sharing a ride to Frankfort. My student companion was heading back to the campus of Kentucky State University, and I was going to the Holiday Inn to spend the night.

My visit to Kentucky State was rewarding in many different ways. It was there that I learned how insidious the separation of the black and white races was in the South. I was told that Kentucky State University was a predominantly black school during the day and a predominantly white school at night. I also learned that the university was chartered in the late 1880s as the State Normal School for Colored Persons. It was Kentucky's second state supported institution of higher learning. In 1890 it became a Land Grant College, and in 1902, the name was changed to Kentucky Normal and Industrial Institute for Colored Persons. The institution underwent three additional name changes before becoming Kentucky State University in 1972. That was only three years before my visit.

From my conversations with students and faculty, I was told that, due to a lack of critical resources, the institution emphasized teaching over research. On the first day of my visit, I gave a formal lecture to a large gathering of students and faculty. I talked about my research program at Pfizer, and I told them that there was a possibility that human cancer could be caused by a virus. On the second day, I got an opportunity to interact informally with faculty and students. Everyone was fascinated by my work, and I remember the students being intensely curious about my experience as a research scientist at a major pharmaceutical company. Several of them confessed to me that I was the first black biochemist they had ever met!

At lunchtime, Dr. Ridgel took me to a local restaurant in the city where I had my first taste of catfish. After lunch, she was very generous with her time, showing me sections of the city and the campus. I would later find out that she was so impressed with my work at Pfizer, that she nominated me for an award at the upcoming annual meeting of the National Consortium for Black Professional Development.

Three months later, I was on a plane heading to Chicago to deliver a talk to conferees who had assembled from all across the nation. At the conclusion of my presentation, the meeting organizers presented me with a plaque for outstanding contributions to the Health Professions.

I visited several other HBCUs as a member of Dr. Amos' Lecturer-Recruiter Program, and those trips were beneficial to the student attendees as well as to me. My passionate advocacy for a Minority Undergraduate Training Program at Pfizer was a direct result of the experience I gained from the Lecturer-Recruiter Program. I submitted my request to the Human Resources Director who liked the idea so much that he set aside $200,000 from his own budget to support the program.

As Manager of the Pfizer Central Research Minority Undergraduate Program and as the Division's Liaison to Minority Institutions, I traveled all across the United States, establishing relationships with faculties and administrators that were committed to transforming science education at their campuses. I remember visiting Hampton, Morehouse, Morgan State, Meharry, North Carolina A&T State, Xavier, Norfolk State, Clark Atlanta, Morris Brown, and the University of Texas at San Antonio. I also used funds from my program to forge strategic partnerships with Hampton, Howard, North Carolina A&T, Morgan State, Meharry, Morehouse, Clark Atlanta, Morris Brown, Elizabeth City State, Florida A&M, and the University of Texas at San Antonio.

One major spin-off from the strategic partnerships initiative that I started was the beginning of Pfizer's first Minority Undergraduate Summer Internship Program at the Central Research Division. That program brought an average of twelve minority undergraduates to our Groton campus annually to conduct mentored, hypothesis-driven research with Pfizer scientists. I also became Pfizer's representative on the Board of the National Consortium for Black Professional Development, headquartered in Louisville, Kentucky, and served as an active member of Pfizer's "Science and Math are Really Terrific (SMART)" Program. SMART was established to support middle school students and their teachers. Pfizer scientists served as "Liaisons" to middle schools in Southeastern Connecticut. I was assigned as the Pfizer "Liaison" to the New London Middle School.

My work with students was so satisfying that once again, I began to seriously consider returning to academia. This time, it would be a permanent move that took me into a completely different world. A world in which I was able to make many lifelong friends, and attract a large number of undergraduate and graduate students to careers in the biological sciences and biotechnology.

While I was a research scientist at Pfizer, I made several trips to Florida A & M University in Tallahassee. Although I liked the university, I never thought of that institution as a place where I would one day want to hold a faculty position. I was in a relatively enviable position when I explored the option of moving to Florida A& M University. I still had my full time job at Groton. I also had a tenured faculty position at City College that I could return to if I so desired. Additionally, Pfizer's very generous retirement policy would have allowed me to take early retirement after twenty years of continuous service.

I had also considered the possibility of returning to Barbados to teach at the Cave Hill Campus of the University of the West Indies. After spending more than thirty years in the U.S., I was no longer upset by the way I had been treated by the Barbados Ministry of Education when I sought their help to get my student visa three decades earlier. Moreover, the Cave Hill Campus was relatively new, and I was confident that I could make a difference as a member of the faculty at that institution. Eudine was not impressed when I talked about a possible return to Barbados. We had too much invested in family, especially our own children, to leave the U.S. at that time. She was acutely aware of the possibility that almost anytime one or both of our children would meet their better half and settle down in the U.S. to raise a family.

With Cave Hill out of contention, Florida A&M University began to look like a reasonably attractive option for a move. After gaining Eudine's support, I began to explore the possibility of joining the academic team at Florida A&M University. I placed a call to the Dean of the College of Arts and Science and talked to him about my desire to seek a faculty position in the Biology Department. He was amused by my expression of interest in joining the faculty, and could not believe that I was serious. He even said that the university would not be able to meet my salary expectations. I expended much effort trying to convince him that salary was not my highest priority in seeking a position there. I informed him of my intention to take early retirement from Pfizer, and of the fact that I was eligible to participate in the company's retirement program.

When the Dean finally realized how serious I was about joining the faculty at Florida A&M University, he agreed to discuss the matter with the president. President Humphries was a very charismatic individual. At close to seven feet tall, his very imposing figure cast a huge shadow across the entire campus. I had a great deal of respect for him, and that was a major reason for my strong desire to become a member of his team. Upon learning of my interest in moving from Pfizer to Florida A&M University, he invited me to Tallahassee for a face-to-face meeting. We spent most of the time in that meeting talking about the unique role HBCUs played in the education of black youth. He was particularly interested in extending that role to the sciences. He told me that he had obtained his Ph.D. degree in chemistry from Pittsburg University. While a student there, he had the unique opportunity of working at Pfizer's Groton Plant as a summer intern. It was obvious to me from the way his eyes lit up as he spoke about that experience, that he had benefited immensely from being a Pfizer summer intern. Our meeting concluded with him assuring me that he would support my candidacy for the faculty position that I was seeking.

My next telephone conversation with the dean was businesslike, and I could sense that he was genuinely interested in my candidacy. He told me that he wanted me to return to campus for a formal interview. He further informed me that he had made arrangements for me to meet with key members of the faculty and administration. On the day of my interview, as I toured the campus after an exhaustive schedule of meetings, I realized that Florida A&M Alumni held most of the top administrative positions at that institution. Before I left the campus for my flight back to Connecticut, I met with the dean to ensure that we had satisfactorily completed the negotiation process. When I received Florida A&M University's formal offer of a tenured professorship in the Biology Department, it was not difficult for me to accept the position without reservation.

The day I left Niantic in August 1994 was a day that I will not forget for as long as I live. Eudine and I had gone to the Crystal Mall on the previous weekend to purchase a cell phone. Cell phones were just beginning to become available in Southeastern Connecticut. There were not many choices then, so I bought what was called a bag phone. I went about the task of planning for the trip to Tallahassee in a very organized fashion. I prepared a check list, and I packed a suitcase with all of the essentials for my long road trip to Florida. Because I needed to be at Florida A&M University in time for the beginning of the fall semester, Eudine and I agreed that I would travel to Tallahassee alone. The plan was for her to remain in Niantic to wrap up her work at the Mall, and coordinate the sale of our home with the real estate agent.

It was a calm, clear New England morning in August 1994. I loaded my 1987 beige Honda Accord with a large suitcase and other personal effects and began the first leg of my trip to Tallahassee. I carefully selected what I thought I would need to tide me through at least two months of isolation from my main base of support. Eudine and I embraced in much the same way that we had done prior to me leaving on one of my routine business trips. Neither of us wanted to admit that the trip I was about to take was vastly different from any of my previous business trips. We acknowledged that difference exclusively through our non-verbal communications. I can still see her standing behind the storm door of the family room as I backed the car out of the long driveway. I could feel my heart getting heavier and heavier when I rounded the corner and our home receded into the background.

The route I chose that day took me south on Interstate-95, across the George Washington Bridge in northern Manhattan and south on the New Jersey Turnpike. After crossing the Delaware Memorial Bridge, I continued south on Interstate-95 through Maryland to Virginia where I picked up Interstate-85 just south of Richmond. I stopped in Durham, North Carolina to spend the night at Peggy's home. Peggy invited a few of her friends over that evening, and we ate, drank, and generally had a good time. It was a most effective way to keep me from focusing on the second leg of my trip to Tallahassee.

The next day I was on my way again heading south towards Atlanta, Georgia. At Atlanta, I picked up Interstate-75 south that took me through Macon, Cordele, and Tifton Georgia. At Tifton my route took me onto State Road-319, which was the most difficult segment of the trip. I was traveling across rural Georgia through small, sparsely populated towns like Moultrie and Thomasville. For the first time I felt a real sense of isolation from family and past. There was an uncertainty in the air that was palpable. One half of me remained convinced that I was heading south to begin a new and exciting chapter in my life. The other half of me, after reflecting on what I was really doing, was incredibly apprehensive about the wisdom of the decision I had made. I was acutely aware, however, that it was much too late to alter the course of the action I had already taken. Those conflicted thoughts left me even more unsettled as I entered a cell phone-silent area of rural Georgia.

Up until the time I reached Augusta, Georgia, I was able to keep my promise to Eudine that I would call her every hour on the hour. Those conversations were very important to me, as they reconnected me to my base of strength. She was the one person in the world who understood what I was doing and why I was doing it. My need for that reassurance increased dramatically as I headed further south. After what seemed like an eternity, Tallahassee loomed on the horizon as dusk approached. I entered the city limits tentatively, hoping that I could postpone the inevitable–checking in to the extended stay hotel that would become my temporary residence in Tallahassee. I was able to maintain my composure as I pulled into the parking lot and eased my car into the space that was closest to the management office. The reservations clerk was expecting me, and check-in was swift and painless.

I sensed a deep feeling of anxiety after I moved all of my belongings into the one room, first floor suite and closed the door. The silence was unnerving! There was a rush of emotions. I thought of Pfizer, Niantic, separation from family and friends. I felt as though I was a stranger in a strange land. I was really not sure that I would be able to adjust. Those fears were assuaged when I called Eudine to let her know that I had arrived safely and that I was beginning the process of settling in. Practical thoughts flooded my mind. They ranged from questions such as what would I eat? Where would I go to wash my clothes? To whom would I turn if I really needed help?

Chapter 20

Making A Difference

Somehow I survived that night and awoke the next morning prepared for my first day on my new job as Professor of Biology at Florida A&M University. When I arrived on campus I had a strange feeling that I was going to be challenged in ways that I had never been challenged before. My first encounter with that reality came as I pulled my car into one of the large parking lots on the main campus. It was obvious to me that this was going to be a hostile environment for new faculty members. Every parking space had a sign posted to indicate that it was reserved for some upstanding member of the university community. Special decals were required for anyone who wanted to park in those spaces. I couldn't believe that there were no signs that indicated where it was safe for a new faculty member to park. To make matters worse, I had no idea where to go to find out how I could obtain a decal that would enable me to park within easy walking distance of the Biology Department.

I thought of how much easier it would have been if someone had taken the time to send me a survival kit to help me negotiate the obstacles I would face during my first day on the job. There was no information desk, no human resources office to consult, nothing but the threat of having my car towed if I left it in the wrong place. I was angry with myself for being there, and I remember feeling like turning around and driving back to Niantic. I realized however, that circumstances would not have allowed me to consider a return to Connecticut as a serious option. I was eventually able to get the parking problem resolved, and soon was on my way to officially join the faculty of biology.

The Biology Department was housed on two floors in Jones Hall–one of the grand old buildings on the Florida A&M campus.

In 1994, there were twelve regular faculty members in the department, ten of them held the terminal degree. There were six hundred majors with an ethnic distribution of ninety-one percent African American; seven percent Caucasian; one percent Asian; and one percent Hispanic American. Those students could choose between five-degree tracks that led to the baccalaureate degree. They included: BS in Biology; BS in Pre-Medicine and Pre-Dentistry; BS in Teacher Certification: BS in Molecular Biology; and BA in Biology. The general education sequence for the first two years was the same for all five tracks, however, requirements varied as students transitioned into their junior and senior years.

The department also offered a master's degree program. That program was launched in the fall of 1990 and was designed to develop competencies in teaching as well as research. The four areas of specialization for the master's degree were Cell and Molecular Biology; Physiology; Ecological Science; and an interdisciplinary program in Space Life Sciences.

The Department of Chemistry occupied the third and fourth floors of Jones Hall and offered programs of study leading to the BS and MS degrees. It had nine full-time faculty members. All of them held the Ph.D. degree in chemistry and taught at the undergraduate and graduate levels. Five of them were research-active, providing thesis research support for graduate students as well as research experiences for undergraduate majors. Faculty specialties included biochemistry, synthetic organic chemistry, and physical chemistry. There were ninety-six undergraduate majors and sixteen graduate students in the department.

At the undergraduate level, chemistry majors could choose from one of four baccalaureate degree programs. These included pre-medicine, pre-dentistry, pre-veterinary medicine, and molecular chemistry.

At the graduate level, students were able to obtain the MS degree in chemistry, after completing thesis research in any of the traditional areas of chemistry. The graduate program also provided options for students to become trained for research careers in industry or for teaching at the community college or university.

Check-in at the Biology Department was a far cry from what happened when I checked into the extended stay hotel. The office was on the first floor. It was a small, unpretentious space that was occupied by the chairman and the department's only secretary. As I entered the door, I was greeted by the secretary. She was a young African American woman, who, from her tough exterior, seemed battle weary from having to counsel the endless procession of students that sought her support. She also had to deal with a significant number of disgruntled parents who kept the department's single telephone line busy all of the time. And she routinely had to assist the faculty who came to the office to pick up their mail or to search for classroom supplies.

After a brief meeting with the chairman, I was escorted to my office. The faculty occupied a large room across the hallway from the chairman's office. I noticed that the door to the faculty offices was secured by two locks. The room was divided into multiple cubicles. The carpet on the floor was worn and water-stained. It looked like it had been installed years ago. The high humidity level of the Tallahassee area had taken its toll on that carpet, and it emitted a musty, moldy odor that made the air difficult for me to breathe.

My cubicle had a beat-up wooden desk that the department's assistant had recovered from surplus storage. He also retrieved an old swivel chair from surplus storage that he saved in anticipation of my arrival. There was no telephone, no computer, not even a book shelf to store anything. I had been warned by a senior faculty member in the department when I first visited the campus, that I had no idea what I was getting into by accepting the offer from Florida A&M University, but I never imagined that it would have been that bad. I sat quietly at my desk and surveyed the space. The ceilings were warped and water-stained, appearing likely to collapse at any moment.

I still cannot believe that on the first day of my arrival at Florida A&M University, I would have been asked to teach a class! Thank God I did not need any time to prepare to teach Molecular and Cell Biology. Shortly after checking in with the chairman, I was given a copy of the official text for the course, and told that the students were in the second floor classroom awaiting my arrival. My years of working as a biochemist, and my familiarity with the theory and practice of modern biology had prepared me well for such a challenge.

I began that first lecture by asking the students if they knew anything about how a molecular biologist could earn a living in the City of Tallahassee. I urged them to imagine that they had already completed a degree in molecular biology, and then I challenged them to think about how they could use such training to be gainfully employed. The key question I asked was, "where would you be going to work this morning if you were an expert molecular biologist?" It definitely caused them to come to grips with how little they knew about the practical ways in which they could apply their classroom training in the real world of work. Having the opportunity to interact with students on my first day at work was all I needed to be convinced that I had made the right decision to return to academia.

Florida A&M University had done an outstanding job of attracting black students from all across the U.S. There were students from as far away as Alaska. Many of them were National Merit Scholars, attracted to the campus by the generous packages that the president offered. I felt like I was in a gold mine, and I wanted to gather as many of those precious nuggets as I could. When I look back on my tenure at Florida A&M University and the different programs that I initiated there, nothing stands out more prominently than the work I did to establish the University's first Howard Hughes Undergraduate Training Program in the Biological Sciences.

Shortly after arriving on campus, I realized that I could use my extensive experience as a biochemist and molecular geneticist to make a difference in the lives of the biology and chemistry majors. Highest on my agenda was a desire to work with the faculty to strengthen the science curriculum, and to garner the support necessary to develop a competitive undergraduate research program in the biological sciences. The Howard Hughes Medical Institute afforded me the opportunity to accomplish both of these objectives.

For several years, Florida A&M University had been invited by the Howard Hughes Medical Institute to compete for funding to strengthen and expand its undergraduate science program. In

1995, not long after I joined the faculty, I learned that the university had not been successful in any of its previous efforts to procure funding from that prestigious institute. That year, when the Director of the University's Office Of Sponsored Research received "the request for proposal" from the Howard Hughes Medical Institute, he asked me to serve as chairman of a planning committee and principal investigator of the grant application. I was confident that I could assist with developing a competitive proposal. The reason for my optimism had much to do with the research and administrative experiences I gained at Pfizer and City College. I had designed and implemented a successful undergraduate summer research internship program, and I had established a number of strategic partnerships with universities that enabled Pfizer to recruit some of the brightest and best students. I had also managed a major research institute at one of New York City's flagship institutions.

Drawing on that record, I drafted the framework for the grant that I proposed to submit to the Howard Hughes Medical Institute. I entitled the application "Florida A&M University Access to Science and Technology" or the FAST Program. I indicated that FAST would seek to enhance the quality of undergraduate programs in biology and other scientific disciplines as they related to biology. I pointed out that FAST would place significant emphasis on recruiting high school seniors, community college graduates and freshman undergraduates. I reasoned that this was the most effective way for the university to attract minority students to careers in the biological sciences. I identified that component of the program as the Pre-college Intervention Initiative. It was designed to expose high school seniors to college level science; encourage community college students to select science as a career path; and offer a subgroup of both sets of students an opportunity to have a laboratory research experience with a research-active faculty member.

I also pledged that if funded, FAST would sponsor career development workshops, small group study sessions, and special courses for freshmen students. Additionally, I stressed the importance of developing an intramural Summer Research Fellowship Program that permitted students at all classifications to work in the laboratory of a research-active faculty mentor. I also promised that FAST would work diligently to develop strategic partnerships with industry.

I included a parallel effort in the application that was directed at creating a biotechnology core laboratory within the Biology Department. I knew that such an initiative would require modification of one of the teaching laboratories, and I was confident that any improvement of the existing infrastructure would positively impact student training. I also requested funding to support the recruitment of an additional research-active faculty member. I envisioned that new faculty hires would help to broaden the scientific expertise of the Biology and Chemistry Departments. I was convinced that this could: stimulate collaborations across departments and disciplines: provide the necessary impetus for new course development; create additional opportunities for student participation in research; and enable the administration to increase the release time allocation for research-active faculty.

I specifically proposed to invite a cohort of the incoming freshman class to participate in a five-week summer enrichment program. Faculty from the Biology, Chemistry, Physics and Mathematics Departments would assist with engaging the students in coursework, seminars, special projects, library/study periods, field trips and other science-related activities. I wanted it to be a residency program that would involve the students in coursework as well as organized research.

I proposed to organize field trips to the Institute for Molecular Biophysics at Florida State University; the National High Magnetic Field Laboratory located at Innovation Park in Tallahassee; and the Biotechnology Center at the University of Florida. I also arranged for evening and weekend sessions so that students could use the library and participate in study groups. I made arrangements to have some of the scheduled activities coincide with events sponsored by the Florida/Georgia Alliance For Minority Participation, a highly successful program directed by one of my colleagues in the Biology Department.

I included a freshmen enrichment component in the proposal in order to stimulate student interest in choosing a science discipline for their major. It was designed to provide first year students with a framework of support that would facilitate cooperative learning. Program staff and faculty mentors were expected to keep those students fully informed of the academic program path they had chosen and the support mechanism available to help them cope with the demands of the freshman year. Tutorials and small group study sessions would be arranged to assist them in making the transition from high school to college. I arranged for all members of the freshmen class to be assigned a faculty mentor and a peer mentor. Weekly meetings between first year students and their faculty mentors were structured to enable those students to discuss progress in academic areas and identify potential issues that could adversely impact their performance. Faculty mentors were expected to help students establish goals and timelines, and review progress towards achieving those goals. Peer mentors would be selected from upper class students who had successfully completed a similar process. Each peer mentor would be responsible for a maximum of two to three students.

The sophomore through senior year intervention components of the program would require faculty advisors and program mentors to rigorously monitor the progress of sophomores, juniors and seniors to ensure that curriculum objectives were completed within projected timelines and that students were maximally utilizing the research-related resources provided by FAST.

The final draft of the FAST application was favorably reviewed by the Howard Hughes Medical Institute's Office of Grants and Special Programs. I received funding for all components of the program, and had no problem attracting the first cohort of students for training in the summer of 1996. Research-active faculty from the College of Pharmacy, and the Biology and Chemistry Departments generously agreed to serve as mentors, and I hired a couple of coordinators to assist me with program implementation.

The Mathematics and English Departments were particularly helpful in providing access to their well-organized summer courses. I couldn't help commending those dedicated faculty mentors for their willingness to sacrifice so much of their valuable time to such a worthy cause. HBCUs have always been branded as institutions that have traditionally served as nurturing environments for their students, particularly those from under-represented minority groups. I was beginning to learn first hand why these universities have earned such a reputation.

Prior to launching the Summer Enrichment Program, I had given little thought to what I would do to keep the students engaged on Saturdays and Sundays when there were no classes scheduled. Movies, pizza, and visits to the malls were thought to be reasonable options, provided that proper precautions were taken to ensure that every student would return to the dorm safely.

The day the program was officially started, I learned that it was impossible to think of everything that could go wrong. After checking in the student participants, I discovered that one of them was disabled. He had a serious kidney ailment and needed to make periodic visits to the hospital for dialysis. I was amazed that our Program Coordinator did not even complain about the extra time she had to spend going back and fourth to the hospital with that student, sometimes in the middle of the night.

For me, the most exciting part of the summer experience for those students was their participation in structured research activities. Each student was paired with a Florida A&M University mentor, and was required to pursue an hypothesis-driven research project. At the end of the internship, each trainee was asked to present his/her findings at a formal meeting attended by members of their family, faculty, and their peers. I arranged to videotape those sessions. The students were simply magnificent! The talent they displayed was unimaginable. It convinced me that it was right for me to cling to the belief that minority students could be attracted to science if provided with the right exposures.

That evening after the program concluded, Eudine and I drove over to campus and waited outside the dorm to ensure that every student had signed out and was picked up by a relative. We returned home exhausted but satisfied. Around eleven o'clock that night the telephone rang, and the female voice on the other end did not hesitate to let me know that she was upset. "Dr. Harewood," she said, "where is my daughter?" I could not believe what I was hearing. "I am here in Atlanta at a friend's house, and I have not heard from my daughter yet." I immediately panicked. I was sure that I had checked the roster at the dorm and knew that every student had been picked up. I was now wondering if someone had played a trick on us by posing as the student's parent when in fact that wasn't the case. All sorts of thoughts raced through my mind.

Eudine was listening to this exchange and she began to hyperventilate. "What could have happened to that student?" she asked, "do you have the Program Coordinator's number? Call her right away!" I could not believe that I would have been able to reach the coordinator at that late hour, but when I heard her voice I was somewhat relieved. I told her as calmly as I could that I had received a call from an irate parent inquiring about her daughter, and I asked her if she knew what had happened to that student. "Oh," she replied, "she is spending the night at my home." Those were the most comforting words I had heard for that entire day. What seemed like a nightmarish event ended with a very sober admission from the coordinator that she was still on the job hours after the program had officially ended.

Our Academic Year Student Support Program was equally successful. I recruited fourteen student participants, and matched each of them with a Florida A&M University faculty mentor. Most of the mentors I selected were from the School of Pharmacy because the majority of research-active scientists held their appointments in that college. I was able to negotiate shared space in an old trailer located on the east end of campus close to the Environmental Science Program's temporary facility. There were two additional programs in our trailer, the Minority Access to Research Careers program, and another program run by a retired Florida A&M University administrator. Access to the trailer was through a low-lying patch of grass where water would accumulate, transforming that narrow walkway into a muddy mess every time it rained. I never let the venue get in the way of effective program implementation.

I assembled my tutoring team of students in one of the three rooms assigned to the FAST Program, and installed a bank of Macintosh computers into what would become the computer laboratory. I hired four undergraduates, Mohammed

Azim and Yolanda Hawkins served as tutors, and Jamal Robinson and Sabrina Suber served as Program Office Assistants. Eudine agreed to help me run the office and manage all fiscal matters.

My weekly meetings with the students helped to keep the lines of communication between my office and the undergraduate trainees wide open. The students and mentors attended those meetings on a regular basis, and contributed constructively to the discussion. I was convinced that I had the full support of the participating faculty, and remained confident in my ability to meet all expectations.

It was now two years since I left the security of my corporate job to take on the challenge of preparing students from under-represented minority groups for careers in science. I was pleased with the progress that I made in that short period of time. The weekly seminar that was held in the very expansive Lee Hall Auditorium was attracting a very distinguished group of speakers from across the country. I was purposefully including scientists from the major pharmaceutical companies in the seminar schedule to constantly remind students that science was a business.

I learned from the Dean of Florida A&M's successful School of Business how she motivated students to attend the school's weekly seminar sessions. Gentle coercion always worked. The tactic I employed was to have each student present a three-by-five card with his/her name and seat assignment to the Program Coordinator as he/she entered the auditorium. Taking note of empty seats and calling students into the office to let them know that their absence was recorded, always convinced them that we were monitoring their attendance. They knew that failure to adequately justify their absence would have negative consequences on their status within the program. Those and other actions were extremely effective in helping to change the culture. Students were beginning to engage with the visiting scientists, and our guests were also realizing that Florida A&M University students were as talented as students at any majority institution, and were poised to become major contributors to the world of science.

Many students benefited from the FAST Program and went on to achieve great things academically and otherwise. In their professional lives they are now giving back to their communities as research scientists, physicians, community workers, teachers, and professors.

In the summer of 1994, soon after my arrival at Florida A&M University, I met a colleague from the School of Pharmacy. I had worked long and hard trying to persuade the Chair of the Biology Department to provide me with wet laboratory space so that I could begin my research program. I brought a sizable grant from Pfizer to Florida A&M University to support a number of student training initiatives. That plan had to be placed on hold because the department was unable to assign me adequate laboratory space. I took my case to the Dean of the College of Arts and Sciences and to the Provost without much success. Then, the Chair of Biology informed me that he was in the process of cutting a deal with a member of the faculty. The deal involved having the faculty member give up the laboratory that he was using as an office in exchange for a new office when ongoing renovations to the building were completed. The deal worked, and I finally had the type of space I needed to launch my research program.

I then had to deal with the reality of trying to purchase equipment and supplies for my laboratory. I soon found out that the department was not organized to support such activities. The paperwork was overwhelming. The requirement for multiple signatures was unbelievable, and to obtain those signatures I had to take the documents to administrators' offices and wait for them to be signed. Sometimes I had to make several trips across campus in a single week! I suffered silently until one day as I was exiting the laboratory to go home, I came face to face with a faculty member who was locking the door to the laboratory just across the hall from where I was standing. We greeted each other with the usual handshake and when he stated his name I knew right away that he was Jamaican.

He told me of his struggle to get laboratory space for his research program. He had developed a rodent model for Parkinson's disease and was making significant progress in identifying key biomarkers associated with the development of that debilitating condition. It was a powerfully persuasive story the way he told it. With two major grants and a highly successful program, he was still unable to convince his administration in the School of Pharmacy to assign him adequate space.

We bonded quickly, sharing stories and pledging to help each other work through the logistical nightmare that we were facing. That weekend, I joined my colleague and his family for lunch. They had recently moved to Tallahassee, and like me, they were busy trying to learn their way around town. They were a major resource to me during the first three months I spent in Tallahassee.

Chapter 21

Tallahassee Lassie

In October of 1994, I purchased a one-way ticket back to Niantic. Our real estate broker and neighbor had finally identified a buyer for our home and I needed to be back in Niantic for the scheduled closing date. Over the three months that I was away in Tallahassee, Eudine did an incredible job of juggling the demands of her work and her commitment to the real estate broker. Finally, we had an attractive offer in hand and did not want to waste any time before closing the deal. I was also looking forward to the move to our new home in Tallahassee.

The closing was uneventful, and I was on time for our appointment with the movers. After the last item was loaded onto the moving truck, we bade our Connecticut friends and neighbors farewell, and began the long drive to the Florida Panhandle.

Our new residence on Gardenview Way, in the Killarne Gardens Development of Tallahassee, was an all-brick ranch style home. I loved the house as well as the community. The lot was elegantly landscaped with beautiful magnolias, and camellias, hydrangeas, azaleas, and oleanders. I enjoyed my early morning walks in the neighborhood with Eudine, and she got to explore the nearby park with one of our neighbors. Everything seemed to be close-by, Wal-Mart, Home Depot, Publix, Brunos, Lowes, as well as many of our favorite restaurants. It was such a welcome change. Beautiful blue skies, flowers and butterflies everywhere, and nice, friendly people. I remember one day, Eudine and I were in the parking lot of the Brunos supermarket. I loved shopping there because they stocked a variety of products from the Caribbean. As I walked across the parking lot towards the entrance to the store,

I did not notice a car approaching. The driver politely brought his car to a stop, leaned out of his window, and with typical southern hospitality said to Eudine, "What a beautiful lady!" I often tease Eudine about that incident. From that day her new name was "Tallahassee Lassie."

From our home in Tallahassee, I could easily explore the Panhandle as well as the entire Gulf Coast of Florida. One of my favorite places to visit was St George Island. I had never heard of St. George Island before I moved to Tallahassee. One day when I was speaking with my neighbor, who was a member of the faculty at Florida State University, he told me about the island. He said it was his favorite place to vacation with his family. I made a note of that conversation, and decided that I would try to visit the island at the earliest opportunity. Soon after that conversation I got my first chance to plan a trip to St. George Island. Eudine's sister Gloria and her daughter Dara were visiting with us, and I considered that to be an ideal time for a day trip to St. George Island.

I set out from Tallahassee and headed south driving through some small towns until I reached the Gulf Coast. The trip took me along the bay into Apalachicola–a tiny, picturesque community of less than three square miles located at the mouth of the Apalachicola River. After crossing the four-mile long causeway that separated Apalachicola on the mainland from St. George Island, I headed east along a narrow coastal road, driving mile after mile through an expansive landscape of sand dunes until I reached a beautiful park. We pulled into the parking lot, unloaded our picnic bags, and spent a glorious time relaxing under the shade of an immaculately maintained hut. We thoroughly enjoyed the park with its white sand beach that is characteristic of the Florida Gulf Coast. We spent about two hours enjoying a sumptuous lunch and watching Dara gather shells at the water's edge. On the way back, I couldn't get enough of the charming towns. We stopped at one of the popular restaurants where we were able to enjoy some of the best seafood that is available along the Florida Gulf Coast.

Although we did not have time to visit Wakulla Spring, I knew that it was one of the popular tourist attractions in the Panhandle region of Florida. It is about fourteen miles south of Tallahassee, and is believed to be one of the longest and deepest submerged freshwater cave systems in the world. The most interesting thing I heard about the Spring at Wakulla is that it is still possible to see the remains of Mastodons and other fossils at a depth of around one hundred and ninety feet!

I found Tallahassee to be an excellent hub for exploring the rest of Florida and the neighboring southern states. I could conveniently drive to Gainesville, Jacksonville, Orlando, and to cities along the west coast such as St. Petersburg, Clearwater Beach, Panama City, Pensacola, Sarasota, and Naples. My trips to neighboring states took me to Nashville, New Orleans, Thomasville, and Atlanta.

Everything seemed to fall into place while I was in Tallahassee. For example, my first visit to St. Michael and All Angels Church felt like I had worshipped there all of my life. I even knew the Rector. He was a Barbadian, who was a student at Codrington College when I was a youngster growing up in St. John. Many of the members of the congregation were from countries in the Caribbean like Guyana, Jamaica, Barbados, and St Thomas. There was also a significant contingent of worshippers from Ghana, and Nigeria. I served as a member of the Vestry, and Eudine became involved with the Episcopal Church Women's Group. Several members of the Florida A&M University faculty also worshipped at St. Michael's, and their involvement in the life of the church enriched the quality of the musical performances at the Sunday morning services.

I learned from members of the Vestry that the St. Michael and All Angels Church began its history in 1882 as a Mission within the Diocese of Florida. They told me that it was not until 1947 that the congregation was assigned its first permanent minister. That was the year when the Reverend Father David Brooks became Vicar. He also served as Episcopal Chaplain of Florida A&M University. It was obvious to me that based on its proximity to Florida A&M University, St. Michael and All Angels enjoyed a remarkably close relationship with the university. I found out that this was particularly true during the period of extreme racial segregation in the State of Florida. As the only predominantly black Episcopal Church on that side of town, St. Michael and All Angels was a magnet for students seeking spiritual guidance and a nurturing environment while they were far away from home.

Our Pastor was a very interesting man. He was approaching retirement, and was inclined to be very direct and candid with his pronouncements. Very often the congregation had no idea when he was going to say something from the pulpit that was not politically correct.

I served on the vestry with several prominent church elders whose dedication and devotion to the congregation and the pastor could not be questioned. The senior warden was from Jamaica, and my colleagues on the Vestry included an eclectic group of individuals that included Florida A&M faculty, an attorney-at-law, a principal, and several community leaders. The group also included a state representative who was an aggressive advocate for matters related to the building and parish. His commitment to serving was unquestionable. Another vestry member for whom I had considerable respect was the brother of the famous actor Ossie Davis. He was a remarkable person who went on to become one of our most highly respected lay preachers.

During the three and a half years I spent in Tallahassee, I worshipped regularly at St. Michael's and All Angels, and made many lasting friendships. In 2007, when the congregation celebrated the church's one hundred twenty-fifth anniversary, Eudine and I were proud to travel back to Tallahassee to join our friends on that memorable occasion. The weekend began on the Friday night with a formal dinner held at one of the local hotels on North Monroe Street. I drove our rented car on Monroe Street past Lake Ella where Eudine and I spent many a Sunday morning walking around its perimeter, and watching the many families that converged on that very popular recreational spot every weekend. The venue for the banquet was approximately one mile past Lake Ella. I can still feel the excitement that welled up inside me as I made my way from the parking lot into the room where everyone was gathered. There were so many of our friends in attendance that up until the time of our departure, we were not able to make the rounds of all of the tables.

Then on Saturday the Florida A&M University Marching Band performed on the grounds of the church at a reception for members and friends. The next day, we were back at St. Michael's and All Angels sitting in our favorite seat, and for a fleeting moment believing that little had changed since we left Tallahassee. And then reality set in. Most of the familiar faces were not there, several of them had passed on since we left, and many of those still present had slowed down considerably, attesting to the fact that father time was steadily marching on.

Every chance I got during that weekend, I took time to revisit many of my favorite places. I drove by our former home on Gardenview Way, and made a sentimental trip to the Florida A&M University campus. As I traversed the many familiar streets on campus, it was impossible for me to forget how much that institution meant to me during the three years I served as a member of the faculty of Biology.

My colleague from Jamaica always told me that Tallahassee was the first city in the United States that made him feel like he was back in the Caribbean, and I have a similar feeling about the city. Tallahassee was a small and effectively managed city. There were three governments battling to outdo each other to keep the city clean. They included Leon County, the City of Tallahassee, and the State of Florida. The network of roads was well-maintained, and the medians were always decorated with crepe myrtles, roses, and azaleas. The recycling policy was citizen-friendly, and there was no state income tax that we had to contend with. We loved the simple lifestyle of Tallahassee and considered it to be an ideal place for retirement. There was absolutely no reason for me to even think of leaving. Then one day, the telephone on my desk at work rang, and the caller was asking me to consider a job opening in North Carolina. I was not in the least bit inclined to consider such an option.

I was deeply immersed in my work as Director of the University's Howard Hughes Undergraduate Program. Eudine was a regular in the office helping me to take care of important budgetary matters. It was very much a normal day at the office until the phone rang. It was a former colleague from Pfizer on the line, and he was obviously vacillating about an important decision he was getting ready to make. He was in the market for a new job and was considering offers from a University in Texas and from a small university in North Carolina. He had reached a critical decision point and was leaning heavily toward accepting the offer from the University in Texas.

He briefed me about the position in North Carolina, stating that it involved directing a new institute that was under construction, and he respectfully asked me to allow him to provide them with my contact information. He went on to say that he thought that I was even better suited for that job than he was. After all, I was deeply immersed in academic life, and furthermore he felt that I would bring a wealth of valuable corporate experience to the position. I listened quietly and waited for him to finish his pitch. My response was clear and to the point. “Thank you for still believing in me, but I am really not interested in moving at this time.” That was obviously not the answer he wanted to hear, so he continued to make his pitch. This went on for more than ten minutes before I conceded by saying that it was OK for him to give them my contact information.

The moment I hung up the telephone it started to ring again. The caller was Gloria Haynes, a senior administrator at North Carolina Central University (NCCU), and she was calling to invite me to visit their campus as a candidate for the institute director’s position. I couldn’t believe what was happening. I asked her to hold for a minute and turned to Eudine and said, “this is NCCU calling. I am not interested in going there to look at any job!” I expected her to agree with me so that it would make it easier to say no. Instead, her response was simple and straightforward; “it can’t harm to go and take a look.” So I agreed to go to Durham, North Carolina for the interview.

My trip to Durham took place shortly after that brief conversation. I arrived at the Raleigh Durham International Airport, confident that there was little my host could do to persuade me to leave Tallahassee. The ride to my hotel was routine, and as I settled in for the night, I was confident of my intention to “look but not leap.”

Gloria Haynes, my NCCU host joined me at my hotel for breakfast the next morning. We talked about the day’s schedule, and left for the short drive to the campus. I had a full schedule that day. I gave a seminar about my research program, and I participated in a formal interview with the members of the Search Committee. I then met with deans and faculty members for one-on-one interview sessions. My last interview that day was with the Chancellor of the University Julius Chambers.

I had heard of Julius Chambers and his long and successful struggle during the Civil Rights era for fairness and equality. While he was a law student at the University of North Carolina (UNC) at Chapel Hill, he played a pivotal role in opening up that institution and the university system to broader minority participation. Later, as a Civil Rights lawyer he fought successfully to integrate the schools in North Carolina. He was also known for his untiring efforts to break down the barriers to freedom both nationally and internationally. He is an individual of enormous stature and achievement, and here I was in his presence talking about a position of leadership in his administration.

He began the conversation by telling me that he was aware of my work as a scientist. He then stated that he was interested in attracting someone like me to help him develop more competitive science programs for NCCU students. He told me that NCCU was located in the shadow of institutions such as Duke, Carolina, and NC State, the three research universities that participated in the founding of the Research Triangle Park (RTP), and in spite of its proximity to the RTP, NCCU still had not earned a reputation as a center of excellence for biotechnology training. I remember him saying that too few NCCU students were being recruited to fill the more than two-thousand entry-level positions that were created each year in the Park. He went on to say that he felt that the best way to prepare NCCU students for jobs in the emerging knowledge economy was to create a research institute at the university's Durham campus. I remember sitting there in total amazement as he briefed me on his plan to reform science education at his alma mater. I knew that he was aware of the fact that RTP had become a major hub for biotechnology in the state, and that HBCU leaders like him needed to respond to that challenge by integrating research into the undergraduate and graduate curricula.

He went on to tell me that he had managed to persuade the North Carolina State Legislature to appropriate $12.2 million to enable him to construct a state-of-the-art research institute on campus. His eyes lit up when he indicated that construction of the building that he planned to call the Biomedical/Biotechnology Research Institute (BBRI), was already underway. After gaining legislative support for constructing the building, he said that his next step was to develop a formal proposal to plan the institute. To accomplish this, he indicated that he sought the advice of Triangle area scientists, research administrators, business, and community leaders. He then got representatives from that distinguished group of leaders to serve on five Advisory Committees that he established to assist with the planning process. Each committee submitted its report to him in writing, and he had a select group of NCCU faculty and staff review those reports, identify the key recommendations, and incorporate them into the comprehensive Building Committee Report. The final design plan for the institute was drafted with the assistance of The Freelon Group Inc, an architectural firm that at that time was headquartered in RTP. The proposal to plan the institute was approved by the UNC System Board of Governors in 1996. Construction of the building began shortly afterwards, and the projected date for completion of the construction phase was August 1998.

I was deeply moved by what I heard during my meeting with Chancellor Chambers. I was particularly impressed by his vision and obvious commitment to science. What struck me most about my interview with this iconic figure was the modesty that he exuded. He spoke confidently but softly, choosing his words carefully, and at the same time engaging in a playful exercise that involved using his right hand to stretch a small rubber band over the extended fingers of his left hand. Chancellor Chambers concluded our meeting by simply asking me what it would take for him to attract me to join him in the effort to develop the BBRI, adding as a cautionary note that he did not expect me to provide him with my response immediately.

During my ride back to the airport after an interesting but exhausting day, the Chairperson of the Search Committee in his inimitable style wanted to let me know that “we are interested in your candidacy and hope that you are serious about this position. If you are not interested you should let me know now because I don’t want to waste your time nor mine!” I was so tired that my response was calm and controlled. “I cannot tell you anything definitive now,” I said, “I was certainly impressed by today’s visit, but need to reflect on everything, and have an in-depth discussion with my wife before I could give you an answer." He respected my position and indicated his willingness to be more patient.

Over the next several days, I engaged all of my family members in a deep discussion about a possible move to NCCU. Eudine and I weighed the pros and cons of staying in Tallahassee versus relocating to Durham. We both knew what the stakes were, and for the second time in just over three years we were again faced with making a major decision. Our children Dionne and Kevin weighed in, providing their thoughts and support as we struggled to work our way through that difficult issue.

In one conversation, Kevin asked me the following question. "Dad, after leaving Pfizer, if you had to design a job that would draw on your corporate and academic experiences, do you think that you would come up with a job like this?" Kevin was very insightful, and his question went to the heart of the issue under discussion. That day I knew what my decision would be. On my next conversation with Chancellor Chambers, I requested a follow-up meeting so that I could have an in-depth conversation with him about the job and the responsibilities of the new institute director. It was at the conclusion of that visit that I knew I would have his unwavering support if I took the job.

Soon after accepting Chancellor Chambers' offer, I received my first assignment from him. He needed me to draft a document to establish the institute. That was the fall of 1997, and he was hoping to submit the proposal to the UNC System Board of Governors before the end of that year. As director designate, I agreed to take on the awesome task of developing the proposal.

I organized the application into separate sections that addressed the BBRI's mission; research programs; administrative structure; core facilities; funding; and future space needs. I captured the institute's mission in a simple statement that read as follows: The BBRI's mission is to create a high quality research program that addresses the health, research, and training needs of underserved minority communities. I selected cardiovascular disease, cancer, drug abuse and addiction, and infectious diseases as the BBRI's major research programs. I chose those diseases and disorders because it was common knowledge that underrepresented minority groups were disproportionately impacted by them. I knew that once established, the BBRI could join forces with other NCCU academic units and relevant departments to collaborate with universities, government, and private organizations to achieve its mission. I firmly believed that the mechanism-driven research focus that I proposed, combined with the utilization of the project team mode of operation would provide a framework for the eventual development of a "Center of Excellence" at NCCU.

I next addressed the issue of the BBRI's administrative structure. I recommended the recruitment of a Principal Investigator to head each of the research programs. I specified that each program leader should hold a Ph.D. and/or an MD degree. I felt that candidates seeking those positions should have a proven record of scientific accomplishment as evidenced by peer reviewed publications and grants awarded. I also thought that BBRI program leaders should be experienced teachers and mentors who would be committed to working collaboratively. The organizational chart that I proposed indicated that the program leaders would report to me as Institute Director, and that I would report to the Chancellor. Program leaders were responsible for recruiting faculty, staff, and students to their respective disciplines. I devoted a major section of that draft proposal to identifying and describing the roles of senior administrative and technical staff needed to assist with the day-to-day management of the institute, and the support staff I needed to assist me with managing the various internal and external committees that would be created to provide guidance and oversight.

I recommended the development of four core laboratories that would provide routine as well as sophisticated technical support to the research programs at no cost initially, and on a fee-for-service basis as the institute matured. Additionally, I provided operational budgets to show how all programmatic activities would be funded over a five-year period. I concluded the proposal by drawing attention to two critical issues that needed to be addressed by university planners in a timely fashion. The first involved establishing a Technology Transfer

Office to encourage the creation of technology-based intellectual property at NCCU, and assist with the commercialization of such technology. The second related to the development of a plan to meet future research space needs. Based on realistic growth projections, I was worried that space allocated to support the institute's research and training activities would be exhausted within five years.

My proposal was carefully reviewed by a team of academic and corporate leaders drawn from across the RTP, and it was submitted to the Office of the President of the UNC System in December of 1997, one month before my arrival at NCCU. Permission for NCCU to establish the BBRI was officially granted in September of 1998.

Chapter 22

Durham North Carolina

I moved to Durham, North Carolina in January of 1998. Leaving Tallahassee and the friendships that I had cultivated there was a difficult and painful experience for me. Eudine and I traveled out of the City by car, following the same country roads that I used when we moved to Tallahassee from Connecticut. Our plan was to try to make it to Durham before nightfall so that we could be there to meet the moving truck the following morning. The trip to North Carolina was long and uneventful, with overcast skies all along the way. There was a weather report on the radio predicting the possibility of snow flurries in North Carolina, but I didn't assign it any credibility. After all, everyone that I talked to in Durham had told me how mild the winters were in North Carolina. As I approached the Durham city limits, the clouds began to look more ominous, and then it started to snow. I couldn't believe it! I had not driven in snow since I left Connecticut in 1995! Although it was a light snowfall with no visible accumulation on the roadway, it still caused me to question the wisdom of my decision to move away from Florida.

I found it convenient to lease a four-bedroom home in Treyburn Park, an upscale development in northern Durham. It was about a thirty-minute drive to the NCCU campus. Treyburn was like most gated communities, isolated from the surrounding neighborhoods, and more like a museum than a place where people lived. The loneliness we experienced in that development was palpable. The nearest shopping center was seven or eight miles away, and there was hardly any evidence of human existence within that community. Two months after moving into that rented house, the owner informed me of her desire to sell the property. Under different circumstances I would have been outraged by her blatant disregard for our lease agreement, instead I saw her decision as an opportunity to escape from an existence that we thought was too confining.

Instead of trying to find another house to lease, we started to look for a permanent place to live. After a short search, we found a home in south Durham that met most of our expectations. The newly constructed house was within easy driving distance from NCCU's campus, and it was large enough to accommodate Kevin and his wife Lisa who were planning to relocate to Durham from Richmond Virginia.

On my first day of work, I drove my Honda Accord into the Hoey traffic circle at NCCU, filled with optimism. Just like my first day at Florida A&M University, no one had made arrangements for a parking space for the new BBRI Director, and it would be some time before I would be assigned a reserved space. Much to my surprise, the university had not yet located a suitable space to serve as my temporary office. Thank God for Gloria Haynes and her administrative assistant Angela who helped me resolve my parking and office problems.

Gloria found me a temporary office in the Jones Building that once housed NCCU's Law School. It was a sparsely furnished space with a large picture window. An old wooden desk was pushed up against the wall near to the entrance, and a freshly painted radiator was visible in the adjacent corner. There was no telephone or internet connection, and it was obvious to me that this space had not been used as an office for a very long time. Fortunately, I remembered my first days at Florida A&M University, and was better prepared to deal with the situation. Armed with my personal notebook computer and cell phone, I was able to begin to construct in outline form the narrative for the grant applications I planned to submit to the National Institutes of Health during the first quarter of 1998. Although those were less than ideal circumstances, I was able to remain focused on the task ahead.

My occupancy of that office was brief. When I arrived at work the second day, I noticed that someone had unplugged my computer and moved it from the desk to the radiator in the corner of the room. I called Gloria on my cell phone to express concern about what had happened. She responded by asking me to remain in the office while she explored other options for office space in the main administrative building. About an hour later, she was ushering me into a very tiny office on the second floor of the Hoey Administration Building. In spite of the cramped quarters, it became my first official NCCU address for over one year and a half!

Within my first few months on the job, I successfully campaigned for an administrative assistant whom I identified through a temporary employment agency. She was an NCCU Alumna who had little experience with office management. Nevertheless, she was able to help me with answering the telephone and ordering office supplies and equipment. Then one day during that first month, I received a call from an NCCU staff member who worked in communications. She told me that she wanted to volunteer the services of her daughter, an NCCU graduate who was experiencing some serious health problems. She was confident that her daughter would enjoy assisting me with filing and answering the phone. I agreed to have her daughter join my fledgling team.

The building that would house the BBRI's programs was still under construction. During the remainder of the construction phase, I was informed that it was my responsibility to conduct periodic walkthroughs to ensure that the work was proceeding satisfactorily. That was a very hectic time for me. I was writing grant proposals and progress reports. I was single-handedly trying to establish partnership arrangements with neighboring universities, and I was deeply involved in the recruitment of BBRI faculty and staff. Looking back, I am still amazed that it was possible for me to address all of those important priorities with the limited help available.

Thursday, September 2, 1999 is a date that I will always remember. It was the day of the formal dedication of the BBRI. It was a most impressive event, complete with the presentation of the Colors by the NCCU Color Guard, and a Ribbon Cutting Ceremony. Gloria and her team organized and coordinated all aspects of the program. The formal presentations were held in the Miller Morgan building, just across Nelson Street from the main entrance to the institute. The large auditorium was filled to capacity with NCCU faculty, staff, students, alumni, friends, and other supporters.

Those in attendance were welcomed by the Interim Provost Dr. Eugene Eaves, the consummate educator and academic administrator. Mr. William Smith, Chairman of the NCCU Board of Trustees spoke about the Occasion, and recognized special guests. Mr. Daniel Blue Junior, a member of the North Carolina House of Representatives; Ms. Molly Broad, President of the UNC System; Mr. Robert Ingram, Chairman, Glaxo Wellcome Inc., and Mr. Clifton Gray President of the NCCU Student Government Association were next in line to speak. The Keynote Speaker Dr. David Satcher, Assistant Secretary for Health and U.S. Surgeon General was introduced by Dr. John Ruffin who at that time was serving as the Associate Director in the Office of Research on Minority Health at the National Institutes of Health.

As I approached the podium to address the packed auditorium, I realized that I was presented with my best opportunity to make the case for the institute. I entitled my remarks "The BBRI Vision." I began by telling them that the BBRI represented an important addition to the research infrastructure of NCCU, the UNC System, and RTP. I said that it symbolized the beginning of a new era of achievement for NCCU, and equally important, it was the perfect way to celebrate NCCU's tradition of good science. I reminded them that NCCU's tradition of good science spanned several decades, beginning with Dr. James Lee whose pioneering studies on cell structure were first published in the October 1941 issue of the Journal *Science*. I also cited the work of one of the chemistry professors who designed and synthesized a novel class of lipid lowering compounds.

I talked about how the combination of good science and the unprecedented advances in biotechnology and information technology that helped to create the BBRI. I went on to state that with its research projects strongly aligned with NCCU's mission, the BBRI was destined to become an integral part of the chancellor's campus-wide initiative to broaden faculty involvement in scholarly research. I reviewed the strategic plan for program development, faculty recruitment, and grantsmanship, and I concluded by reminding everyone that through hard work, strategic partnerships, and unwavering commitments from NCCU and the UNC System, the BBRI would become a national model for student training and faculty development. Chancellor Chambers was the last person to speak that day, and after he concluded his remarks the venue changed to the ribbon cutting ceremony.

The landing at the Nelson Street entrance to the BBRI was the perfect setting for that ceremony. After a rendition of *the Impossible Dream* by Ms. Dana Williams an NCCU student accompanied by the NCCU Jazz Ensemble, everyone was invited to a sumptuous reception under a large air-conditioned tent that was pitched on the BBRI parking lot. Official tours of the building were conducted for those interested in learning more about the institute's research programs.

I could not have imagined how supportive the leadership in Durham would be for me as a new administrator and faculty member at NCCU. The welcome I received from academic, government, and corporate sources in RTP was most impressive. The Vice President for Research at Duke University Medical School was one of my most visible supporters. I met with him on a monthly basis to explore ways in which our two institutions could partner, especially in the areas of research and student training. He was a reliable and resourceful mentor to me during the first phase of development of the institute, and I deeply appreciated all of the help that he provided. His counterpart was the CEO of Duke Health Systems. He had grown up in Brooklyn, N.Y. and when he learned that I had lived in Brooklyn, that became part of the glue that strengthened our relationship. I would always remember the formal reception they hosted for my family and me on the Duke University campus. The reception was complete with a string quartet and plenty to eat and drink. I was deeply moved by their genuine expression of support.

The Wall Street Journal was the first major national media outlet to send a reporter to campus shortly after I arrived. The young reporter who was assigned the task of conducting that interview was very candid when I asked her what was the motivation for the newspaper's interest in NCCU. She told me that it was all about Chancellor Julius Chambers and his stellar reputation as a civil rights lawyer. She also wanted to write about his struggle to obtain the funding needed to build a new research institute. When her story appeared in the Wall Street Journal it attracted considerable attention to the chancellor and to the university. It provided an in-depth account of Mr. Chamber's career, including the landmark civil-rights case he successfully argued before the U.S. Supreme Court in 1971 when he represented the Swann family against the Charlotte-Mecklenburg School System. That was the case that forced the use of busing to integrate the North Carolina School System. Her article also referenced the work done by Chancellor Chambers to win support for developing the institute that I was recruited to manage. In order to illustrate how frustrating the process was to get the institute off the ground, the article included the following paragraph, "And the research institute which Mr. Chambers pledged in 1993 would be operational in two years, has taken longer than expected. He got the State General Assembly to approve the money to build it in 1994, but a cumbersome planning process delayed the start of construction until November 1996. The institute's new executive director, Ken Harewood, who Mr. Chambers recruited away from Florida A&M University's molecular biology research laboratory still doesn't have a phone three weeks into the job..."

One of the most important lessons I learned after having spent twenty-three years in the Pharmaceutical Industry, was that success in research is largely driven by good ideas, teamwork, and strategic partnerships. It was not surprising therefore that I wanted to devote as much time as possible during my first year as director to fostering relationships with academic and corporate leaders.

My first major research collaboration was with the Lineberger Comprehensive Cancer Center at the UNC at Chapel Hill. I was fortunate to meet the Cancer Center's Director during my first visit to NCCU. He was a member of the Search Committee, and in that capacity he got to interview all of the candidates for the director's position. From our first meeting on the day of my interview, I was aware of the fact that we both had a passion for cancer research. It did not take long therefore for us to begin talking about the possibility of starting a pilot project on breast cancer research. That initiative blossomed into a full-fledged partnership that subsequently received multi-year grant awards from the National Cancer Institute, and the National Center on Minority Health and Health Disparities.

During that period, I met many of the directors, presidents, and CEOs who were providing competent and effective leadership for many of the scientific organizations in RTP. The leaders I targeted included those from the Environmental Protection Agency; the National Institute of Environmental Health Sciences; GSK; BD Diagnostics; Biogen; the Research Triangle Institute; the Chemical Industry Institute of Toxicology; the Burroughs Wellcome Fund; and the North Carolina Biotechnology Center. I also got to meet several of the chancellors and presidents of the public and private universities within North Carolina.

Some of my initiatives paid immediate dividends. For example, the Glaxo Wellcome Foundation responded positively to my application for three-years of funding for the BBRI. The Burroughs Wellcome Fund, the North Carolina Biotechnology Center, and the Schering-Plough Corporation were also generous in their response to my requests for funds to support student scholarships and infrastructure development.

Those early successes attracted considerable attention to the institute, and I was soon invited to serve on several Boards and Advisory Committees. My Board involvements included the Board of Directors of the North Carolina Biotechnology Center; the North Carolina Board of Science and Technology; the Board of Governors of the Research Triangle Institute International; and the Advisory Committee of the North Carolina Supercomputer Center.

Forced by a grant from the National Heart Lung Blood Institute to identify and hire the Program Leader for the Cardiovascular Disease Research Program within a twelve-month period, I had no choice but to assign that task highest priority. That was a challenge I knew I was accepting when I signed on to become Director of the BBRI. The ideal candidate needed to be an experienced scientist with a record of publication and funding in the cardiovascular disease area. Teaching experience and demonstrated leadership ability were important criteria for selection. Finally, acceptance by the administrator of the National Heart Lung Blood Institute's program grant was a major requirement.

The first advertisement I placed in one of the national journals attracted few qualified applicants; instead it triggered responses from headhunters. One in particular was very aggressive. That experienced university professor was the president of a consulting company that specialized in helping small colleges like NCCU fill senior leadership positions. In spite of much arm-twisting, I resisted the temptation to enter into any contractual agreement with his company. Instead, I sought the support of a trusted network of scientists and administrators to assist me with this important recruitment effort. I attended American Heart Association Meetings to ensure that I was covering all possible bases. Soon, my efforts would pay big dividends. A young, accomplished scientist who was a member of the faculty at the University of Texas Medical Center at Galveston, saw the advertisement and submitted an application. He turned out to be the person I was looking for. In spite of his limited knowledge of NCCU, in particular and HBCU's, in general, he was excited about having the opportunity to shape a program that could make a difference in students' lives. We talked at length about our vision for the institute, and I urged him to seriously consider relocating to NCCU. It was a perfect match, and when he accepted the offer to become Program Leader for the BBRI's Cardiovascular Disease Research Program, NCCU became the first of the four National Heart Lung Blood Institute supported universities to have identified and hired a Program Leader. He was the perfect choice to provide leadership for the BBRI's Cardiovascular Research Program. We worked well together to implement the goals and objectives of the program. We hired new faculty, wrote competitive grants, established important collaborations, and strengthened the graduate curriculum in biology. I still cannot believe how quickly our efforts began to transform the research culture of that small, comprehensive, teaching institution.

After the Principal Investigator of the BBRI's Cardiovascular Disease Research Program got his laboratory up and running, he recruited the first post-doctoral trainee to the institute. It proved to be a difficult undertaking because the university had never had a post-doctoral program in its entire history. Chancellor Chambers supported our fledgling effort and was very receptive to developing NCCUs first Post-doctoral Training Program.

The framework for that program was first drafted and incorporated into a grant application that I submitted to the National Cancer Institute. The goals and objectives of the program were also spelled-out in that grant application. The duties and responsibilities of the trainee, the mentor, the principal investigator, and the sponsoring institution were addressed in considerable detail. The reviewers deemed the plan meritorious, and the National Cancer Institute provided necessary budgetary support. That plan was subsequently refined and later embodied into NCCU's official Post-doctoral Trainee Policy.

With African Americans serving as mentors and in visible roles as post-doctoral trainees, it became less difficult to attract undergraduates and graduates to the BBRI's Education and Training Program. Financial incentives were a pre-requisite to student recruitment. Those included generous stipends that were competitive with those provided at majority institutions; tuition waivers; books; and travel to local, national, and international meetings. In exchange, students were required to make time commitments to their BBRI mentors. For undergraduate students the time commitment was at least ten hours per week working in their mentors' laboratories conducting hypothesis-driven research. Graduate students were required to be in their mentors' laboratories when they were not attending formal classes.

The Education and Training Program had a rocky beginning. The first two graduate students recruited did not have stellar academic credentials. That made it almost impossible for them to function effectively in a laboratory setting. I found this to be exceedingly challenging, because administrators within the Biology Department were not sympathetic when I sought their counsel. To compound matters, one of the scientists that I recruited from a pharmaceutical company in RTP, collaborated with me in selecting the next two graduate student trainees. Neither of us was prepared for what happened after the students signed on to the program. Persistent delinquencies complicated our relationship with those students, and almost every week we had to reprimand them for poor attendance. The word quickly spread across campus that the BBRI was insensitive, and that we were treating students harshly. That was such an outrageous claim that I chose not to dignify it with a response.

It was against that backdrop of rumor and innuendo that I struggled to repair the BBRI's image. Fortunately, Chancellor Chambers and I were invited to a symposium at Wake Forest University School of Medicine. Their campus is in Winston Salem, approximately one hundred ten miles southwest of Durham. Chancellor Chambers and I took advantage of that opportunity to meet with the University's President. We told him of our interest in exploring a strategic partnership with scientists at his campus, and he pledged to support our initiative. That chance contact between the leaders of the two universities resulted in the creation of a Masters to Doctoral BRIDGE initiative that benefited NCCU graduate students immensely. Our grant application to the National Institute for General Medical Studies was successful; and the first BRIDGE Program in which NCCU was the lead institution was launched.

With well-defined criteria for student participation, and the prospect of a seamless transition from the masters program at NCCU to the doctoral program at Wake Forest University, the BBRI's graduate students got a second chance, and it quickly became an attractive way for NCCU graduate students to earn a doctoral degree at one of the state's premier research universities.

The BBRI Undergraduate Fellows Program was equally successful. Fashioned after the Howard Hughes Undergraduate Program that I ran while at Florida A&M University, it quickly attracted funding from corporate and government sources. Unlike most other student support initiatives, the BBRI Undergraduate Fellows Program admitted students throughout the entire academic year. All NCCU undergraduates who were full-time enrollees were eligible to participate. All participants were expected to devote at least ten hours per week working with a BBRI mentor on a medically relevant research project. Students were encouraged to participate in all research and research-related activities sponsored by the BBRI. Those included weekly seminars, journal club meetings, and project team meetings. Additionally, the BBRI's Education Director and I met with the student trainees at least once a month, to track their progress and answer any questions they wanted to raise.

I next developed the BBRI's Pre-college Summer Internship Program. It was NCCU's first summer internship program that offered high school students an opportunity to be trained in biotechnology and the biomedical sciences. It was a natural outgrowth of the successful Undergraduate Student Training Program sponsored by the BBRI. The Pre-college Summer Internship Program was much more flexible than the Undergraduate Student Training Program. It reached out to high schools from across the state of North Carolina. It was run in conjunction with the Summer Ventures Program that was ably managed by a member of the Geography Department. He was one of a handful of dedicated NCCU faculty with whom I was privileged to work. His commitment to student training was unwavering, and he was a tremendous resource for helping with program logistics.

Chapter 23

Engagement and Outreach

Within two years after the launch of the BBRI, Julius Chambers announced that he would retire from the position of chancellor. That was shocking news to me as well as to the members of the institute's research programs. We were all filled with uncertainty about what the future would hold for the institute and its unique organizational structure. I watched with considerable apprehension as the university went about the process of finding a new leader.

The search for a replacement for Chancellor Chambers was comprehensive and timely, identifying a bright, energetic, and charismatic individual to lead the University. The new Chancellor, Dr. James Ammons was a familiar figure to me. He served as Provost at Florida A&M University during the brief time I spent there as a professor in the Biology Department. Although our interaction then was limited, I got to know him as an administrator and as a person. I knew of his passion for student training, and his desire to provide high school graduates with greater access to a high quality college education. His warm and friendly demeanor and his reputation as an excellent planner had endeared him to the students, staff, and faculty at Florida A&M University. I considered him an excellent choice to lead the university during a time of unprecedented growth.

He proved to be the perfect choice. He literally hit the ground running, displaying a keen sense of what his role should be as chancellor, and demonstrating an unwavering determination to be the best chancellor that he could be. He became an ardent supporter of the BBRI and the research agenda that his predecessor had fought so courageously to establish. One of his first actions was to establish a "Think

Tank" comprising NCCU faculty and a cross-section of RTP corporate leaders. He asked that group to help him develop priorities for improving university/industry relations. The outcome of those deliberations was the formation of the NCCU Business and Industry Cluster. Biotechnology, information technology and pharmaceutical companies signed up for membership in significant numbers, and their representatives visited the campus annually to discuss best practices for student training and faculty development. Almost overnight, the Business and Industry Cluster became a major vehicle for exposing the campus community to the best practices exemplified by our corporate partners. I was impressed by the number of NCCU students signing up for summer internships at member institutions, and by the professionalism they displayed when they returned to campus and shared their experiences with their peers and others at the annual meeting of the Business and Industry Cluster. There was no doubt in my mind that the Business and Industry Cluster was beginning to change the culture at NCCU.

Our BRIDGE program was satisfying all of its objectives, and the number of undergraduates participating in our academic year program had reached an all-time high. The best way to describe the mood in the BBRI is to say that it was upbeat. Our scientists and their student trainees were generating lots of exciting data on a gene that we believed to be involved in blood pressure regulation, and we were eager to share our findings with our colleagues at an international meeting that was scheduled for the fall of 2001.

Then, on Tuesday, September 11, I was in my dentist's chair for a routine visit to have my teeth cleaned. My 8:00 am appointment had lasted for one hour. At the end of the session, I left the dentist's office and drove to the BBRI. When I entered the building, I noticed something very strange was happening. My staff was huddled around a small television in the first floor conference room and they were absolutely glued to the screen. I considered that behavior to be highly unusual. Everyone knew that the television in the conference room was meant to be used by our graduate students. We wanted them to review pharmacology and physiology lectures that our partners at the Wake Forest University School of Medicine provided to us on videotapes. Before I could enquire about what was happening, my cell phone vibrated and it was Eudine on the line. She was so shaken that she could hardly get the words out. "Two planes just crashed into the World Trade Center buildings in New York," she said, "It's being shown on television right now!"

After hanging up from that disturbing bit of news, I turned on the radio in my office to try to get a better sense of what was transpiring in New York. Without the benefit of video, the first impression I got was that a small plane might have accidentally crashed into one of the World Trade Center Towers. What I couldn't understand was why a second plane would make the same mistake? I soon learned, along with the rest of the nation, that what was happening in New York was not an accident but a terrorist attack. It was unbelievable. Several questions raced through my mind. Who was behind this? What would happen next? Would this trigger a nuclear holocaust that could lead to the end of life as we knew it? I wondered if I should be heading home to be with Eudine during such a period of uncertainty. I did have the foresight to call her back to talk about the situation, and that conversation helped to calm her nerves as well as mine.

As the news reports continued, the full scope of the attack that occurred on that day began to emerge. The event is now referred to as 9/11. On that morning, nineteen members of the terrorist group known as al-Qaeda hijacked four U.S. commercial jet liners and crashed two of them into the Twin Towers of the World Trade Center in New York killing everyone on board along with almost 3,000 other individuals, most of them workers in that massive complex of buildings. The hijackers crashed the third airliner into the Pentagon in Arlington, Virginia. The fourth plane was brought down in a field in Shanksville, Pennsylvania, after the passengers sought to regain control from the hijackers. That single event would launch two wars, one in Afghanistan and the other in Iraq, and a protracted War on Terror that has seen America retreat from many of its long held principles. This is an outcome that no one would have expected as the new millennium began.

True to form, Chancellor Ammons responded to that very distressing development by scheduling a service to remember the 9/11 victims. As leader of a major university in the state, he wanted to demonstrate support for the nation in a time of crisis. The attack cast a pall across the entire country. The Airline business virtually ground to a halt. Everyone was afraid to fly, including me. I was scheduled to travel out of the country with my colleagues to attend a conference in Cancun, Mexico and I could not bring myself around to going. I called the conference organizers and requested a refund, which they graciously approved.

The next time I traveled was to attend a meeting sponsored by the National Institute of Drug Abuse and Addiction. The meeting was held in Philadelphia, a location that was convenient to reach by car from Durham, North Carolina. My project officer was keenly interested in having me attend that meeting to represent the NCCU program. Eudine agreed to travel with me and we decided to take our grandson Brandon who was only three years old. I requested a room on a lower floor consistent with my practice since watching the horror that occurred at the World Trade Center. Our room was on the seventh floor, and in between meeting sessions, I would hurry back to the room to be with Eudine and Brandon.

On the second day of the conference, I experienced the scare of a lifetime. I was attending a mixer on the second floor when the fire alarms sounded throughout the hotel. I could see the security agents rushing around the lobby with their radios held close to their ears. Then we heard the bad news–everyone was instructed to evacuate the building immediately. Well, I remembered that the last time I saw Eudine she was in the hotel lobby playing with Brandon, so I raced down the stairs to the first floor in an attempt to find them.

After a frantic search, there was no sign of my wife or grandson. That is when I knew that I had to go up to the room on the seventh floor. I undertook this risky trip fully aware that I should have been going in the opposite direction, but I was running on pure adrenaline and was unable to think rationally. I did not find them in the room and was at my wit's end. All of my fears were soon put to rest when I spotted Eudine as she was about to exit the lobby with Brandon in tow. She told me of her ordeal of trying to take Brandon down seven flights in the darkened stairway with the assistance of a lady who was her guardian angel for the day.

As time progressed, I was able to resume air travel, although with considerable apprehension. Traveling out of the Raleigh Durham International Airport was an ordeal. The screening process was onerous and intrusive. Carry-on bags were searched and re-searched. Passengers had to try to keep up with a growing list of items that could not be taken on board. Once seated, it was not uncommon to see passengers studying the faces of fellow passengers to see if anyone fit the profile of a potential terrorist. It was a time of real madness in America. In spite of those developments, Chancellor Ammons and his administration maintained its quest to move NCCU to the next level.

By 2004, approximately three years after Chancellor Ammons' arrival at NCCU, the BBRI's reputation as a Center of Excellence for Health Disparities research and a national model for training students, particularly those from underrepresented minority groups, was well established. The institute had become the driving force for an impressive number of peer-reviewed publications. We authored the university's first Assurance Document that resulted in the creation of an Institutional Animal Care and Use Committee. The latter enabled research-active faculty for the first time in the history of the university to utilize animal models to study human diseases. It also permitted NCCU to hire its first veterinarian, a development that introduced faculty and students to twenty-first century drug discovery and development technologies.

Multi-year budgetary commitments from key National Institutes of Health agencies provided the stimulus for an aggressive faculty recruitment program. For example, by the end of the second year of operation, I had successfully recruited a total of twenty-three employees, including ten Ph.D. level scientists. The roster of full-time BBRI employees increased to fifty-two in 2005, with twenty-seven members of that group being Ph.D. level scientists. Together, those faculty members trained six junior faculty; eleven post-doctoral fellows, two of whom transitioned to tenure-track positions; eight graduate students; and thirty undergraduates. That was possible because the faculty recruitment plan was designed to foster the development of highly focused, productive programs that addressed minority health disparities. This made it easier for prospective trainees to consider the BBRI to be an important disease prevention and science education resource. Those scientists were engaged in an intensive effort to identify and analyze genes implicated in diseases such as cancer and hypertension. They were attempting to better understand how changes in the linear sequence of the genetic information known as Single Nucleotide Polymorphisms or SNPs are able to alter the function of a gene to cause a particular disease. The emphasis on studying the association of genetic change with disease causation was a major strength of the BBRI. It was the glue that brought the institute's research portfolio into general alignment with the research programs supported by the biotechnology industry and the major pharmaceutical companies. It became an attractive way to promote interdisciplinary and inter-institutional collaborations.

One of the BBRI's most impressive achievements was in the area of grantsmanship. I authored several grants that provided more than $30 million of support for BBRI research and training programs. In 2004, I was the recipient of NCCU's largest award ever. It was a grant from the National Center on Minority Health and Health Disparities. BBRI scientists were awarded five RO1 grants during that period, an unprecedented development in the history of the university. RO1 grants are considered to be the gold standard of investigator-initiated research, and those five grants were proof positive of the quality of the research projects that were conducted in BBRI laboratories. One of those grants was awarded to a junior investigator, representing the first time ever that an NCCU faculty member was able to transition from junior faculty to RO1 funded investigator!

The well-documented faculty and student successes combined with the institute's designation as a Center of Excellence for Health Disparities Research helped to propel the BBRI into a position of even greater prominence nationally. In addition to the research and training programs sponsored by the institute, the Engagement and Outreach initiative became one of its signature programs. It was the stimulus for creating a drama-based initiative that proved most effective in the delivery of health education messages to communities served by NCCU.

The BBRI's Engagement and Outreach Program was project team driven with significant involvement of scientists from the institute along with faculty and students from the theater, psychology, health education, and nursing departments. The program's focus was to increase faculty and student involvement in structured engagement and outreach activities. It sought to translate the BBRI's research and training programs into a viable community health education initiative; and it utilized drama-based methods to deliver health education messages. By the end of its fifth year, the program had sponsored plays that increased community awareness of heart disease, stroke, drug abuse and addiction, breast cancer, and AIDS.

Each year's program began with meetings between the BBRI research team and the local organizations that were committed to collaborating on the project. Team members used those meetings to gather information, identify appropriate stakeholders, discuss logistics, hire a playwright, and design culturally-sensitive instruments to facilitate the collection of relevant information. The playwright worked on the script and presented the first draft to project team members for review and modification. The Program Leader hired actors and other production personnel, and identified community groups and expert panelists. The play was widely advertised across the targeted communities, and the performances were held on campus in the university's theater.

The performances were scheduled for two consecutive weekends during the summer, with pre- and post-performance surveys administered by members of the project team. Outcomes included increased knowledge and awareness of the health disparity dealt with in the play; reported intention to change behavior by community participants; increased willingness to discuss health disparity problems with family members; and increased involvement in structured efforts to address health-related issues with community groups.

In addition to its contributions to science, the institute brought considerable distinction to the university by generating three patent applications describing new technologies developed at NCCU; and publishing on average more than forty manuscripts annually in peer-reviewed journals. Unwavering commitment from the NCCU administration and the formation of strategic alliances were prerequisites to the institute's remarkable successes.

There were several other key initiatives undertaken during the Ammons administration, and I had the good fortune of being a major player in some of them. The program that significantly elevated NCCU's image was the successful partnership in a statewide campaign launched by the Biomanufacturing Pharmaceutical Training Consortium (BPTC).

Word of the development of BPTC reached NCCU almost one year after the state legislature had reviewed and rejected a request submitted by North Carolina State University for funding to create such a consortium. The idea made good sense. Its central focus was on workforce development. Realizing that the decline in textiles, tobacco farming, and furniture manufacturing left many North Carolinians unemployed, the state of North Carolina through the newly formed Golden LEAF (Long-term Economic Advancement Foundation) sought to expand its biomanufacturing base by providing incentives to attract new companies. One of the incentives that proved to be most effective was the promise of easy access to a trained workforce.

The state's fifty-eight community colleges and North Carolina State University were key players in the revised proposal, and NCCU campaigned successfully to be included as the third active participant in that major economic development initiative. I wrote the NCCU proposal, and collaborated with the Associate Provost to develop the five-year budget plan. I also conceived of the acronym BRITE as the most appropriate designation for the new program. My initial attempt to convert letters into words was almost effortless, so in less than ten minutes, I was able to fill in the words Biomanufacturing, Research, Institute, and Training. Then I really got stuck. I couldn't think of an appropriate word for the letter E. I wanted to identify a word that best represented the mission and vision of the proposed new institute. In desperation I appealed to the Chancellor's Chief of Staff who was a bright, high energy, hands-on Executive Assistant. Without hesitating, she uttered the word Enterprise, and that was the designation I used for the program in my proposal.

The new Institute was named BRITE as I suggested, forever reminding all stakeholders of NCCU's commitment to preparing the brightest and best graduates for the biomanufacturing industry. The fight for the BRITE program was just beginning. It took months of aggressive action from the NCCU leadership team, in concert with the support of key members of the North Carolina Legislature, before NCCU became a serious contender for membership in the consortium. There were criticisms of our student enrolment projections; our curriculum; our desire to include research in the proposed curriculum; and the size and type of facility that we said we needed for student training and education.

On August 7, 2003, the Golden LEAF Board voted to provide $19.1 million in funding to NCCU to build the BRITE Institute. It was envisioned that BRITE would collaborate with industry and community leaders to develop comprehensive curricula to provide high school and community college graduates with expert training in biomanufacturing. Enrollees in the program could pursue bachelors, masters, and doctoral degrees in areas such as process development, quality control, and quality assurance.

In 2006, because of Chancellor Ammons' aggressive marketing strategies and as a result of the remarkable successes of the BBRI, NCCU was invited to become a partner in a new consortium in Kannapolis, North Carolina. Kannapolis, a tiny community approximately twenty miles north of the city of Charlotte, became a major site for textile manufacturing at the beginning of the twentieth century when James Cannon founded the Cannon Manufacturing Plant there. The company produced many of the sheets, towels, comforters and other textile-based products commonly used in American households. Cannon controlled much of the commercial activity in Kannapolis, and the community was completely dependent on the jobs that his company provided.

Pacific Holdings, a company owned by David Murdock, purchased the Cannon Mills Company in 1982, and four years later the bed and bath operations were sold to Field Crest Mills. Pillowtex acquired Field Crest in 1997 and when that company closed in 2003, more than four thousand workers lost their jobs. David Murdock again came to the rescue when he purchased the company in 2004. In 2006 he demolished the more than six-million square-foot plant, making way for the construction of the North Carolina Research Campus.

Mr. Murdock's vision was that the massive development at the former Pillowtex site would significantly expand and enhance research on food and nutrition within the region and state. He believed that the proposed research campus would strengthen the growing biotechnology cluster in North Carolina. He thought that this would attract additional companies to the state, and their presence could serve as a driver for research and economic development. His dream for the campus included an $80 million, three hundred eleven thousand square foot domed structure to house the David Murdock, state-of-the-art Core Laboratory. He wanted that building to be the centerpiece of the campus, and when completed, he felt that it would provide broad technical support to the many corporate and academic scientists he planned to attract to Kannapolis.

Mr. Murdock also planned to surround the Core Laboratory with more than one million square feet of laboratory and office space to house the research programs of six constituent institutions from the UNC System; Duke University; Lab Corps; and his own company the Dole Food Company. Additionally, he indicated that he would dedicate approximately three hundred fifty thousand square feet to medical offices, residences, a town hall, a movie theater, a hotel, a performing arts center and conference facility, a wellness center, a girls high school for math and science, a community college, multiple parks, and a central green.

I was asked by Chancellor Ammons to draft a strategic plan to create an NCCU Center of Excellence in Human Nutrition at Kannapolis. I saw this as an excellent opportunity to expand the BBRI's research programs in a manner that would foster heightened interactions with many of the scientists that were planning to move to Kannapolis.

The thematic focus of the program that I proposed emphasized the use of zebrafish and rodent models to study the effects of diet and herbal medicines on the prevention and treatment of cancer, diabetes, and cardiovascular disease. I was fully aware of the fact that zebrafish could serve as a unique model for studying human diseases and development.

Their utility had already been demonstrated in developmental biology studies ongoing in the BBRI. Their small genome size, short generation time, optical transparency, and the ease with which their embryos could be manipulated made them ideally suited for the Human Nutrition Research Program. Furthermore, production of fish could be conveniently increased for large-scale evaluation of the effect of any dietary component or metabolite on their growth and development. I requested a suite of laboratories at the Kannapolis site along with funds to hire research personnel, procure equipment and supplies, and support student education and training. My proposal was approved, and NCCU became one of the founding members of the North Carolina Research Campus at Kannapolis.

On October 20, 2008 after intensive planning and development, the new North Carolina Research Campus at Kannapolis was officially dedicated. It comprised more than one million square feet of laboratory and office space, and was constructed at a cost of one and a half billion dollars. Several buildings dotted the landscape of that professionally designed research center. The Core Laboratory building with its more that three hundred eleven thousand square feet of state-of-the-art laboratories anchored the campus. Buildings dedicated to supporting the research programs of the partner institutions provided the space needed to house the nutrition research programs. Companies such as Lab Corps, Red Hat, Carl Zeiss and other biotechnology based organizations were among the early partners.

NCCU's program was housed in the UNC Nutrition Research Building, a one hundred twenty-six thousand sq ft, four-story structure dedicated to supporting research in the area of Human Nutrition. Three other UNC System institutions occupied the building along with NCCU. They included UNC at Chapel Hill, North Carolina Agricultural and Technical University, and UNC at Greensboro. Because of my extensive experience in establishing new institutes and centers, I was able to hire research personnel and launch the BBRI's Human Nutrition Program before the campus was officially opened. Operating out of temporary offices during Phase-1 of the Program's development (April to June 2008), I hired two new faculty and procured relevant equipment and supplies. By

August, the two new hires moved into the building and started their research programs. By the end of that calendar year, those investigators had already been awarded research grants and published manuscripts in peer-reviewed journals.

One day, as I sat in my office on the Kannapolis campus thinking about how exciting it was to be directing a major research program on human nutrition at one of the world's largest research campuses, I remembered what Dad always told me. He would say, "Ken, always remember that a proper diet and regular physical exercise is the best way to stay healthy." How interesting, I thought.

Chapter 24

Honors and Awards

My achievements as Director of the BBRI did not go unnoticed by Chancellor Ammons. He routinely had his public relations office highlight the institute's successes in its weekly press releases. Then in January 2006, he informed me of his intention to nominate me for the Oliver Max Gardner Award. In his letter to the Chair of NCCU's Nominating Committee he cited two examples of my achievements that convinced him that I was deserving of such an honor. The first related to my contributions in the area of health disparities research. He commended me for being a recipient of a Center of Excellence Award, and for developing innovative, culturally-relevant health education messages for delivery to communities within the state.

The second accomplishment he referenced was my contributions to the area of workforce development. He talked about the proposal I authored that resulted in an award of $19.1 million from the Golden LEAF Foundation to create the BRITE Program. He also cited my service on regional and national boards and committees as a compelling reason for selecting me as the 2006 Oliver Max Gardner honoree.

The Oliver Max Gardner Award was the oldest and most distinctive statewide honor given to faculty members by the Board of Governors of the UNC System. Initiated in 1949 by the North Carolina Legislature as directed by the Will of Oliver Max Gardner who was Governor of North Carolina from 1929 to 1933, the Oliver Max Gardner Award is given annually to the faculty member who in the opinion of the UNC System Board of Governors made the greatest contribution to the welfare of the human race.

Friday May 12, 2006 was a beautiful morning in every sense of the word. I arrived at the UNC System Building around nine o'clock. The members of the Board of Governors were already assembled in the large conference room. At nine-thirty, the Chairman of the Board called the meeting to order. With Eudine at my side, our children Dionne and Kevin, and my siblings Joyce, Kid, Peggy, Roger, and Philip, I sat quietly as the citation was read by the Chairperson of the Selection Committee. Then the lights were turned down, and we all got to watch a video that highlighted my career as a scientist. Then, the President of the UNC System asked me to approach the podium where I was presented with the 2006 Oliver Max Gardner Award.

In my acceptance speech, I thanked Chancellor Ammons for nominating me and the Board of Governor for considering me worthy of such distinction. I indicated to everyone gathered in that spacious board room that I was accepting the award with much humility. I reminded them that it was my parents who had nurtured me and instilled in me the value of scholarship and hard work. I told them that I particularly wanted to thank Eudine for the patience she consistently displayed, and the encouragement and support she provided me throughout my entire career. I reminded them about how rapidly the world of science had changed since I was a graduate student. I revisited the time I spent working in the laboratory of my mentor Jack Goldstein, and wanted to let them know that it was he who introduced me to the world of nucleic acids research. I told them that it was at Pfizer Central Research that my research toolbox grew in size and sophistication. That it was there where I was first exposed to the discipline of Molecular Genetics. I recounted my successes with cloning the rennin gene, and the subsequent events that led to the successful development of the first recombinant DNA process for a food ingredient; and I also told them about my involvement in the design and implementation of molecular strategies for discovering novel anti-cancer drugs. I talked about my other mentors and about how they influenced my career development path. I concluded with a pledge to continue to use my skills and experience to help train the next generation of biomedical scientists.

Chancellor Ammons was so proud of the work I had done, and he was particularly appreciative of the fact that I had brought national attention to NCCU's contributions in the biomedical sciences and biotechnology. In order to show his appreciation, he awarded me the highest honor that NCCU could bestow on a faculty member–The Chancellor's Merit Award for Exemplary Service to NCCU in the field of Higher Education. On the eighteenth of October, in the Grand Hall of the NCCU Law School, he sponsored a special dinner, complete with Caribbean foods and trappings. He assembled a group of university administrators, colleagues of mine, and friends of the university, and he had the NCCU Jazz band provide the music. Eudine, Kevin and his wife Lisa, my grandsons Brandon and Jaden, and Phil were in attendance. It was a memorable evening, particularly when the Jazz Band began playing our favorite song *Little Things Mean A lot*.

In June 2007, I was selected by the President of the UNC System to serve as a member of the Scholar's Council. That group of highly distinguished professors was drawn from several of the constituent institutions within the UNC System, and represented some of the best minds that could be assembled to take on the task that they would be assigned by the President. Designated the UNC Tomorrow Initiative, its purpose was to determine how the UNC System could respond more directly and proactively to the twenty-first century challenges facing the state of North Carolina.

The fourteen-member Scholar's Council was first asked to develop "framing reports" that identified the major issues and trends that might impact North Carolina over a period of twenty years. "Framing questions" would then be compiled from information provided in the reports, and used to guide the discussion in a series of public listening forums that were scheduled across the state. Members of the Scholars Council were also required to participate in the regional listening forums along with the UNC Tomorrow Commission–a twenty-eight member blue-ribbon group that included business, education, government, and non-profit leaders drawn from a cross section of North Carolina communities.

For approximately one year, my colleagues and I developed the "framing-reports" and discussed them with the UNC Tomorrow Commission. We then attended the regional forums and collected data on issues and trends after listening to members of the public articulate their specific needs. We drafted a final report that detailed our findings, and identified the changes that we believed the UNC System needed to make in response to the inputs obtained from all stakeholders.

My work on the Scholar's Council was one of the highlights of my career as a tenured professor in the UNC System. I enjoyed interacting with my colleagues whose credentials were so impressive that I was deeply honored to have been selected to serve with such a distinguished group. Their resumes spanned disciplines such as Health Policy, Political Science, English, Information Management, Agriculture, Psychology, Chemical Engineering, Technology and Science; and the Biomedical Sciences and Biotechnology. I made valuable friendships with several members of the Council. I visited them at their home campuses, and was able to gain their perspective on what they felt to be the best course of action the UNC System could take to better align the respective campuses with the unique economic development needs of the regions they were established to serve.

In November, I was once again honored for my contributions to biotechnology and the biomedical sciences. This time it was for high, meritorious service in the field of cancer research, and it was the Government of Barbados that decided to recognize the contributions I made to the War on Cancer effort. The occasion was the fortieth anniversary of Barbados' independence. The award was the Gold Crown of Merit. It was forty-six years since I left Barbados to enter NYU to pursue a career as a scientist. After almost five decades, I was returning to Barbados to be the recipient of one of the honors the Government was bestowing on a select group of its native sons.

The investiture for all recipients of the 2006 National Independence Honors was held in a gigantic air-conditioned tent that was pitched on the grounds of the Governor General's official residence. All honorees were seated in rows of chairs meticulously positioned on a dais in front of an extremely large gathering drawn from a cross section of the privileged classes in Barbados. The interior of the tent was well decorated with impressive banners and large photographs of Barbadian sports personalities. The Royal Barbadian Police Force Band played a number of musical selections. The signal that the program was about to begin came when the Honor Guard and two members of the Barbados Defense Force in their distinctive Zouave costumes took up their positions on either side of the pathway at the entrance to the tent. Amidst considerable pomp and ceremony, the Chief Justice arrived, followed by the Prime Minister, and their Excellencies the Governor-General Sir Clifford Husbands and his wife Lady Husbands. After the Governor-General reached the dais, the Royal Barbados Police Force played the National Anthem in their inimitable style, and the Investiture began.

The Orator that day was Professor Henry Fraser an alumnus of the Lodge School and a longtime friend. When it was my turn to be presented with the Gold Crown of Merit Award, I was signaled to step forward to the platform to face Sir Clifford. As I stood there before the glaring lights of the television cameras, I could hear Professor Fraser clear his throat as he began to read the citation. I was pleasantly surprised when he told the audience that he and I had overlapped as students at the Lodge School. He then talked about my remarkable skills as a soccer player, cleverly weaving some of the history of the rivalry between Lodge and Harrison College into the profile of my career that he shared with the audience. I was desperately trying to maintain a calm exterior during what I thought to be a very hilarious presentation.

When the last citation was read and the formal proceedings of the Investiture ended, the Governor-General and his wife withdrew to the house and the Honor Guard marched off. Sir Clifford returned later, less formally attired to rejoin the honorees and their guests for a cultural presentation. I found the skits to be well choreographed and authentically Bajan. I thought that the young performers were talented and very much in touch with their cultural heritage.

The evening concluded with an official photo session in the dining room of Government House, and everyone was treated to a sumptuous reception on the grounds of the mansion. The crowd was so large that it took me almost an hour before I could locate Eudine and the rest of my family. I remember thinking how fortunate I was to be able to share such a special event with my wife, children, and siblings. Oh how I wished that my Mum and Dad could have been there.

The morning after the ceremony, the telephone in my hotel room rang, and when I picked up the receiver, I realized that it was the headmaster of the Lodge School on the line. He apologized for calling so early, but explained that he wanted to extend his personal congratulations to me as the recipient of a Gold Crown of Merit Award. He went on to tell me that he was so proud of my accomplishment that he wanted to have me address the entire assembly of students before I left the island. He apologized profusely for the short notice, and offered me a choice of either the Monday or Tuesday morning of the following week for my presentation. I thanked him for his thoughtfulness, and told him that I was happy to accept his invitation.

As I hung up the receiver, I couldn't help remembering the time when, as a young student at Lodge, I participated in a similar event. I believe that I was either in first or second form when the porter Mr. Marshall interrupted my class to tell us that the headmaster wanted all students to assemble in the sports pavilion. The occasion, a visit from a very distinguished Lodge School alumnus. My classmates and I walked across the schoolyard until we reached the pavilion where we were asked to sit on the concrete steps awaiting the arrival of our distinguished guest. The headmaster was obviously very proud of the accomplishments of his guest. During his lengthy introduction, he showered him with praise, and reminded us that there was a lot to look forward to after graduating from Lodge. The speaker did an outstanding job that day. He began by telling us about the time when he was a student at Lodge, and what life was like for a student at that time. He then talked about his experiences after leaving Lodge. The one thing I remember best from that speech, was the story he told us about the Boer War. I had known very little about that war, but when he finished his presentation, it was impossible for me to erase the graphic images from my mind of some of the battles he described. I was particularly intrigued to learn about the bravery and strength that was exhibited by the British army Brigade of Gurkhas during that terrible war. His visit impressed me profoundly, and I always thought about how wonderful it must have been for him to return to his alma mater to share those incredible stories with a new generation of Lodge boys.

Now it was going to be my turn to address an assembly of Lodge School students. This was a different time, and the story I wanted to share with the students was one about the future not the past. My wish was that I would be able to make an impression on at least one student in that assembly, just as I was impressed by the speaker more than a half of a century ago!

I arrived at Lodge just before 8:00 am on December 4, 2006. The campus had changed significantly since my departure in 1958. I parked my car in a small parking lot on the perimeter of what used to be the second-eleven field. The building that housed Prep form in 1948 was still there. I took the short walk to the headmaster's office that occupied the building that was once used as the boarding master's residence. I sat in the reception area for a few minutes before a slim gentleman of modest build emerged through the doorway to greet me, it was the headmaster. He extended his hand and indicated that he deeply appreciated my willingness to be the guest speaker for that morning's assembly. After a brief exchange, I was on my way to meet the students.

As we approached the Assembly Hall, I noticed that unlike the time when I was at school there, the students had gathered in the paved area in front of the Hall rather that inside of the building. I was standing on the steps in front of the Hall where we met annually to have our official photographs taken. When I looked out over the large gathering of students, the first thing that struck me was that Lodge was now a co-ed institution. The sight of so many girls at assembly was something I needed some time to get adjusted to. The number of students in attendance was a clear testimony to how much the school had grown in enrolment since my days as a student there.

The headmaster was very generous in his introductory remarks, and the moment I had waited for had finally come. I began my talk by briefly reminiscing about my time as a Lodge School student. I recalled the time when I was in their position listening to an alumnus come back to tell his story. I told them how that talk has resonated with me over the years. I talked about Lodge's exemplary past, and about the many different ways my life was shaped by my experiences as a Lodge School student. I talked briefly about my work in cancer research, and about how well my teachers at Lodge had prepared me for the career I chose. The message I tried to leave with them that day was that mentorship and hard work are key ingredients to good career planning. I told them that their success in whatever career path they chose would depend on their willingness to listen to their mentors, work hard, and dream big dreams.

After assembly, the headmaster invited me to meet in the Boardroom with a group of faculty, staff, and student leaders. The Boardroom was located on the other side of campus in the building that once housed the school's sanitarium. We met at a large table and engaged in a very constructive conversation over sandwiches and fruit juice. I talked about the Pre-College Program that I had initiated at NCCU and I told them how effective that program was in helping to broaden student exposure to careers in the biomedical sciences and biotechnology. I challenged them to identify two students that they believed would benefit from participation in such a program. I told them that if they could submit the names of those students to me on or before May 2007, along with their completed applications and a letter of recommendation from the headmaster, I would be able to expedite the reviews and could notify them of our decision immediately after the reviews were completed. I cautioned them to select the best-qualified students whom they felt could serve as exceptional ambassadors for their institution.

I did not feel that it was necessary for me to tell them that I had developed this passion to give back based on the positive inputs I had received from several kind and caring individuals during the course of my life. The lesson I learned from my family, and from mentors like Mr. Gittens, Mr. Tobin, Jack, and others was that it is critically important to remember that one good turn deserves another.

I was delighted when I discovered that the headmaster shared my feelings and was keenly interested in having his students participate in the NCCU program. He liked the idea of providing them with an international summer internship experience, because he was convinced that it would give them an entirely new perspective on the world of science and technology.

Two sixth formers, Cherish and Verol-Ann were the first Lodge School students to apply. They were both highly qualified students, and my Education and Training Committee lost little time in admitting them to the 2007 Pre-College Summer Internship Program that began on June seventeenth and ended July eighteenth.

Like the other student trainees, they were required to live on campus in one of the residence halls. Their day typically began with a lecture that was held in the BBRI's auditorium, and presented by one of the research-active scientists. At the conclusion of the lecture, they, along with their American counterparts, joined the BBRI's project teams to work on a research project of their choice. Every afternoon, Cherish and Verol-Ann were required to attend a forum that was co-sponsored by the BBRI and the University's Summer Ventures Program. Those forums exposed them to a range of academically strengthening activities.

The combination of didactic teaching and basic research introduced Cherish and Verrol-Ann to some basic principles of biology and chemistry, and showed them how a combination of the two could help a scientist to solve a real-world problem. At the conclusion of the formal program, Cherish, Verrol-Ann and their American counterparts presented their findings at a research symposium that was attended by faculty, mentors, and peers. I was extremely proud of their performance at that symposium. I was convinced that the expenses incurred for their round-trip travel to Durham, room and board, and scholarship check were completely worthwhile.

Word about the success of the Pre-College Summer Internship Program, and about the positive experiences of Cherish and Verol-Ann quickly reached the secondary schools in Barbados. I believe that the news was spread by the Honorable Edward Bushell who, at that time, was serving as the Barbados Consul-General in Miami, Florida. On one of his visits to North Carolina, he requested and was granted a tour of the BBRI. I remember telling him about our Pre-College Internship Program, and I could tell that he was impressed by what he saw and heard. He became one of the program's most vocal supporters.

Three Barbadian students applied to the program in 2008. Two of the applicants were students at the Barbados Community College and the third was from the Lodge School. One of the Community College students withdrew for religious reasons, and we accepted the other Community College student, Samira. Delacia, a sixth former at the Lodge School, was the other student selected that year. The Education Director did an outstanding job of managing and flawlessly coordinating the various academic and extracurricular activities for those two students. Delacia and Samira thoroughly enjoyed the experience at the BBRI, particularly Samira who became so fired-up that she could hardly wait to begin her career as a pharmacologist in the fall. Delacia's plans included enrolling in the undergraduate program in biochemistry at the University of the West Indies, Cave Hill Campus, Barbados. Both students were provided with the same perquisites as their American counterparts.

By 2006, because of its well-documented achievements in the areas of grantsmanship, publications, and scholarship the BBRI was gaining regional and national attention. I had raised more funds from private foundations, corporate sources, and government agencies than all departments within the College of Arts and Sciences. The number of manuscripts that BBRI scientists published in peer-reviewed journals had reached an all-time high, and there was a concomitant increase in the number of research citations. Patenting of new discoveries had increased dramatically; and I had successfully launched the university's first Post-doctoral Program. Based on these indicators, it was clearly evident that NCCU was about to join the ranks of a small group of state institutions that had the potential to earn the designation of research university. Many of my colleagues in the biotechnology industry and in academia also shared that view.

Chancellor Ammons in his inimitable style wasted little time in capitalizing on those developments. He created a Doctoral Degree Task Force and named me as its chairperson. My charge was to develop a proposal for NCCU's first Doctoral Program in the Biomedical and Pharmaceutical Sciences. My committee went to work immediately assessing needs and defining the key objectives of such a program. Within three months we had completed the first draft of a proposal. Everything we proposed was doable within the projected timelines, and I genuinely believed that it would just be a matter of time before our proposal would be submitted to the UNC System Board of Governors for review and approval.

The Board never got a chance to review that proposal. While the Task Force was busily crafting and refining the document, we learned that Chancellor Ammons was being considered for the job as President of Florida A&M University. It was a shocker, but there was little that we could do but wait. Rumors were circulating all across campus that he had already been named as Florida A&M University President, and that had a chilling effect on the Task Force's efforts, causing important decisions to be placed on hold. It did not take long before the rumors were confirmed, and it became official that Chancellor Ammons would be leaving NCCU to become the President of Florida A&M University.

The Ammons years at NCCU were the glory years for promoting and supporting biomedical science and biotechnology. That was what attracted him to NCCU, and like Chancellor Chambers he was firmly committed to transforming NCCU from a teaching institution to a research center with the capacity to contribute significantly to workforce and economic development within North Carolina, specifically and the nation, generally. NCCU's Public Relations Office was a major resource that Chancellor Ammons used effectively to promote his message of positive change to all stakeholders across the RTP and beyond.

Chapter 25

Change Is In The Air

In February, I attended a special meeting sponsored by the American Association for Cancer Research. The title of that meeting was "Molecular Biology and Therapeutic Strategies: Cancer research in the 21st Century." The venue was Hawaii with all of the scientific sessions held in Kaanapali, Maui. It was a memorable meeting featuring exciting science presented by American and Japanese cancer research experts. I was pleased to learn how far the field had come in the years since I worked on the Cancer Drug Discovery team at Pfizer.

I met a faculty member from Tuskegee University at that meeting. He was a talented, young African American biochemist who shared my passion for training the next generation of minority scientists. He and I talked at length about our successes and the challenges that we faced in trying to increase minority participation in the science, technology, engineering, and mathematics disciplines. I talked to him about the Task Force that I was chairing, and about NCCU's desire to establish its first doctoral degree program in science. I returned to Durham energized, and further convinced that we were moving in the right direction. It was good to know that there were others who felt the same urgency that I was feeling about the value of having a strong doctoral program at an institution like NCCU.

When Chancellor Ammons left NCCU to assume the presidency of Florida A&M University, I felt that NCCU had lost a golden opportunity to develop its first Ph.D. program in a science discipline. It was Chancellor Ammons who had pushed aggressively for a Ph.D. program. He was completely aware of the fact that a bold initiative such as that would require involvement of and unwavering support from the Chancellor's office. Although I was aware that a change in administration could further delay the application process for the Ph.D. program, I did not spend much time worrying about that possibility. What concerned me most was the overarching need to maintain the integrity of the institute's reporting structure and method of operation.

Chancellor Chambers and I had fought long and hard to obtain Board of Governors approval for the existing reporting structure, and I couldn't even entertain the thought that a new administration might want to tinker with it. I still felt confident that the roster of prominent supporters that I developed within the corporate and academic communities would assist me in neutralizing any assault on the institute's organizational structure and stability. Several of the BBRI's friends had reassured me that it would be virtually impossible for anyone to even think of doing anything that could compromise the institute's record of success. After all, the BBRI had earned national recognition as a Center of Excellence for Health Disparities Research. Its unique reporting structure was always considered by NIH peer reviewers to be among its greatest assets.

A Search Committee was impaneled and charged with recruiting the next NCCU Chancellor. I was chosen to be a member of that committee. Before long, the campus was caught up in the ritual of selecting a new leader. Like everyone else on the committee, I desperately wanted to find someone with clear ideas about how to build on the successes of the Chambers and Ammons administrations. From that vantage point, I was able to get a good sense of the quality of the individuals included in the candidate pool. As expected, they all said that it was NCCU's reputation in science and law that was the driving force behind their decision to seek the position of chancellor.

In order to preserve the confidentiality of the process, the committee was sequestered in a hotel fifty miles away from campus. The list of questions that we used for the interview process was developed from information that the committee gathered from focus group meetings conducted with a cross section of NCCU stakeholders. It was a thorough and fair process that was coordinated by one of the nation's leading search firms. After a week of interviews and deliberations, the committee reached a decision, and submitted an unranked list of three finalists to the President of the UNC System. The President reviewed the list of finalists and selected NCCU's next chancellor. In August 2007, NCCU welcomed its tenth chancellor.

In his installation address, the new chancellor shared his vision with the campus community. He told a packed gymnasium that he desired to have NCCU keep up with the rapid pace of globalization. He felt that NCCU should strive to be "...among the best comprehensive, public, liberal arts universities in the southeast, graduating students who are prepared to live and lead successfully in the global world." He promised to implement three Ph.D. programs within the next six years, "beginning with a multidisciplinary Ph.D. program in Biomedical and Pharmaceutical Science" that he felt would "build on the strengths of the BBRI and BRITE initiatives." The other two doctoral programs he proposed to develop included one in Library and Information Sciences and the other in Communication Disorders.

The lengthy speech entitled "In Pursuit of Excellence: a Return to Basics," seemed to be well received by the large gathering of students, faculty, alumni, and friends of the institution. I remember how I couldn't help wondering what was meant by the phrase "a Return to Basics," and hoped that it did not in any way signal a departure from the policies and practices of the Chambers and Ammons administrations.

It did not take long before the new chancellor announced the creation of a position called the Vice Chancellor for Graduate Studies and Research. The job description indicated that the successful candidate for that new position would have budgetary and scientific control of the two institutes, and my instincts told me that the voices that were clamoring to have the institute's faculty assume heavier teaching loads were gaining traction within the new administration. It was also clear that administrative responsibility for managing the BBRI and BRITE was about to change.

Ironically, that was a time when the UNC System had rolled out its UNC Tomorrow initiative. The President of the System was pressing all chancellors to better-align their programs and policies with the needs of the state. He wanted universities like NCCU to become drivers of workforce and economic development. The draft of the Ph.D. program that we developed before Chancellor Ammons left, was designed to do just that. But with the changes that were being proposed in the new administration, the clock was about to be reset on one of the most important initiatives the university was about to undertake as it approached its hundredth anniversary.

After much self-searching, I thought it best to take a break so that I could get away from the day-to-day grind of managing the institute. After all, I had spent more than ten years establishing and running a high-demand institute that now had a roster of more than fifty full-time employees. During that period, I had devoted 100-percent of my time to ensure that all of the institute's programs met the highest standards of excellence. I felt that I had earned the right to get away for at least six months, so I submitted a request for that long-delayed sabbatical. On January 6, 2009, I took my first official leave from NCCU.

As I left the campus late that January evening, I found myself reflecting on the enormity of the task I assumed in 1998, and I was filled with pride when I thought about how profoundly science education had changed at NCCU as a result of my efforts. I remembered my first conversation with Chancellor Chambers about best practices, and the need to establish a reasonable balance between teaching and research. In that dialogue, the chancellor and I agreed to follow the lead of the major U.S. research universities. That model places a high priority on recruiting the brightest and best research faculty possible, and providing them with the infrastructure and resources necessary for success. In those settings, release time and research space are allocated based on a formula that rewards outstanding performance. Investigators with the largest budgets are awarded release time and space consistent with their ability to pay. It is no secret that arrangements such as I just described are largely responsible for the phenomenal success of America's research universities.

I thought about the struggle I went through to convince my colleagues at NCCU of the wisdom of adopting such a practice. The argument Chancellor Chambers and I made seemed so obvious, that I simply could not understand why some of my faculty colleagues were reluctant to support it. Why was it so difficult for them to see that the university desperately needed to modify some of its arcane practices if it truly desired to embrace research as one of its major priorities. The answer, I would later discover, had more to do with tradition than with rational thinking.

The record shows that HBCUs were initially established as teaching institutions or Normal Schools. Their primary goal was to increase literacy rates among the descendants of slaves. For decades they focused on preparing the priests and teachers that were desperately needed to educate the masses. Waves and waves of graduates from those southern Normal Schools migrated north and made significant contributions in educating blacks who were trapped in the ghettoes of the large cities. It was therefore not surprising for me to understand why many HBCU administrators would be reluctant to talk about research in the same way that they talked about teaching. I remembered that the faculty at NCCU was divided into two camps: the progressives who wanted reform, and saw the BBRI as an instrument for such change; and the traditionalists who felt threatened by the administration's desire to make research a permanent part of the university's mission. These were the staunch supporters of the status quo. While the progressives instantly saw the value of research and campaigned actively for the proposed change, the traditionalists countered by warning that research was much too expensive, and an unnecessary burden on a faculty already strapped with heavy teaching loads. They felt strongly that the university's limited resources should be directed exclusively to support its teaching mission.

I reflected on the many times that I found myself trying to compare the research culture at NCCU to the culture I experienced in the pharmaceutical industry. One notable example that I often cited to show my colleagues how industry differs from academia was the occasion of the publication of the Human Genome Sequence. On February 15, 2001, the Journal *Nature* published the complete sequence of the Human Genome. The following day the Journal *Science* carried a banner headline–The Human Genome. *Science* adorned its cover with a DNA chain assembled from the faces of a diverse group of individuals; while *Nature* displayed a segment of the DNA double helix against a background constructed from innumerable human faces.

In its editorial page, *Science* boldly stated–"we have received a powerful tool for unlocking the secrets of our genetic heritage and for finding our place among the other participants in the adventure of life." The commentary section of the journal *Nature* warned that, "the complete sequencing of the human genome ... threatens to throw the patent system into disarray!" That was a heady time, and I could hardly contain the excitement that welled up inside me.

I thought of how my colleagues in industry would have reacted to those groundbreaking reports. Project teams would have been hastily convened to pour over the sequencing data. Senior management would have appointed a taskforce comprising experts drawn from different disciplines, and that group would have been charged with determining how the published information could be used to advance ongoing discovery projects, or aid in the identification of novel biomarkers for disease. There would have been intensive discussions about reagent procurement; consultancy arrangements; patents; secrecy agreements; and new opportunities. That was how industry would have reacted to such an important development. At NCCU however, no special meetings were held; no one called to discuss the implications of those groundbreaking reports; and no exploratory projects were set in motion. The reason for such a tepid response had little to do with money and much to do with attitude. I will always believe that the university's reaction in February 2001 represented a missed opportunity for students and faculty alike.

During the first week of my sabbatical, I spent some time reflecting on what it would take for NCCU to consolidate the gains that I had made over the past ten years. I incorporated my thoughts into a document that I entitled, "Four strategic imperatives for strengthening and enhancing research at NCCU."

The first involved continued support of the BBRI as a Center of Excellence with oversight for all of NCCU's health disparities research. The second required an unwavering commitment to the project team mode of operation for all the institute's programs and projects. The third called on the administration to retain the unique reporting structure of the institute. And the fourth advocated for a continuation of the policy to have panels of experienced scientists review all BBRI research programs on an annual basis.

While the number of faculty members conducting organized research within the Biology and Chemistry Departments remained unacceptably low, it was important for NCCU to support the Centers of Excellence model conceived by former Chancellor Chambers. The BBRI was the appropriate vehicle through which all of NCCU's health disparities research could be channeled.

The Project Team mode of operation provides a critical link between discovery and development. This mode of operation is essential to research productivity, and serves as an effective student recruitment tool. As an innovative model that fosters and supports research and student training, the BBRI should be encouraged to continue to use the Project Team mode of operation to promote inter-disciplinary research across the various NCCU schools and colleges. The combination of rigorous standards with this proven mode of operation can be a powerful force for change, and should be maintained as an integral part of the university's strategic planning process.

The basis of much of the BBRI's remarkable success over the first decade of its existence has been the university's unwavering commitment to its unique reporting structure. Most HBCUs are reluctant to commit to an administrative structure in which the director of a research institute reports directly to the president or chancellor. To many, such a reporting structure is viewed as compromising the provost's role as Chief Executive Officer and Chief Academic Officer. To a large extent, faculty who have been steeped in that tradition are unwilling to engage in an objective discussion of the merits of considering an alternate reporting structure. The fact is that in an institution such as NCCU with a Carnegie Classification of Masters Colleges and Universities Large Programs, and a recently established College of Science and Technology, it is unrealistic to expect to build and sustain a Center of Excellence Program without having a critical mass of highly productive scientists.

Departmental and institutional politics, rivalries, and petty jealousies do not augur well for the success of such an arrangement. Additionally, budgetary constraints simply will not permit a provost to reallocate funds from teaching to research. Finally, the most strident voices within science departments tend to be those of faculty members with the longest service and the greatest influence within the faculty senate. Most of these politically connected professors are no longer research-active. To many of them, any attempt to innovate is viewed as undermining the traditional values of the institution. Bold leadership is therefore needed to ensure that research is supported at HBCUs in ways that complement and supplement teaching activities.

As NCCU approached its centennial anniversary, I felt strongly that the university should continue to align its programs and policies with its unique mission and vision. In that regard, the efforts of Chancellor Chambers to make the BBRI the driver of collaborative, long-term, health disparities research should be central to all future planning. The institute should remain the primary vehicle for bringing basic and translational scientists together to design and develop appropriate, culturally relevant instruments for conducting health disparities research. Other key roles for the BBRI include assessing community disease education and assistance needs; developing effective, culturally-specific communications to address those needs; and evaluating the extent to which community-directed health communication messages are accepted by minority groups.

The institute should also continue to develop its core facilities and expand the university's infrastructure in a manner that is appropriate to ensure the success of the research programs that it sponsors. The BBRI's research programs should continue to involve minority students in conducting hypothesis-driven research; stimulate and promote faculty and student exchanges; and increase health disparities awareness through sponsorship of workshops, focus group meetings, and formal seminars.

Finally, subjecting a body of work or ideas to scrutiny by a group of external experts from the same discipline is a key element of the peer review process. It is widely utilized by NIH and by industry, and when buttressed by the appropriate legal instruments, it does not compromise secrecy or ownership of any intellectual property. External reviewers provide objective inputs that invariably improve the quality of the program or activity that they are charged with evaluating. Since its inception, the BBRI has been uncompromising in its quest to have all programs reviewed by External Advisory Committees comprising experts drawn from the respective program disciplines.

Each External Advisory Committee conducted an annual review of a specific program and prepared a written report that was distributed to the chancellor as well as to the agency that funded the particular program or activity. That process proved to be highly valuable to the scientists whose projects were subjected to the committee's scrutiny. It was also very instructive to program leaders as well as to me as Director of the BBRI. It eliminated petty claims of bias by colleagues or supervisors and it provided an objective basis for assessing the strengths and weaknesses of every program. Exposing student trainees to the peer review process proved to be a very constructive way of broadening their perspectives on how science should be practiced. It provided them with a different model of science education than was afforded by the rigid departmental structure with its silo mentality.

The challenge that NCCU faces to educate the next generation of scientists is formidable. It will require the involvement of all stakeholders as it seeks to re-design science curricula to meet current and future challenges. The university's role in increasing minority participation in the biomedical sciences and biotechnology cannot be over emphasized. Because of its unique history, NCCU is the preferred institution to lead the way in designing appropriate strategies to attract, retain, and graduate minority students in a variety of science disciplines. The BBRI has already demonstrated its capacity to meet such a challenge, and NCCU needs to do all it can to preserve the unique structure and vision of one of its most prized possessions.

Chapter 26

Dreams Do Come True

When Dionne graduated from East Lyme High School in 1984, Eudine and I were the proudest parents in all of Connecticut. We had nurtured her from infancy through the teenage years until she became the accomplished young lady that we saw walking across the stage that day. She was surrounded by a loving family that provided her with the support and protection she needed to be successful in a world that had become increasingly more competitive. Above all, I felt that I had done everything possible to keep her firmly grounded in her West Indian roots. Those investments in her paid off in very substantial ways. Not only was she graduating from one of the best high schools in Southeastern Connecticut, but she was also named among the Top-100 Black Achievers in the entire state. All members of the family showed up for her graduation ceremony, and although Dad was trying to cope with failing eyesight caused by glaucoma, I will always remember how his face lit up when Dionne's name reverberated over the loudspeaker system that announced it was her turn to receive her diploma.

Finding the right college for Dionne to pursue her education was my next challenge. Distance from home, location, cost, and institutional reputation were factors that ranked highest on my list of priorities as I tried to help her make that important decision. She was quite resourceful, and that helped Eudine and me to restrict the choices to universities within the New England region. Because of her outstanding academic record, Dionne was offered opportunities to attend Brandeis, Brown, and Wesleyan universities. She interviewed at each of those institutions. She and I toured their campuses; met with admission representatives; and talked to a number of their minority students.

While we were discussing the pros and cons of attending one of those institutions, Dionne received a letter from the University of Connecticut (UConn) at Storrs, informing her that she had been granted early admission to that campus. Their offer was based on the fact that she had been named as one of the state's Top-100 Black Achievers. That was considered to be such a high honor, that UConn held an annual "Day of Pride" celebration to recognize the black scholars and their parents. The honorees were treated like movie stars, and each of them got a chance to spend two days on that campus in one of their newest dormitories. The event was so well organized and executed that when we picked up Dionne at its conclusion, she had made up her mind that she was going to attend UConn. I knew that her best friend and classmate from high school was planning to enroll there in the fall, and felt that Dionne's decision could have been influenced by that reality.

Dionne spent just one year at UConn before concluding that it was not the right place for her. She was dissatisfied with the limited access she had to faculty mentors, and was quite upset by the bad advice she received from their guidance office. She communicated her disaffection to me with a simple statement, "Dad, I feel like I am drowning at Storrs, I really need you to come and rescue me." The news did not surprise me. I knew that she was not impressed by a number of things that had happened during her freshman year, and in some sense, I was relieved that she was prepared to take action. In the summer of 1985, Dionne and I were on the road again looking at colleges. This time however, the task was simpler. Dionne knew that she wanted to go to an HBCU. I sought help from some of my HBCU colleagues, but it was my coworker's daughter who provided the information that we were seeking. Like Dionne, she was a participant in the Pfizer Employees Summer Internship Program. One day when she was having lunch with Dionne, she talked at length about the wonderful time she was having at Hampton University. Dionne was enthralled by what she learned about the social and academic life at one of Virginia's most celebrated HBCUs. We wasted little time in submitting an application, and were thrilled when we received a letter informing her that she had been accepted and could begin classes in the fall.

After four years at Hampton it was once again graduation day, and Dad was there when Dionne received her bachelor's degree. He was also present four years later when Dr. Louis Sullivan, President of Morehouse Medical College, presented her with the MD degree.

Dad also got to attend Kevin's graduation from East Lyme High School; and he was able to make the trip back to Hampton University when Kevin was awarded his bachelor's degree in Accounting. Dionne's experiences at Hampton featured prominently in Kevin's decision to pursue his undergraduate degree there. He felt strongly that exposure to the HBCU culture would provide him with the nurturing environment he needed to excel academically. He was right, because it was at Hampton where he met his wife Lisa who was a student at neighboring Norfolk State University. Kevin would later go on to complete an MBA degree at Elon University in North Carolina.

Both Kevin and Dionne are happily married and pursuing careers in pediatrics and banking, respectively. Dionne has three daughters, Lauryn, Mia, and Danielle. Kevin's children, all boys, include Brandon, Jaden, and Evan. Eudine and I consider ourselves fortunate to have been blessed with six adorable grandchildren. Mum was still alive when Brandon and Lauryn were born, and she got a chance to shower them with affection, even though it seemed to be just for a fleeting moment. Dad did not get to meet any of our grandchildren, but I am confident that he would be proud to know that we have instilled in them the same values that he and Mum passed on to us when we were growing up in Barbados.

In 1991, Dad got to realize yet another dream. Over the thirty years that he spent in the U.S., he always reminded us of his desire to live out his last days in Barbados. Over the years, he made several memorable trips there, and was visibly refreshed after each of those visits. Finally, he was about to have his wish come true, he was going home to escape the harsh New York winters, and reconnect with some of his childhood friends. Joyce was the one who made this possible. She purchased a lovely home in an upscale community on the south coast of Barbados. The house was slightly elevated from the water's edge, and the sound of the waves beating against the rocks could be heard throughout the day and night. Joyce took early retirement from her job at Planned Parenthood International in New York City, and moved home to join Mum, Dad, and Aunt Eude who were already there. It was a joy for me to spend summer and winter breaks with them reminiscing about childhood experiences, and probing them for every bit of information about the family that I could extract.

In 1995, the entire Harewood family was in Barbados on a very special trip. It was the occasion of Peggy's marriage, and we were all elated to be back at home together. It was a traditional wedding with Holy Cross Church serving as the venue for the ceremony, and the Marriott at Sam Lord's Castle the site for the reception. The proceedings continued well into the night, providing ample opportunity for everyone to enjoy the sumptuous Barbadian cuisine, and talk about old times with friends and acquaintances.

It was quite late that night when the formal activities at Sam Lord's Castle finally ended, and the entire contingent of Harewood family members along with some close friends agreed to meet at Joyce's home the following evening. This was an extraordinary gathering because it included all of the children, grandchildren, aunts and uncles. It was our first official family reunion, complete with Tee shirts and videographers. I remember it being a grand occasion. We ate, drank, and swapped childhood stories. Around eleven o'clock that night, I was sitting at the kitchen table next to Dad. My siblings were gathered around the table, some standing others seated, and we were reminiscing about the past. Dad was obviously enjoying himself, so I was surprised when he told me that he was getting tired and wanted to go to bed. I helped him up from his chair, and began to walk him to his room, which was on the other side of the house. On the way, I noticed that there was a slight tremor in his right hand, but I did not think that it was cause for concern. After making sure that he was comfortably tucked into bed, I returned to the kitchen and rejoined the group.

When the party finally ended, Eudine and I left for St. James where we were staying. I mentioned to her that I had noticed a Parkinson's-like tremor in Dad's right hand. We both thought that it was possibly due to the fact that we had all had a very long day.

The following morning I got up early, and after breakfast, I called Joyce to find out how Dad was doing. She told me that she had been up all night battling to keep his temperature under control. It was then that I found out that his temperature had spiked soon after I left, and he had a very high fever during the night, and was obviously not doing well. I told her that Eudine and I would try to get there as soon as we could, our only stop would be at the pharmacy to purchase a few items that we knew Dad needed. I left St. James, and after a brief stop at the pharmacy, I drove directly to Joyce's house in Christ Church. When I arrived, I noticed that the wrought iron gate was wide open, and as I pulled the car into the courtyard, I saw Joyce standing in the carport with the most distraught look on her face. I parked, and before I could say anything, Joyce blurted out the words that I have not been able to forget. She simply told me, " Dad is no longer with us!" Dad, gone! three months after his 92nd birthday? Impossible! I couldn't believe it. I rushed into the room where I had left him less than ten hours earlier. He was lying on the bed with his eyes closed just as he usually did. "He isn't dead," I kept telling myself, in spite of the fact that I saw he was not breathing. I didn't know what to say, and I didn't know what to do. I was overcome with grief and a profound sense of loss.

Over the next few days, it seemed to me that the world as I know it had been turned upside down. Commitments I had made to friends and family no longer seemed important. I felt that everyone should understand that Dad's death had exempted me from all responsibilities, personal and professional. Among my many commitments was a pledge I had given to the Barbados Society for the Blind. I had agreed to be their keynote speaker at a meeting that was scheduled to be held at Bethel Methodist Church on Bay Street. The date for my presentation was just a couple of days after Dad's death. The title of the talk I planned to give to that group was "Genes and Disease." They specifically wanted me to explain to them in simple terms the genetics of inherited diseases. It was a talk that I was confident that I would enjoy giving, considering the fact that some of the members of the group were willing to share their own personal stories about genetic disorders in their family. But now, after Dad's death, I was finding it difficult to even conceive of keeping my commitment. After all, my father had just passed away, and I had the responsibility of assisting with the funeral arrangements. The grief and pain that I felt were excruciating.

The answer to the question about me honoring my pledge to give the talk came easier than I expected. All I had to do was to reflect on what I felt Dad would have done under the circumstances. I was confident that he would have urged me to go ahead with my plans to speak. I quickly got in touch with the group and confirmed my decision to proceed, respectfully informing them of my intention to dedicate my talk to Dad's honor. The large gathering in the church hall included several individuals with hereditary disorders as well as some physicians from the Queen Elizabeth Hospital. As I introduced the subject and began my talk, I could feel Dad's presence in the room. The words were simply rolling off of my tongue, and I was able to guide that audience through a very difficult subject with considerable ease. I could sense that everyone was drawing on the energy that I exuded.

The next day, I contacted the airlines and requested an extension of my stay in Barbados so that I could assist with the arrangements for Dad's burial. The days following Dad's death were quite hectic as my siblings and I ran back and forth trying to organize the funeral service. I knew that I would be the one designated to deliver the eulogy at Dad's funeral.

I will never forget July 5, 1995 when I had to stand before that congregation that had gathered in the St. Philip parish church to deliver Dad's eulogy. I remember looking out at the large gathering of family and friends as I began to tell them about the Dad I knew, my father, my friend, my mentor, my role model. I began by telling them about his childhood years and about the pain he experienced as an eight year old when he learned about his father's death in Panama. Then I told them that at fourteen years old, tragedy struck his family again when his older brother Stoddard died. I wanted them to know that during that very difficult time, Dad responded with resolve. As the only male left in the household, he decided that he should try to fill his father's and his older brother's shoes. I told them that I always believed that Dad was a man ahead of his time. I explained how I thought his deep and abiding faith in God, and his dependence on the Bible as the primary source of his spiritual enlightenment provided him with the strength he needed to succeed in life. And how he believed that spiritual development was as important as physical development, and that he felt that both should be kept in proper balance. I also told them that "pride" and "resourcefulness" were two words that best characterized Dad. He was proud of his humble origins and of his loving mother and siblings. He was a problem solver who used his creative energies prudently. He adored his children, and grandchildren, and was impressed by their accomplishments. I concluded by speaking of the despair I felt whenever I confronted the reality of not being able to embrace him ever again, or draw on that vast reservoir of wisdom he possessed. Before leaving the lectern, I recited the words from his favorite psalmist, "...for he shall give his angels charge over thee, to keep thee in all thy ways."

Two years later, we gathered at Holy Cross Church in St. John, Barbados to celebrate Mum's ninetieth birthday. It was indeed a joyous occasion. Mum was absolutely filled with pride as her children and grandchildren celebrated her life, along with a packed congregation. It was a time for reflecting on the contribution of our ancestors, most of whom were baptized and had worshipped in the same building.

On Saturday July 13, 2002, I was back in the Holy Cross Church eulogizing Mum. She had lived the good life and fought the good fight, and now she was tired and ready to go home. My siblings and I were all overcome with grief. Dionne tried to render a solo of the favorite hymn Mum taught her and she was only able to finish the first verse. I was almost finished with the eulogy when I was overcome with a deep sense of sadness. I knew that Mum would have wanted me to complete my tribute to her life, so I took a deep breadth, stiffened every sinew in my body, directed my gaze to the casket containing my mother's lifeless body, and spoke from the bottom of my heart: "your love for God and adherence to precepts of the good book have instilled in us the value of prayer, and endowed us with the ability to have faith in the face of adversity. Mum, we have come here today to salute you for your Job-like patience. It took patience to raise this many children. We are all grown now and can better understand the depth of your commitment. Young and poor, you devoted your life to family, to us. You reminded us daily that it was by the grace of God that we had food on the table, clothes on our backs, and a roof over our heads. It is funny how, despite the many economic challenges, we knew that we were not poor, for we were richly blessed to have a mother whose faith in God and trust in self helped us to ride out the storms of life. We were lucky to have a mother who gave up her dreams so that we could dream."

As darkness fell, and the cortege departed from the cemetery, I realized that we were about to begin a new chapter in the life of the Harewood family. Mum and Dad were now gone, and it was now our responsibility to provide a new generation of Harewoods with the leadership that guided the family's destiny for all these years. It was then that it really dawned on me that I needed to have the courage, fortitude, and wisdom to play the new role that had been thrust upon me.

Seven years after Mum's passing, as I prepared for my trip back to Barbados in 2009, I couldn't help reflecting on the richness that tiny island provided me during my childhood years. I wanted very much to revisit those places where I spent my formative years. I wanted to go back to Society Mixed School and to the Lodge School where I received my primary and secondary education. I yearned to spend some time walking around the grounds of Codrington College and its surrounding communities to find out how much things had changed since I left in 1960; and I also had a strong desire to talk to some of my childhood friends to get their perspective on how much Barbados has changed since gaining its independence from England in 1966.

Society Mixed School still occupied the same building, but it's name has been changed to the Society Composite School, reflecting a dramatic increase in student enrollment. I was surprised to learn that the school has added class five and six and draws students from St. Philip's Boys, St. Philip's Girls, Ebenezer Primary, St. John's Primary, Cherry Grove Primary, and St. Luke's Primary. When Mr. Parris who served as my headmaster retired, he was succeeded by Mr. Bell and then Mr. Moseley. Mr. Carl Springer was next to take the helm and he was followed by Mr. Frank Reid in 1989. Four years later Mr.

Garnes was appointed to head the school. The first ever female head teacher, Mrs. Whitehall, was appointed in 1998. She spent three years in that position before being replaced by Mr. Cliston Burke who was still serving as Principal at the time of my trip. Codrington High School was no longer the segregated facility that it once was. In 2009 it was serving a racially and culturally mixed student body.

There were so many changes in the community in which I grew up that it was difficult at times for me to recognize some of the major landmarks. Several buildings that were prominent structures in the neighborhood when I was growing up were no longer standing. They included the garage that once housed the Simpson buses, and the Brooks and Wilkinson homes. The Kidney and Harewood homes were still there serving as beacons from a distant past. No Kidneys or Harewoods occupied either of those houses. In fact there were no Kidneys living on College Land and there was only one Kidney listed in the Barbados Telephone Directory! The linkage between Codrington College and the people who lived on College Land was no longer as noticeable as it once was, and the influence of that venerable institution on the current residents of my old neighborhood has waned significantly.

The Rawle Institute was also a thing of the past. Many of the young people who resided on College Land were not even aware of its earlier existence. The swimming pool at Codrington College was no longer there, and neither was there any evidence of the spring that flowed on the south of the campus without interruption, providing fresh water for the women to wash their clothes, and the men to take their daily bath.

The hill behind our home, Howard Hill, was no longer accessible due to the dense overgrowth of shrubs and trees. Because the entire community was completely electrified no one needed to use wood for cooking and baking, and the de-bushing of the hill that was an annual ritual was no longer practiced.

The Lodge School had also undergone a radical change. Like the other secondary schools in Barbados, Lodge was a co-ed institution, serving the needs of both male and female students. I found it difficult to adjust to that reality. I prefer to think of Lodge as a boys' school, and Queens College as a girls' school. I have wondered what it would have been like attending a co-ed institution when I was a teenager. Would I have been able to focus on academics without distraction? Would I have been able to hone my skills on the athletic field in a co-ed setting without succumbing to the temptation of showing off to my female admirers? Lodge is no longer a boarding school so it has shed most of the vestiges of its racially-divided past. Since I graduated, there were several black headmasters, and the mix of courses and sporting activities available to the students is much more diverse than at anytime in the school's history.

Barbados was no longer the major sugar producing territory that it once was. In the heyday of sugar production there were as many as twenty-six factories operating on the island. By 1985 that number had declined precipitously to about six. Those included Andrews, Buckley, Carrington, Foursquare, Hayman's, and Portvale. When Haymans, Carrington, Buckley, and Foursquare closed, only Andrews and Portvale remained operational. No one could have predicted that Barbados' major economic engine would grind to a halt within less than three generations! Most Barbadians around my age still cited a remark made by the father of Barbadian independence as a primary reason for the change. The former Prime Minister is alleged to have said that he did not want to see another cane blade in Barbados. Whether it was for that reason or simply because of the pressures of globalization, Barbados' agricultural base is no longer what it used to be. Most Barbadians now believe that sugar is no longer King. That reality was evident everywhere I traveled across the island. Fields that were formerly densely packed with juicy stalks of sugarcane are now either covered with bush or have been cleared to accommodate a residential park with a fancy name, a professional golf course, a polo field, a race track, or more recently, a high-priced gated community.

The grab of beachfront properties and agricultural land that began in earnest during the 1970s, and continued over the ensuing years, has gained considerable momentum, especially within the last ten to fifteen years. I was disheartened when I saw that I could only get an occasional glimpse of the turquoise Caribbean Sea as I traveled north from the capital Bridgetown along the coastal highway that leads to the old city of Speightstown, St. Peter. One additional sign of the rapid rush of

Barbados into the developed world is the horrific traffic problem the island is experiencing. Cars and trucks and SUVs are everywhere, and they all converge at those ubiquitous roundabouts that are popping-up at every major intersection, sometimes choking off movement in every direction.

I have sensed what it feels like to be a returning national. I pay ten dollars for a visitor's permit to drive a car, and the permit expires in two months. I find it difficult to stay in the sun for more than ten minutes at a time, and when I am outdoors on a sunny day, I have to wear a hat. I still cannot believe that with the limited time I spend in the sun, I peel more readily than ever before. Does that mean that my melanin no longer protects me from the damaging ultraviolet rays of the sun? That is a question that could best be answered by studying the biology of melanin. Maybe this is a project that I should have assigned to one of my more inquisitive students.

I have often been told that change is inevitable, and now I firmly believe that this is indeed the case. I have seen it so many times in my private and professional life. What is therefore critical is to create a climate within which change is more readily acceptable. No one was able to do that better than Barack Obama, formerly United States Senator from the state of Illinois and currently serving as the forty-fourth President of the United States.

I remember sitting in my family room in North Carolina on a Saturday in February 2007 watching Senator Obama as he announced his candidacy for president of the United States. It was on a cold winter's day in front of the old State Capitol Building in Springfield Illinois. There was a large crowd in attendance when the Senator addressed the American people. Halfway across the country on the campus of Howard University in Washington, DC, the Black leadership had gathered to participate in "The State of the Black Union" conference, held annually and hosted by a young, ambitious Black reporter and television personality.

It was rumored that Senator Obama had been invited to the conference, and that the Senator was unable to accept because of his planned announcement for the presidency. Some of the prominent blacks at the conference roundly criticized him for declining the invitation. It was clear that they, along with many other political pundits, believed that the young Senator had no chance of capturing his party's nomination.

There was something quite special about Senator Obama's announcement, and about his candidacy. His campaign slogan, "Change we can believe in," resonated with a large segment of the American electorate. Eudine and I were so captivated by him, as well as by the pragmatism of his message, that we decided to volunteer to help his campaign team in Durham, North Carolina. It was a very exciting time indeed. From the temporary campaign headquarters in a strip mall on Fayetteville Street, I made calls to potential voters soliciting their support for our candidate. I was given my talking points, but before I could get into my routine, invariably the person at the other end of the line would express unwavering support for Senator Obama. It was easy to sense that this was no ordinary presidential campaign, this was a movement that the American electorate was witnessing, and it was being flawlessly orchestrated as if by a higher power. I considered myself fortunate to have been a part of it.

Barack Obama went on to win the nomination of the Democratic Party and then to defeat the Republican candidate John McCain for the presidency. I was numbed when the major networks and the other cable television stations announced that Senator Obama would be the winner of the presidential race. As much as I sensed that it would happen, I was still stunned when it did occur.

I was in Barbados on the day of the inauguration of President Barack Obama, and the mood was electric. There were parties organized all across the island to celebrate that once-in-a-lifetime event. I was glued to the local television station that broadcast the entire ceremony. I was very conscious that I was witnessing history in the making. I couldn't help thinking of my father, and my grandfather and I wondered how they would have reacted to the news. I thought of the previous generations of Harewoods, and Hayneses and Kidneys and I was acutely aware of how far we had come as a family and as a people.

Since my return from Barbados, Eudine and I have been blessed with the arrival of our sixth grandchild, Evan. He is an adorable baby with keen reflexes and a cool disposition. As I looked at him all cuddled up in his little infant seat, I couldn't help but think about all those members of the family who paved the way for him to have the freedom and opportunity that he has. He is the latest member of the Harewood family that will carry the torch throughout this century and into the next. I think of him as providing yet another chance to continue the proud tradition that was started so many generations ago by the pioneers of my family. This book represents my effort to try to connect Evan and the other members of the family to the rich past that was forged by their ancestors. I trust that it will instill in them the will to soar beyond their wildest dreams.

www.ingramcontent.com/pod-product-compliance
Lightning Source LLC
Chambersburg PA
CBHW030936150426
42812CB00064B/2941/J

* 9 7 8 0 6 1 5 4 8 5 3 5 5 *